HARD BALL

George Bell
and Bob Elliott

KEY PORTER BOOKS

Canadian Cataloguing in Publication Data

Bell, George
   Hardball

ISBN 1-55013-265-2

1. Bell, George   2. Baseball players – Canada – Biography.   3. Baseball players – Dominican Republic – Biography.   I. Elliott, Bob.   II. Title

GV865.B44A3 1990   796.357'092   C90-094873-6

Key Porter Books Limited
70 The Esplanade
Toronto, Ontario
M5E 1R2

Typesetting: Computer Composition of Canada Inc.

Printed on acid-free paper ∞

Printed and bound in Canada

90 91 92 93 94 95 6 5 4 3 2 1

Contents

"When Boston goes into Toronto they have a thing for George Bell, a favourite among Red Sox pitchers. The plan to throw at Bell was set up on the road trip before, or before the game. They seemed to get off on that. You've got a pitcher with total control — why not make some batters look like wimps when they jump away from a pitch? The Red Sox players all hated George Bell's guts, they said he was the most hated man in baseball."

— Margo Adams in the April 1989 issue of Penthouse *magazine*

"I've known George a long, long time. There's no greater friend, there's no greater teammate and there's no greater citizen of the Dominican Republic. His heart is as big as Casa Bell."

— former Blue Jays shortstop Alfredo Griffin

Prologue

May 2, 1989

It was a Tuesday night at Exhibition Stadium and the Oakland A's, defending American League champions, were in Toronto to start what was for us a tough home stand. This was our first home date after a long trip to the coast and our first game without Jesse Barfield, who'd just been traded to the Yankees Sunday morning, so everyone wanted to get off on the right foot. Our season had started terribly and people were already talking about how Jimy Williams' days were numbered. I didn't care about Williams — I just wanted to win some games.

Dave Stieb was pitching for us that night, and when Stieb is on, his ball moves more than anyone's I've ever seen, except maybe for Mario Soto, who I saw pitch in the Dominican Republic winter league. Stieb's fastball is like a sinker and when Dave has good stuff, his breaking balls dart all over the place. Anyway, in the first inning Stieb threw a sinker to Dave Henderson, the A's second-place hitter. The ball sailed and the pitch hit him in the shoulder. So Oakland was already mad and the game was barely started. I don't know what it is about our two teams, but the last few years something always seems to get out of hand when we play each other.

Then, in the bottom of the first inning, the Oakland starter, Bob Welch, quickly evened the score. Welch retired Lloyd Moseby, and after Tony Fernandez lined the first pitch he saw for a double, Welch hit Freddie McGriff square in the knee. Now when somebody throws a pitch at your knee he wants to hit you — it's the toughest pitch to duck away from — and as far as I was concerned that pitch was intentional. The mood on our bench was getting ugly and the first inning wasn't over yet. I hit a single to load the bases. Welch got Ernie Whitt out, but Rance Mulliniks hit a grand-slam homer. Just like that we were ahead 4-0.

But Oakland kept coming back. In the fifth they scored one run and then in the seventh added three more against Stieb and reliever David Wells to tie the score 4-4. In the top of the ninth inning we were leading 5-4, thanks to an RBI by Pat Borders. Duane Ward was trying to save the game for Wells. Ward struck out the first two batters he faced, but then Luis Polonia and Dave Henderson each singled. So Jimy brought in Tom Henke to try to shut the door. Well, it was one of those nights for big Henk. First he walked Parker on a 3-2 pitch to load the bases. That brought up Mark McGwire, who had never had a hit off Henke. This was also one of those nights for McGwire. He hit Henk's pitch away up into the left-field bleachers for a grand slam and Oakland was ahead 8-5. When the ball flew over my head and over the fence, I thought to myself, "Well, the game's lopsided now; they're going to win."

In the bottom of the ninth Rick Honeycutt was pitching in relief for Oakland. Just like Ward, he retired the first two batters. Then Oakland's manager, Tony La Russa, brought in Gene Nelson, a right-hander, to pitch to me. Nelson had hit me once when he played for the White Sox and I hadn't forgotten. Since there were two out and nobody was on base, I went up there trying for a homer to cut the lead to two runs. This wasn't a one-run lead La Russa was trying to protect. I didn't really understand why Honeycutt couldn't have worked one more hitter since even if I hit a homer they would still be up by two runs and we were still down to our last out.

On the first pitch Nelson threw me a fastball up and away and I swung and missed. I fouled off the next one — strike two — and then he threw me a slider down and away, trying to set me up for something high and tight. Just as I expected, he came inside with the next pitch. As I pulled back and tried to duck away, it just missed my face but hit me hard in the chest. It was like he was aiming square at my helmet. Right away I knew that what Nelson had done was deliberate. I thought to myself, "No way." I paused for a second and then out I ran to the mound to show him there's no way he can treat me like that and get away with it.

I hit him a good one right in the nose and he was bleeding. Third baseman Carney Lansford and catcher Ron Hassey and half the guys on our team were around us trying to break up the fight. By this time Nelson and I were wrestling around on the mound and I hit him another one. Later when they pulled the two of us apart, I said to him, "First time a ball can get away from a pitcher, the second time there's no way — it's intentional." I said quite a few other things that weren't nearly so polite. We kept yelling at each other, and guys from both teams joined in. Dave Parker was doing a lot of yapping.

Later Glenn Hubbard of the A's said I was pulling Nelson's hair, which isn't true. The next day Tom Henke said some of the A's were trying to pull him down by the hair and he joked that Oakland was trying to make him look like Ernie Whitt. Ernie doesn't have a whole lot of hair left.

That was the end of the game for me. Davey Phillips was umping and he kicked me out. We lost 8-5. Later the American League suspended me for three games. But the thing with Nelson was he was trying to intimidate me. I don't think he'll try that again.

That wasn't the first time I was hit by a pitch and it won't be the last. I had my jaw broken when I was playing at Syracuse, and in Milwaukee in 1987 I got hit in the nose with a pitch and wound up with a fracture. Since 1984, my first full season as an everyday player, I've been hit 30 times with pitches. You have to figure there were twice as many pitches I just got out of the way of. Sometimes I wonder why I get thrown at so often, but I've learned that when you play hardball like I do, it goes with the territory.

1

Growing Up in the Dominican

"What do you think a Dominican name is anyway? George Bell?"
— *Mets minor leaguer Valdimir Perez,*
brother of Dominican dandies Pascual and Melido,
January 8, 1990, Sports Illustrated

I REMEMBER WHEN I WAS SIX YEARS OLD BEING THE bat boy for my dad's baseball team. The sugarcane factory where he worked had a ball team and every Sunday it would play a doubleheader. My dad was the manager, but he would also play — anywhere he was needed: usually in the infield, but sometimes if the team was in trouble he would pitch or, if a guy didn't show up, he would catch. Most Sundays he would play third base in the first game and second base in the second game of the doubleheader.

Sometimes now in the winter when we sit around at home talking, my dad still argues he was a better player in his day than I'll ever be. There weren't any scouts around San Pedro when my dad was young. In his day he probably was better, but I always tell him, "Maybe then, but not now" and we laugh. He showed the same encouragement and support with my younger brothers as he did with me. The number-one reason for my family being active in baseball is my dad — he was everything growing up and he still is.

One day when I was about five years old, there were kids in the street begging for money from American tourists. I saw what they were doing and did the same. I came home with a few pesos and showed them proudly to my parents. But instead of congratulating me, my dad spanked me. He explained that if I needed or wanted money I should ask for it, but "George Bell will never beg for anything."

I saw a lot of baseball in those days. You'd have trouble finding a play I haven't seen. Now that I'm in the big leagues I'll sometimes be in a game and something funny will happen, like a rare play, and I'll remember seeing the same thing happen years and years before when my dad's team was playing. Like when two runners wind up at third base, or when a guy starts his slide too late and, even though he beats the throw for a stolen base, overslides the base and gets tagged.

At that time there were only about 4500 people in the whole town of Santa Fe, in the Dominican Republic where we lived, but about half the town came out to those Sunday afternoon games. To us this was the major leagues, even though none of the players were paid. Not everyone had TV sets and the only professional game you could get was the Saturday Game of the Week. Baseball was our main entertainment. There was real excitement; maybe it was like the high school football championships in Texas I always hear people talking about. When my dad's team played, everyone wanted to say, "Our team is better than yours, our factory is better than yours and our village is better than yours." They played for fun and for bragging rights. There were six teams in the league, the Circuit de Los Ingnios, and they played a 30-game schedule. The league was made up of factory teams from little towns around our area on the eastern end of the island. Players had the names of the factories on the front of their uniforms. This was back when the sugarcane factories were still the kings of the Dominican people. Now the Dominican economy is worse than when I was a child.

Whichever team won the factory league playoffs advanced to play the winning team from the league in San Pedro de Macoris, the biggest city in the region, only a few miles away. My dad allowed me to be the bat boy only for the home games; he said it was too dangerous being on the bench when the team was on the road because you never knew when there would be a fight during the game. Dominicans take baseball very seriously. So when the team was away I'd stay at home and try to stay awake waiting for my dad to come back with the news from the games. Even though he was tired, he'd always tell me who had the important hits, how we scored our wins, who played well in the field and how we got our wins.

When my dad's team won the league he allowed me to go to the games they played in the playoffs against the winner of the San Pedro league. They won in 1970, when I was 11; they won again the next year, too. I remember that 1971 playoff really well. Each day of the series the players and their families piled into the new blue factory bus for the drive to the Tetelo Vargas Stadium in San Pedro. For those games my dad would make me sit in the grandstand. I always learned more sitting on the bench because in the seats with my mom I was too busy watching people.

In the playoffs there would be twice as many fans as on a normal Sunday, maybe 9000 people. The people from the other small towns who were against us during the season now cheered for us against the team from the city. Vendors sold fried bananas, hot dogs, ice cream, beef sandwiches, Coca-Cola, bottles of rum and ice. Fans from each town sang and cheered for their side. There were often fights over a foul ball. If people were upset at a call the umpire made they would throw empty bottles onto the field. I had never seen people so excited before. When my dad's team won, the bus was loud and noisy with people singing, drinking rum and toasting the star of the game.

Sitting there as a bat boy during regular season games in the factory league, I saw a lot of fights between players. In the Dominican Republic, guys fighting on the ball field is not a big deal like it is in North America. If a batter was beaned once by a pitch he would keep his anger in until he was hit a second time and then away he'd go: he'd charge the mound to fight the pitcher. If a base runner had a chance to take out the second baseman or the shortstop he would. If the infielder didn't like it, chances were pretty good he'd start swinging. It seemed there was a fight every other weekend. Baseball has always been like that in the Dominican.

My dad was my favourite player, but I had a few other players I enjoyed watching and I guess I modelled myself after them: third baseman Juan Turner, shortstop Cachimura Richardson and centre fielder Miguel de los Santos. The three of them all played the same way. In those days I thought of them as cool, *mano suave*, yet if you were a player in the big leagues and you saw someone like them you might call them "hot dogs." They did a good job, they knew how to play and they made playing look easy. But they were flashy. I think they could have been professionals, but at that time it was not easy for a Dominican to become a professional ballplayer. There weren't as many scouts around, so only the very, very best were signed.

I began learning how to play the game from watching those factory league games, from being around older men. That's different from most American and Canadian kids who learn on their Little League teams with kids the same age. My dad taught me how to throw and catch and how to hold the bat, but I learned about baseball from being around his team. I was very lucky. And I was proud sitting on the bench with these men, my dad's friends. When I was beside those older players I learned more than just baseball. First off, I learned I had to behave myself. I owed the players my respect because they were older than I was. They really cared about baseball and they cared about my dad, so I had to repay them by treating them properly.

The most important thing I learned about baseball then is if you don't have enough guts to play there's no way you're going to be a good ballplayer. If you're afraid of getting hit by the pitcher you'll never do well; if you're intimidated, you're not going to get a hit; if you're afraid to break up a double play because the shortstop might punch you in the face, you'll never be able to slide. You have to play the game hard! Like hockey, football or rugby. People think baseball is different, a more easy-going sport, because the pitcher and catcher play catch and all you have to do is hit the ball. Well, sometimes they don't play catch. Sometimes they throw at your head. I learned back then that if a team wants to take you out of a really important series, the pitcher will throw at you.

Another thing I learned really early was how to control my emotions. Everyone thinks I have a hot temper and can't control myself. Well, one time when I was about eight years old my dad was pitching batting practice to me. He was trying to make me a switch hitter, so I was batting on the left side of the plate. He threw a pitch, I didn't duck, and it hit me square on the temple on the right side of my head. I went down in a pile — and oh my head ached — but I didn't cry. My dad told me that the pitch was accidental and he explained that when I was playing I would sometimes get hit with pitches. Most would be unintentional but some would be deliberate. It was up to me to tell the difference and over the years I did. If it was intentional I'd sometimes charge the mound; other times I'd keep my feelings in control. It depends on the situation. The time I went after Bruce Kison of the Red Sox, there was no hesitation. He was asking for it, and he got it.

Some people think that in the Dominican we are all born wearing a baseball glove. It is true that baseball is very important in my country. Not only do we love the game, we have a passion for it. But when I was born my parents weren't thinking about baseball, just how happy they were to have their first child. That was October 21, 1959. I was born in the hospital at San Pedro de Macoris at 7:05 on a Wednesday morning. I weighed seven and three-quarter pounds and they tell me my skin was white, yes white. I was so white no one believed I was my dad's son. Later my grandparents told me I was as white as a little rat, that you couldn't even see my eyebrows or the nails on my fingers. After about a month I began to get darker and darker.

My dad's name is George Vinicio and he named me George Antonio. I'm the oldest of five kids. You may wonder how come a Dominican has a name like Bell. If you go back long enough in history you're going to find my ancestors came from Africa. Same for a lot of people who came to the Caribbean. When Spain and England were in control, they would ship slaves over on boats to work on plantations, exactly as the Americans did in the South. Nowadays I bring workers over from Haiti or Puerto Rico to work on my farm — except I pay them to do the work and they can leave any time they want. I guess I also have some Spanish blood, but the real descendants of the Spaniards, the Dominican Spaniards, live in the northern part of the island near Santiago. Mostly, though, I'm Dominican, a proud Dominican.

My dad's father and mother came to the Dominican from English islands in the Caribbean. The story goes my dad's father came to Santo Domingo, our capital city, from the island of Anguilla to buy a machete for cutting sugarcane. Back then Anguilla was still a British territory. When he realized the island was bigger and more successful than the one he had left behind, he decided to stay. He got a job cutting sugarcane and moved to San Pedro. My dad goes back to Anguilla once in a while to visit his sister who moved there when she was about seven years old.

My dad's mother came to the Dominican from Montserrat, which also used to be a British colony. She meant to take a boat to England, but she got on the wrong one and wound up in Santo Domingo. I laugh when they tell that story. If my grandmother had boarded the right boat I'd probably be a blue-eyed soccer or rugby player. And I'd be one of the best, making a million dollars a year.

My grandmother was gorgeous. She had the same complexion as people from Guyana or Trinidad, much fairer skin than I have, with dark, straight hair. Everyone who knew my grandmother says I look a lot like her but more like my mother. My grandmother's last name was Bell and she and my dad's father never married. My dad kept my grandmother's name. That's quite common in the Dominican. English names have always been a tradition in our family.

On the east side of Santo Domingo, the capital of the Dominican where my father's parents lived before moving to Santa Fe, you can still find a lot of people originally from different countries. Because of the many rivers emptying into the ocean there, this was where the traders in the early days came to make camp and trade merchandise. My dad and mom were both born in San Pedro. When they married they moved to Santa Fe where my dad worked for the sugarcane factory.

The small town of Sante Fe, where I grew up, is about four or five miles outside San Pedro. When I was a kid the roads in and out of Sante Fe were paved, but that was about it. The three-bedroom house we lived in was owned by the sugarcane factory. Pretty soon the bedrooms were full. There was my dad, my mom, Juanita, my three brothers, my sister and myself. Jose Vinicio was born a year and a half after I was; next came my sister Marisela; then George Vinicio, who everyone called Rolando; and last was Juan, the youngest. Everyone calls Juan by his middle name, Tito. My mom and dad slept in one room, Jose and I shared another, and my sister was in the third room with the two babies. It was crowded, but we kids didn't notice. All our friends lived the same way. It was the only way we knew.

Back then I was close to my mom. I wasn't tough at an early age and was always at my mom's side. My mom is one of the sweetest people to be around. She never argues with anybody, she's never mad, she's always happy, she likes to work hard. Everyone has a temper on my island, but my mom was very slow to show hers. Mostly when she became angry she wouldn't say a word but just walk away, like I try to do most times. My dad is more hyper. I'm close to both my parents, but I get along better with my mom. I can tell her things I need to talk over. Like secrets.

I was pretty quiet until I was about 10 years old. There were so many different people from many different parts of the country coming in to work at the factory and some of the new kids would try to show they were tough. They would try to take advantage of me at school or when we were playing marbles in the street. You had to fight. If you didn't, you lost all your marbles. My dad didn't want us to fight, but we were only trying to survive.

Nowadays in the Dominican you seldom see two brothers hanging out together. Kids are always with their friends from school instead of with their family, but Jose and I were always together. We both did really well in school. We played ball together, went to birthday parties and to the cinema too. Our dad would drive Jose and me into San Pedro to the Cantiflaus theatre any time it rained and we couldn't play baseball. Our favourite was Mario Moreno, a Mexican comedian. He was our Bob Hope. Moreno was a typical Mexican actor: big old hat, big old moustache and big old cowboy boots. We thought he was funny as hell. When dad took us to the movies our treat would be vanilla ice cream.

When we went to school my brothers and sister and I had to write the date on a page in our blue notebooks every day. For years we didn't know why we had to do it, but every night our dad checked our books. Years later our dad told us it was because he wanted to make sure we were in school. He figured if we wrote down the date and what we did that day we wouldn't skip school. My dad was pretty tough. He would have spanked us and not allowed us to play baseball if we hadn't gone to school. Jose and I never skipped school until after grade nine, but a lot of kids did. I remember my friend Juan Reyes coming around to copy down what I'd written and he'd write down the date at the top of his page too so that he could fool his father.

The sugarcane plant where my dad worked was shut down three months a year and it would open in October. The plant would operate for six months straight until the harvest was completed in the fall, then shut down completely for two months and then it would reopen so the people could come in and fix the equipment. My dad was an engineer in the processing plant, but he would also do mechanical work like fixing the engines of the diesel locomotives and repairing wagons if they broke down. He would work dawn to dusk to make enough money to keep the family going. Even so, sometimes when the plant was shut down life was pretty tough. My dad would take an odd job here or there for 10 days to make extra money. And my mother ran a take-out restaurant out of our kitchen. She made lunches to sell to the factory workers. At the peak time she had three or four employees working for her making lunches. My mom was busy even when the plant was closed because people still had to eat. So we were never short of food, unlike some people. Every month my mom would take in about 2500 pesos and put the money in a bank account. We never touched that money, even when the factory was shut down. I guess in Dominican terms we were middle class, even though a Canadian or American would look at the way we lived and say that we were poor.

When I think back to those days it seems as if my mother was always cooking. She would get up before us to start breakfast. In the Dominican we eat really heavy in the morning: chocolate milk with *yaniques* (tortilla shells made with flour), *plantinos*, bananas fried in a batter, and yucca roots. For dinner she would cook rice, beans, and chicken, shrimp or fish from the Caribbean. Filet of sole was my favourite. But the best meals were on Saturday nights — as long as Jose and I didn't get home late from the ballpark. There would be my dad, my mom, my dad's two sisters, Jose, Rolando, Tito, Marisela and myself. Jose and I were close, but my family was raised right — we were all close. My mom would serve a big dinner and we'd all take turns telling my dad what had happened in our day. Whoever had the most hits that day got to go first. I went first a lot.

We watched some games on the television my dad bought for our house in 1971, but sometimes we'd watch games at other people's houses. When I was growing up, my favourite teams were the San Francisco Giants, the Houston Astros, the Cincinnati Reds and the Los Angeles Dodgers. We cheered for the Giants because of Juan Marichal and the Alou brothers — Felipe, Matty and Jesus, who are all still active in baseball. Felipe still manages the Escogido team in Santo Domingo in our winter league. We all liked the Astros because of Cesar Cedeno and Rafael Batista; the Reds because of Cesar Geronimo, Dave Concepcion and Pedro Borbon and the Dodgers because of Manny Mota. Every morning at 7:30 the radio commentators would tell us what the Dominican and other Latin players had done the night before. There weren't as many Latins in the major leagues then as there are now.

I wanted to grow up to be like Rico Carty. He was my idol. This was long before he played for the Blue Jays. He hit 25 homers with the Braves in 1970. In 1978, he came to the Blue Jays from Cleveland and hit 31 homers. Now there was a bat with a lot of pop. Rico is from San Pedro too. He was a childhood hero of most of the guys I played ball with.

In 1972, things were a lot better for my dad. The workers signed a collective agreement that guaranteed they would be paid all year — not just when the factory was operating.

In 1972, the three-bedroom company house in Santa Fe had become too small for Papa Bell's growing brood. And thanks to his wife's thriving year-round business and his rising income, the family had saved enough money for a down payment. That year construction began on a new, larger house in the east end of San Pedro de Macoris.

Two years later, when George was 14, the house was ready and the family made the move from the small town to the big city (then a population of 80 000). Senor Bell continued to work at the sugarcane plant. Now there were four bedrooms. George, Sr., and Juanita were in the master bedroom. Marisela had her own room; Rolando and Tito shared another; and George, Jr., and his younger brother, Jose, shared the fourth room.

It was in San Pedro, playing sandlot baseball with other teenagers his own age and older, that Bell began to blossom. He may have learned his primary lessons from a bunch of factory workers, but he was already better than some players years his senior. San Pedro sandlots served as the Dominican Republic's "Field of Dreams" and in the next decade earned the city the nickname "the Shortstop Factory." Alfredo Griffin, Tony Fernandez and Manny Lee are just three of its products.

So picture in your mind, if you can, a pick-up game between two groups of youngsters on a corduroy-like diamond where a ground ball with a true hop is a rarity: nine skinny kids are on the bench picking out a bat to do some serious damage when their turn at plate comes. In the field are a pitcher, a catcher, a first baseman and five prospective shortstops fighting for territorial rights between third base and second. In the outfield all by himself is a slender George Bell — different from the others.

I wasn't always an outfielder. When I first started I used to play third base — just like my dad. Sometimes I would pitch, play shortstop or second base. I had been playing against older boys since I was 12 or 13, so I improved faster. My last game as an infielder was at second base. A guy hit a hard hopper at me, it took a bad bounce and hit me in the collarbone on the right side. The ball knocked me down and knocked me out. When I came to, I told everyone that was it for me and the infield. I didn't play for about two weeks and when I came back I switched from playing the infield to being a right fielder. Partly it was an excuse. My heroes were all outfielders and my dream from when I was little was to be one of the great Latin outfielders. But my first game left a bad impression.

In those days we played on a small softball diamond with palm trees behind the outfield fences. In right field was a concrete wall. My first game back, about the fourth inning I was chasing this long drive and I ran into that wall and knocked myself out — again. But I was going to stick with right field. I decided I'd stay away from the wall. A few games later, at the same park, I hit the ball over the left-field fence to help us win a game. That was the first time I hit a ball over an outfield fence. Even if it was a softball diamond, it felt good.

When I moved to the outfield Cesar Cedeno was the player I wanted to be like. The first time I ever saw him I was about 11 years old and Cedeno was 19. He came to the ballpark in Santa Fe and my dad took me to see him play. He was already a minor leaguer with the Houston Astros, but he was still living in Santa Fe in the winter. They played a pick-up doubleheader. He pitched one game, even though he was an outfielder, and played centre field in the second game. The way he had developed was amazing. He could do everything you would ever want to do on the ball field: hit for average, run, throw accurately, field, steal bases and hit with power. He was a complete ballplayer and he had become good by working hard.

The best thing about growing up in Santa Fe and San Pedro was we had plenty of baseball facilities. My dad and other men built a diamond in Sante Fe. We could play baseball any time we wanted and we didn't have to pay for the use of the field. Every weekend and days when there wasn't any school, we'd play baseball eight or nine hours a day. Of course if you added up all the time we spent arguing whether a guy was out or safe or a ball was fair or foul, it would probably subtract at least two hours from our playing time. We loved to argue — safe or out, fair or foul. Even our pick-up games were hot. Sometimes there would be fights. But for all the scraps I've been in the one that left the worst mark happened when I was still playing on the sandlots in Santa Fe. Someone threw a bat, I jumped to miss it, landed on another one and fell headfirst into the bench. My right eye was black. The doctor said I might have a permanent discoloration as I do to this day. Every spring as a pro, guys who don't know still ask me about my black eye and wonder what kind of fight I've been in.

We'd arrive at the diamond ready to play about 8:00 A.M. In the morning the ball diamond was a beautiful sight: the grass still had dew on it at the start of a new day. We'd leave at two in the afternoon to go home for lunch. At three o'clock we'd all be back to play until six at night. If Jose and I came home late for dinner, our dad would whip our butts, but sometimes it was hard to leave. Everyone wanted one more at bat. Some days it felt like we could play forever.

Since my dad was still manager of the factory team I was usually able to get a baseball and my brothers and I were able to get gloves. The ball my dad gave us would never be new but it would last six or seven days unless it got wet from the rain — then it would last only a day or two. When the stitching came undone and the cover began to fall off, we'd cover the ball with electrical tape — now you're really talking hardball — so the ball would really sting your hands when you caught it or if you hit it off the end of the bat. I can still feel the sting when I think about it. If we could have, Jose and I would have played baseball all day, every day.

It was our dream to make the majors and be another Rico Carty. But my parents allowed us to go to the park only on Saturdays and Sundays because they wanted us to concentrate on school. We went to a private Catholic school, Gaston Fernando Deligne High School. I always had grades in the eighties and nineties in elementary and high school. I had to do well because of my dad and because of the nuns. The nuns were mean. They yelled and screamed at me more than umpires ever did. You couldn't talk in class, you had to sit straight. If the nuns caught you doing something wrong, they'd make you stand in the dark corner of a closet for 15 or 20 minutes. And if they caught you turning around then they doubled your time. Sometimes they'd give you a rap on the knuckles for not paying attention.

But I enjoyed life — there wasn't anything to worry about. If I hadn't made the major leagues, I probably would have grown up to be an engineer or an architect. I think it would have been the thrill of a lifetime to build a bridge on my own. I did well in math even when I was in grades five and six. I'd see an adding machine or a calculator and I'd get excited. It was always fun to work on problems.

There were tough kids all over when I was growing up, but there were a lot more of them when we moved to San Pedro. Life was a little bit harder for me when we moved there. There were some neighbourhoods where we couldn't go after 9:00 P.M. because it was dangerous. Not that there were gangs but close to it. There wasn't any shooting like in New York City, but if someone saw you in the wrong neighbourhood they'd wear out their fists beating on you. So Jose and I went everywhere together. That way the two of us would have a chance when challenged. That was another thing Jose and I did together. We got in trouble together.

Once in grade 10 the principal phoned my dad and told him they were going to kick me out of school for fighting. We were playing basketball — three-on-three — and this one guy on the other team kept calling me *maricon, maricon*, Spanish for "faggot." I told him to stop, but he didn't. He kept poking me with his elbow. So when we were underneath the basket, I elbowed him right in the jaw. He came down, put up his guard and we went right at it. I beat him up. He didn't call me a faggot any more.

I used to play a little basketball, soccer and volleyball. I was pretty good at spiking because I used to jump pretty high. And I was pretty good at rebounding, but I was never a fanatic about any sport except baseball.

I was about 15 years old when I first met Tony Fernandez; he was only 12 then. We played baseball together and against each other. Like me he was learning fast by playing with older people, but Tony lived really close to Tetelo Vargas Stadium in San Pedro. He was always hanging around practising fielding ground balls. It was easy to see Tony was going to be a good player. Even when he was little he was smooth at fielding the ball no matter where it was hit. Tony had a bad leg at the time, but he had an operation that fixed the problem. After that everyone was sure he'd be one of the best.

By the time I was 15 we were playing more organized games on the diamonds. Weekends the kids in our neighbourhood would usually play a team from another neighbourhood in a best-of-five series of three-inning games. Each team would put up 20 pesos — that was about four dollars Canadian in 1975. The losing team had to buy everything for the winner at the victory party: Coca-Cola, fruits from the roadside stands and ice cream. Those are good days to remember — being on the winning team and getting a base hit to drive home your brother with the winning run. Jose played some infield, but most of the time he was our catcher. Then we'd celebrate with oranges and Coca-Cola. Just like major leaguers, we thought. After the game, both teams would sit around, each teasing the other.

Those games were a lot of fun, but we took them seriously — for most of us it was the first time we'd ever played a game with something at stake. And those pesos we contributed meant a lot — no one wanted to lose his money. If your team lost, all you could do was sit and watch or go home because another team was always there waiting to play the winner in half an hour. We didn't have any coaches, but someone came up with the idea of picking a spectator to umpire the games. Still, there were a lot of arguments and I was involved in quite a few of them. Sometimes, if the game was close, you'd stand around and watch an argument go on for half an hour. There were days when the umpire would just get bored and go home.

At that time we weren't paying umpires anything but then a guy came up with an idea to cut down on the arguments. At the beginning of each game each team would give its 20 pesos to the umpire to hold. Then if one team argued too long, the umpire could take the money and go home. If we played the whole game and the umpire stayed he would get four pesos. Some games there were still fights. Guys would be upset about too hard a slide or a batter would be angry over being knocked down. Hell, there are even fights in organized Little League games in the Dominican. It's always the same thing. The pitcher hits someone in the head and the batter charges the mound. It's always the pitcher's fault; pitchers start everything.

The next year I moved on to play in the juvenile league. We had coaches and umpires for every game. But pitchers were still the same. Often pitchers would get all puffed up. The guy would be walking around high school saying, "I struck him out. I hit him and he didn't do a thing." Next time you could bet on it: there were going to be fists flying.

Pro baseball had been a dream of mine ever since I was old enough to dream, old enough to fall in love with the game. So, I always had a good attitude about working hard and playing hard. And by 1976 I knew I was a prospect. I was throwing the ball well and hitting line drives non-stop. I wasn't hitting any homers, not over the fences anyway, but I was hitting one line drive after another into left field. Scouts were watching our games and I was working out in the mornings at the complex the Philadelphia Phillies had.

The Dominican Republic was fertile, virgin soil in 1977, unhindered by restraints of the amateur, free-agent draft which in the United States, spread the available talent evenly — provided the ball club had a good scouting system. In the Dominican the hardest-working scouts signed the most players. It was as simple as that.

If a scout had a keen eye for projecting talent and carte blanche *when it came to handing out a signing bonus, he could fill his yearly quota quickly. For the well-connected ones with big bankrolls it was like shooting fish in a barrel, quite a contrast to the draft process in the United States where a team gets one out of each 26 draft selections. In the Dominican it was first come, first served.*

It had been that way in the United States until 1965. In those days, popular legend has it, a scout driving to a ball game could spot a youngster idly firing rocks at a passing railway car, notice the strong right arm, jam on the brakes, make him an offer and sign him on the spot.

In the Dominican in 1977, the year before George Bell signed his first contract, a scout named Epy Guerrero was already making his presence felt. Guerrero, who had signed the smooth-fielding infielder Damaso Garcia to a contract with the New York Yankees, had joined the Blue Jays well into their first year of operation at the invitation of executive vice president Pat Gillick. He and Gillick had worked together before with Houston and the Yankees. Now Guerrero was touring the island spreading the Blue Jays gospel: it was the best team in baseball because of room for quick advancement. George Bell listened to Guerrero but wasn't convinced.

I expected I would sign with a major-league team. It was just a question of when and which one. Scouts from a number of organizations told me I was a prospect because of the way I hit so many line drives. For almost a year I had been working out with the Atlanta Braves and the Houston Astros and the scout from Atlanta said they were really interested and one day he said he was going to phone me. The call from the Braves never came.

But most of the time I had spent working out with the Phillies. They were the first team to build a complex. Quiqui Ascebevo, who scouted for the Phillies and lived in Santo Domingo, showed the most interest in me. He and I talked baseball a lot after workouts and he would give me pointers. So I wasn't surprised when he called me over one day after a workout, but I was surprised when he said the Phils wanted to sign me if it was all right with my dad. It was certainly all right with me. Quiqui said I had to work out in front of a scout from Philadelphia before we could sign.

The day the scout came, Quiqui hit me fly balls in right field and I threw to the bases. Then he pitched batting practice and I hit a couple out, but mostly it was one line drive after another. I was introduced to the man from the Phillies, but he didn't say too much. I guess he was observing me. He must have liked what he saw, because after he and Quiqui had a talk by their car, Quiqui came to my house to wait until my dad came home from work. When my dad walked through the door, I wanted to jump up and tell him the big news but as soon as he saw Quiqui sitting there he knew what was happening.

From the time of Quiqui's visit until I actually signed took 20 days. Quiqui is a good man: he respected my parents and treated me fairly. To this day we still have a good relationship, but the whole process was dragging. I didn't know whether they still wanted me. Quiqui kept in touch. He talked to my father every day about the contract. He also signed Juan Samuel, Julio Franco and Carmen Castillo, who all made the majors.

Near the end of the 20 days, after long talks between Quiqui and my dad, I had to work out again for another Phillie scout. The Los Angeles Dodgers and the Blue Jays entered the picture the final week. The Dodgers didn't offer as much, probably because they thought they were Latin America's team and I would sign for less for the honour of playing for them. Even though Epy and the Blue Jays offered me more money than the Phillies, I felt that they had jumped in too late. I thought I owed the Phillies some loyalty. In the end the Phillies agreed to give me a signing bonus of $3500 American. I would earn the standard first-year contract of $500 a month, which added up to $2500 over the season. Even though I weighed 148 pounds soaking wet, Quiqui and the Phils thought I projected as a power hitter.

I was excited when it was finally over. The scouts helped me improve as a ballplayer, spending a lot of time with me. This was in late September of 1977. They couldn't register my contract until March when my contract expired with Escogido in the winter league. Even after I signed in March, my dad kept me in school until I had to leave.

I spent a couple of hundred dollars of my bonus money on new clothes, but I didn't buy a car the way a lot of guys do. I put the rest in the bank and left it there for my dad so that he could use it to help raise my younger brothers and my sister. In a way I was repaying my father who'd always dreamed of having one of his sons play in the majors just the way he used to dream about playing himself. Of course, like most sons, I'll never be able to repay my father for everything he has done for me.

When I turned professional, the thought never entered my mind that I could make as much money as I make today. I still play baseball the same way I used to play when I was a kid: for fun and because I like it. A lot of people don't believe that, but that helps explain why I come to play whether I'm hurt or in pain, no matter what. That's the way I learned to play when I was a kid — and the fact I make two million dollars a year hasn't changed that. Baseball has always been a part of my life for as long as I can remember. When I think of growing up in the Dominican, baseball is what I remember most: being bat boy for my father, playing on the sandlots with Jose, playing on the diamond my dad and his friends built, watching Rolando and Tito get better, those weekend series with the ump walking down the road jingling our pesos and 15 kids begging him to come back and promising never to argue again.

That winter I met an infielder named Alfredo Griffin, who was from San Pedro and playing for the Estrellas club in San Pedro, which is in the Dominican League, our pro league. We hit it off right away. We had personalities which seemed to mix from the start and we're still best friends today. In those days Alfredo was playing in the Cleveland organization and he told me what I could expect in the United States — the bus trips, staying in hotels and how hard it was to make it all the way.

My last few months in San Pedro were important for other reasons than baseball. For one thing I finished my grade 12; for another I met my future wife.

One day at recess, in February of 1978, Rafael Ramirez showed up. I knew him from playing with him in the juvenile league the year before. Rafael had already played a year in the Atlanta Braves organization and was on his way to the big leagues. He was a shortstop who could turn a double play and make the throw from the hole. Anyway, when Rafael and I were sitting out behind the school and I was asking him questions about life in the United States, a girl called him over to say hello. Her name was Maria Peguero and she was Rafael's first cousin. She asked when he was going to spring training with the Astros. Maria and I were looking at each other so he introduced her. The two of them did most of the talking. I just kept looking at Maria and thinking she was special. Then the bell rang and recess was over. That afternoon I didn't go back to school. Rafael and I went for a walk and I remember saying, "Your cousin looks pretty good." He said he knew where she lived. I never really thought, "This is the girl I'm going to marry." When you are a teenager you don't really think about getting married, but I knew I wanted to get to know her. In a few days Rafael took me to her house to meet her mother and father.

Maria and I were both pretty young and liked each other a lot. She used to argue all the time. I don't mean raising her voice, but Maria had strong opinions. For instance, we always saw each other on Sunday. Sometimes I wouldn't show up Monday; sometimes I wouldn't show up Tuesday. Then when I did show up, she'd start complaining, saying I should pay her more attention. I'd say, "Wait a minute, I don't get paid for this." Then she'd get really angry.

Maria's coming into my life was good for me. To know a woman who really cared about me was different. She didn't change my life or anything: I didn't need to be changed. The only way my personality is different since I met Maria is that I'm not as shy. When I met Maria things started changing — for the better. So I saw Maria often in the five months before I left for the U.S.

March arrived and I didn't get the call to the Phils' spring training complex in Clearwater, Florida. So I didn't think I'd be playing with a pro team until 1979. I didn't know anything about the "short-season, rookie-class leagues" that go from early June until the end of August. I thought you were supposed to go to Florida, try to make the Class A team and then your team would begin play in April. I thought Class A was the lowest rung on the ladder, but they had found a lower one to start me off — the Pioneer League, which was rookie class.

At the end of May the Phillies told me to fly to Helena, Montana, and report to the Helena Phillies to begin play in early June. When it was time to leave I packed a few pants and some shirts, but I used some of my bonus money to buy a sports jacket for my first plane ride. I had to get a new baseball glove too. My dad was sad to see me get on that plane, but he knew I had to leave if I was going to become a major-league baseball player. My mom, my three brothers, my sister and Maria came to the airport to see me off.

Pro baseball was my dream but I never dreamed of Helena, Montana. My dream was the big leagues. That first plane trip — my first time off the island — was an experience. As kids growing up we'd be playing in the sugarcane fields or eating oranges in the orange groves and we'd all stop and watch the planes coming into and taking off from Santo Domingo. We used to wonder where they were going and imagine how important the people must be.

Now I was going to find out where all those people were going. As the plane left Santo Domingo it headed east, and I remember looking down at the lines of orange trees and the kids in the sugar-cane fields. That was me down there I was leaving behind.

2

The Phillies

"Leaving George Bell unprotected and losing him in the major league draft wasn't the worst mistake the Phillies ever made while I was there. I'd say losing Mike LaVailliere to St. Louis in '85 was the worst. George Bell was a close second."

> — *Hall of Fame scout Hughie Alexander,*
> *former Phils executive, now of the Cubs,*
> *July 21, 1987, Arlington Stadium*

WHEN MY PLANE ARRIVED IN HELENA, MONTANA, I'D been travelling for 17 hours and it was pitch dark. I took a cab to my motel, checked in and crashed into bed. The next day when I woke up, I looked out the window and the first thing I noticed was that there weren't any palm trees. Not that I was expecting tropical plants. I thought I knew about Montana because as a kid I'd read all those Gene Autry comic books, and I was expecting cowboys riding horses, people wearing cowboy boots and plenty of guns. On my way to the ballpark that morning I did see guns, shotgun racks on most of the trucks driving around town, and I did see a few Stetsons, but not too many cowboys riding horses. Gene Autry wasn't anywhere to be seen. One of the players told me Autry owned the California Angels but at first I thought he was kidding. What would a cowboy be doing with a baseball team? Everything was so strange I could have been on a different planet.

The Helena Phillies had players from all over. There were alot of guys who had been at the Phillies' camp in Florida and had stuck around there for extended spring training after the team had left to start the season. So they were all ahead of me. Others were in their second year of pro ball and a third group were high school players. But we all had one thing in common: we believed we could make it to the big leagues. I was earning $500 a month like all the other first-year players.

I had a strong notion about the English language from my parents and from school, but I could speak English only a little. In the Dominican we get two years of French and then two years of English in high school, but I couldn't carry on much of a conversation. Unless you've lived in a foreign country where you don't know the language, you have no idea how tough that can be. When I arrived, there was no one my age I could sit down with and have a long talk in Spanish. Our manager, Larry Rojas, spoke Spanish, so that helped.

But I made friends. Right from the start I hit it off with Ryne Sandberg, who like me was a first-year pro. He was a high school draft from Spokane, Washington, so he wasn't that far away from home. He was the guy who really helped me with my English when I first arrived. If people spoke slowly I knew most of what was going on, but with slang words and English baseball jargon I needed help. For instance, when I first heard someone yell "BP in ten, hurry!" I had no idea he meant we were going to be taking batting practice in 10 minutes. And if you missed your turn you lost it for the day. Then there were baseball expressions like "moving the runner over" and "going the other way with a pitch." Those weren't expressions I'd learned in English class at Gaston Fernando Deligne High School in San Pedro. Back then, Sandberg was playing shortstop before they converted him into a second baseman. Bobby Dernier, who later made it as an outfielder, was the back-up shortstop. Dernier was pretty cocky because he knew he was fast, but he was a good guy. He said he'd be the first one to make the majors. (He was — the Phils called him up in 1980.) We also had a pretty good catcher in Ed Hearn.

The Helena Phillies' ballpark, Kendrick Legion Field, had only about 2400 seats — less than a third of Tetelo Vargas Stadium in San Pedro with around 8000 seats. But the green grass made the park attractive; it wasn't burnt yellow from the sun like at home.

We worked out for about seven or eight days before opening day of the Pioneer League season — that was my spring training. Those workouts were very different from the way we practised in the Dominican. At home, we'd mostly just play. When we did practise we'd talk and relax a bit. In Helena, Larry Rojas would run one drill after another: throwing to the bases, taking fly balls, hitting cut-off men, escaping rundowns, sliding into second and going over the signals until we got them right. Playing in the Dominican we'd never had indicators for steal, bunt, hit and run. It was complicated, but I learned fast.

After the June draft the Phillies signed some new guys and they sent us more players, three of them Latins. First, Francisco Berenguer, a pitcher, arrived from Panama City. Then came Luis Santos, a pitcher from Puerto Rico, and finally Alejandro Vidana, a Mexican player. Suddenly I wasn't as lonely.

The ball club helped the four of us find a furnished house to rent. It was a really old place built back about 1870 and now in a bad part of town. The people of Helena didn't appreciate dark-skinned baseball players living in the nicer neighbourhoods. The other players on the team called our place a "witch house" because it was so old it looked haunted.

So there we were, rooming together — a Mexican, a Panamanian, a Puerto Rican and a Dominican — and each one of us thought his country was the best in all of Latin America. We were a bunch of innocent kids. This was the first time away from home for all but one of us and we were all single. Most of the high draft picks on the team were in fancy apartments and driving big fancy cars bought with their bonus money.

Early in the season we came back from a road trip to find there wasn't any hot water in our house and the power had been turned off. I thought maybe there was a power failure; we have a lot of power failures in the Dominican and most houses have their own generators. We called the landlord and he told us we hadn't paid. He said, "You're responsible for the bills." That's how much we knew. We thought the ball club would look after things like that. We'd never had to pay for these things living at home. The next day, when we got to the ballpark, we explained our problem to Larry Rojas and he arranged for the power to be turned back on and then for us to pay what we owed the companies.

Of the four Latins, the guy I was probably the closest to was Luis Santos. He could also speak a little English, but mine was better. So when we went to the supermarket or a restaurant, I usually did the talking. Berenguer was struggling with his English. It was easy to see he had a big head. His brother Juan, who later played for the Blue Jays and is now with Minnesota, was at Tidewater Triple A that season and then the Mets called him up for a while. Francisco thought he was better than the rest of us but *he* never made it to the majors.

The four of us were always together. The people in Helena knew we were baseball players. Of course I was easy to spot because I was always wearing my Phillies warm-up jacket. I'd never had a lined jacket and you needed one even on summer nights, it was so cold. But I couldn't afford to buy one of my own that first year. Also, I was dark-skinned and the only way you would see a black man in Helena was if he was with the Phillies or one of the other teams that came to town. Most of the people, the baseball fans, would appreciate us and talk ball when we'd bump into them downtown — easy stuff like "Who are you guys playing tonight?" or "You guys sure were tough on that starter the other night." But they never went further than that.

When we could afford to eat out we'd usually have the basics, like chicken with rice or spaghetti or "amburgessa" (that's the way we say "hamburger" in the Dominican) and ice cream. The $500 a month was barely enough to live on. Seldom could I afford a steak. When the scouts talk to you about signing they always say you are serving an apprenticeship like a plumber or an electrician and when you ask for more money, they tell players, "That's all we can give you right now, but the sky is the limit."

Going out for dinner could also be scary at times. We would sometimes have to make a couple of stops before we found a place that would serve us. We had A LOT of trouble, even just going for hamburgers. I don't mean trouble communicating, but problems with the owners. Often they didn't want to serve us. The guy in the restaurant would say, "What are you bunch of niggers doing in here? Get the hell out. NOW!" That sounds bad and it was; I'm not making it up. We survived all those nights and learned the language, but sometimes I felt like giving it all up and going home where I knew I was welcome.

This was the first time I had run into such open racism. In the Dominican racism exists but it's different. Mostly it's directed towards the Haitian people; most Dominicans despise Haitians. That's because our two countries fought each other and at one time Haiti ruled the Dominican. The other kind of racism in the Dominican goes way back in history. Christopher Columbus might be a good name in America, but he's bad news in the Dominican. He discovered our island and named it Hispanola on December 6, 1492, but the Spaniards he brought to the island were bad for our country.

The Spaniards wanted to live in Santo Domingo, so they made the Indian people live in the jungle. They treated the Taino Indians terribly. They made them work like horses, stole their gold, abused their women. Over the years they killed them all. I'm not a fanatic, but most places you go in Central America, in North or South America you will find plenty of native Indians. Canada has native Indians, as does the United States. Not the Dominican. In school, the history books taught us the Indians were a peaceful race, one of the best-looking, attractive Indian nations in the whole world. They were tall, fair, with long straight hair. Now you would have to look long and hard to find anyone with Indian blood in my country.

In the forties the cities in the Pioneer League would have been labelled Class D in baseball's alphabet. Years later when major-league baseball shuffled the deck of minor-league classifications, A, B, C and D were exchanged for Triple A class, Double A, Class A and rookie league. Triple A became the highest level of the minor leagues, just a phone call away from the show. Each major-league team has one Triple A club, a Double A team, two or three teams in Class A and at least one affiliate in the rookie league.

Whereas the other minor-league levels open a few days after the start of the major-league season in April and run until the end of August, the rookie-league season starts in early June and concludes at the end of August — three months rather than five. The Pioneer League straddles the U.S.-Canada border in the northwest with teams in places like Calgary, Lethbridge and Medicine Hat in Alberta, and Great Falls, Billings, Butte and Helena, Montana, as well as Idaho Falls, Idaho.

First- and second-year professionals only were allowed to play in the rookie classifications. If after two years you weren't good enough to move up, you moved on. Normally a player who breaks in at rookie league is four or five years away from making it. If he is a skill-position player — catcher or shortstop — and he finds himself behind an established star on the major-league level, he often lingers in the bushes much longer. Unlike in junior hockey, where a player can be drafted in the first round and open the next season in the National Hockey League, a pro baseball player may sign with a club one day and not see the city he signed with for more than half a decade. Obviously, it is far more difficult for the baseball scout who signs a young player to project a player's talent that many years down the road. The odds of Bell or any of the rest of the Helena Phillies ever making the major leagues were 20 to 1.

It was 24 games into the season before I got to play. Larry Rojas never told me why, but I guess he figured I wasn't ready. I'd take batting practice, then sit and watch the games. I wasn't used to that. There were a few guys who were older than me. Earl Neal, the Phillies' second-round pick in '77, was playing ahead of me. The high draft choices, I soon learned, get every opportunity to play. Finally, after more than three weeks of sitting freezing on the bench in the coldest weather I'd ever experienced, I told Larry I was going to go home. I wasn't staying around for any more just watching. Not that I was homesick, but this was a waste of time. Rojas told me to be patient — it wouldn't be much longer — so I told him I would stick it out a while.

I got along with Rojas, but he wasn't anything like I thought my first manager would be. I expected my first manager to be just like the first manager I ever met — my dad. But Rojas never talked to me patiently as my dad had. I guess he was concerned about the guys who were playing regularly. It didn't matter to him that I was only 18 and in a strange world. I guess I have to give him credit for one thing, though; he eventually got me into the lineup every day.

After I talked to him he must have phoned the farm director in Philadelphia because a day later he stuck me into the game as a pinch hitter. My first professional time at bat wasn't much to write home about. It was against Billings, a farm team of the Cincinnati Reds. Tom Lawless, that little midget we have on the Jays now, was playing for Billings. It's okay for me to call him a midget because that's what I call him to his face — besides he beats me at cards too often. Anyway, his team had this big, tall left-hander, Larry Jackson, and he struck me out in my first at bat. Jackson never made the majors.

The next night against Billings turned out to be something different. I went three-for-four, my best game of the year. I hit a single, a double and a triple. After that I was in the lineup for the rest of the season, batting seventh and playing right field. I don't know what would have happened if I hadn't gone to Rojas and complained about not playing.

I wrote Maria to tell her I had finally started in a game and had some hits. We wrote often. I found myself thinking about her a lot.

The Pioneer League was a wild way to break in. I don't know how many times I thought, "I hope every year of pro baseball isn't going to be like this." Some road trips, for example Helena to Lethbridge, Alberta, we would ride the bus from 11 o'clock at night after a home game until 10 o'clock the next day. We'd check into a motel, sleep for a few hours and then we'd be off to the ballpark. I was only a rookie, but to me this was a crazy way to make a living. I didn't play cards then, so most of the trip I'd spend talking to the Latins or sleeping. An outfielder named Will Cumer, from Nassau in the Bahamas, was on our team. He was a carbon copy of Boston's Jim Rice: big shoulders, muscular arms and a great swing. Sometimes when we sat around talking on the bench or on the bus, we'd play a game: name the top three prospects from our team who would make the majors. I'm sure they do the same thing on every minor-league team. Whether we were talking in English or Spanish or regardless who was playing or who had had all the hits that night, Will was always on everyone's list. On some he was even ahead of Sandberg. Early in the year I never made the list, but in the last month guys mentioned my name some nights.

Sandberg always treated me fine, but some of the other Americans gave me a hard time — like Earl Neal who was always calling me a Puerto Rican. When I'd say I wasn't a Puerto Rican and explain that I was from the Dominican Republic, he'd say, "Same thing." We had a pitcher named Martin Shoemaker and he was nasty. We'd walk into the clubhouse or pass him on the bus and he'd say, "Hide your money, guys, here come the Puerto Ricans."It wasn't good-natured teasing.

Once, after a road game in Great Falls, Shoemaker went too far. The dressing room wasn't that big and the showers were even smaller, so you had to wait your turn for a shower after the game. Shoemaker finished, yelled "Next" and a few of us moved in under the water. But, as he was leaving, Shoemaker turned the tap to hot, hot enough to burn us. About three of us were jumping around naked trying to get out of the way of the scalding water. I was so upset that I wanted to fight him right there. Sandberg was angry too, getting scorched by the water. I was 148 pounds, but a guy named Randy Greer stepped in between us. He was Shoemaker's size, about six feet, 195 pounds. That ended the argument. I appreciated the help from Greer because Shoemaker was tall and I was scared as hell. I was the baby on the team.

We only drew about 500 or 600 fans a game but a lot of guys in the league went on to make the majors. The Blue Jay farm team was at Medicine Hat and that was where I first saw Lloyd Moseby. Lloyd was exciting to watch in those days because you never knew what he was going to do. He might make a mistake on a ball but he was so fast he could usually outrun his mistake. Centre field was not his normal position, so he was out there learning as he went. The Blue Jays converted him from first base.

At Helena I hit well, a .311 batting average, and drove in 14 runs in 33 games, but I didn't have a single homer. I didn't make many errors and I was known as a good outfielder. Sandberg hit the same, but he had one homer and 23 RBIs. We finished the season in sixth place with a 30-38, 20 games out of first place.

When I went home at the end of August, my brothers, my dad and my friends were excited. They met me at the airport and wanted me to tell them everything that had happened in North America and how many cowboys I had seen. I told them as much as I could on the drive home to San Pedro and then over one of my mom's big meals, but after that I was off to see Maria. We spent the evening at her place with her mother and father, catching up on all the news about San Pedro.

Two weeks later I was in Clearwater, Florida, for six weeks at the Phillies' instructional league. Sandberg was there too. That was a big deal, to get invited to instructional league. It meant they considered you a prospect because they invited only about 30 players. In Clearwater we worked our rear ends off — we'd practise all morning and play games in the afternoon. I was hopeful I'd be promoted to Class A for the following season.

When I went back to the Dominican after instructional league, Maria was going to college, the University of Central East, in San Pedro. We went out a couple of nights a week since I wasn't playing winter ball that season. I really liked Maria, but at that point she was a lot more serious about our relationship than I was.

That December of 1978, Alfredo Griffin was traded from Cleveland to Toronto for a pitcher named Victor Cruz. When I heard the news I was upset. Dreaming of making the Phillies some day, I had hoped that if Alfredo was ever traded it would be to a National League team so that we could play against each other. But Alfredo was happy. Toronto was a young team and now he would be playing every day.

In March of 1979 I left for Florida for my first spring training. I was really looking forward to it. Now I would be there with all the other minor-leaguers and able to compare myself with the other right fielders rather than with just the five guys we had had the year before in Helena. And maybe I'd catch a glimpse of the Phillies' stars like Mike Schmidt, Steve Carlton or Greg Luzinski we all talked about in the minors. It was certainly different, all right, but not in the ways I expected. Unlike at Helena and instructional league, there were enough players running around to fill out five teams. The Phillies had only four minor-league clubs, so some players were going to be sent home and some would be asked to stay for extended spring training. They made us work twice as hard as I'd ever worked before, with one drill after another. They had so many coaches that as soon as one guy got tired of hitting fly balls another one would take over.

Despite all those extra bodies and the fancy facilities, some things were just like at Helena. The guys who had been around were always tough on us new guys. It's not surprising, I guess, since we rookies were a threat to their jobs. I don't suppose the Phillies' training camp was any different from that of other teams. It wasn't that much different from the way Blue Jays' camps are now, except now it's my turn to make fun of the rookies. But I would never be hard on someone because of his colour or the way he talked.

The worst park of the four was at the Carpenter complex, the one the American players called Vietnam, a smaller diamond with a rough infield right up against Highway 19. Everybody used to hate that field. In the clubhouse it was always easy to tell which team was just back from Vietnam. We'd be undressing in the locker room with guys from Triple A, Double A and the two Class A teams, but the ones who had been to Vietnam had cut lips or puffy eyes where they had been hit with a ball after a bad hop.

I had a pretty good spring, and when it was over, I was assigned to Spartanburg in the Western Carolinas League (Class A) for my first full season. That was good news. After playing only 33 games the year before, I could have been sent back to Helena. This was the next step up on the ladder.

South Carolina is a lot closer to the Dominican than Montana is and there are quite a few black people living there, but I didn't feel any closer to home. The people in Spartanburg were even less friendly than the people in Helena. First, they would look at me thinking I was a black ballplayer from Mississippi, Tennessee or New York. But after they found out I was from the Dominican, their attitude would change. They would become more talkative. Still, it was difficult getting to that second stage. But then people would ask about my island and I would talk on and on about how it is the most beautiful island in all of the Caribbean, how they should come down for a visit to see our lovely white beaches and the water — more shades of blue than you will ever see anywhere else. I would talk so much I'd start to get homesick. At least in Spartanburg the mail delivery from the Dominican took only seven days to arrive instead of a month, as it had in Helena. Maria wrote often.

Bill Dancy managed the Spartanburg Phillies and I thought he was a great guy. I think players and managers got along well at Class A because at that time big money was not involved. All that mattered was ability and Dancy knew I could play. The only time money entered into it was that he would fine me $20 just like anyone else when I'd miss a sign. When you're earning $650 a month and you get fined that much you learn the signs fast.

There were quite a few familiar faces on that 1979 team. Ryne Sandberg was there. So were my old pals Earl Neal and Martin Shoemaker, but they didn't bother me so much this time around. My best friend was Sandberg — we spent a lot of time together that year. Ryne would often come up to me after a game and ask if I wanted to go out for something to eat. We both liked to eat the same things. After the game we'd go for a sandwich.

After two weeks I was hitting only .143. That's when Granny Hamner came to Spartanburg for one of his visits. Granny was a roving minor-league hitting instructor with the Phils and he would visit each of Philadelphia's minor-league clubs to see how everyone was doing at the plate. I'd met Hamner at Clearwater in instructional league the previous November and he was the first guy to show a lot of interest in me. Of all the guys in the Phillies organization, he was behind me more than anyone else. Right from the start Hamner respected me. He'd shake his head, flick the ashes off his cigarette and say, "Never seen a guy so little with so much power." I weighed about 152 pounds at the start of my second season. I was hitting the ball hard, driving pitches off the wall, but there was something wrong with my swing. I couldn't get any lift. This one visit turned my season and my career around.

Granny watched our game from the bench the first night. The next day we had batting practice at 10:00 A.M. and he must have spent 45 minutes with me alone. I'd be in the cage taking my cuts, come out and get back in over and over. All the time he was talking to me — talking and chain-smoking cigarettes. Players told me he was a smart batting coach but what I liked about him was that he was patient and a soft talker.

That day Hamner said I had pretty quick hands and good hand-eye co-ordination, but I had to develop a lift to my swing. I was so quick with my bat that if I could try to stay back and keep my shoulder closed I'd do well. He didn't want my left shoulder pulling off the ball — opening up — before I started my swing. He wanted me to keep my weight on my back foot and not commit my swing too early. If I committed too early then the only power I had was from my wrists and I needed power from both my legs and my wrists if I was going to hit home runs. The key was my left shoulder. That would be a check point for getting both parts of my swing — the legs and arms — going at the same time. Granny told me I should try to hit the ball to right field more. That way I'd still get base hits even if I was jammed inside. He had probably seen guys take 10 million cuts at fastballs, so he knew what he was saying.

Each time I got back into the cage he'd say, "Stay back, don't fly open," and I'd drive the ball. I'd get out and we'd go over it again. And again he'd say, "Stay back, don't fly open." He told me to keep saying it to myself because he was in town for only a few days and then I would be on my own again. The more times in the cage, the better I was. We worked all morning until my hands were sore.

That night the pitchers didn't get me out once and — I'll never forget it — I went 11 straight at bats with 11 base hits: 11-for-11. And on the eleventh at bat I hit a line drive to left field to bring in a run and the bat broke. When I got to the majors I heard players say how a bat "died with honour." Well that was my first lucky bat. Some hitters start to worry when they're going real good and they break their hot bat, like they're jinxed. I wasn't. I kept remembering what Hamner had taught me. Even today when I step out of the box, sometimes I'm saying to myself, "Stay back, don't fly open."

After that, anytime I heard Hamner was coming into town I'd get to the park early. It got so he expected to see me, and every time he repeated the same message. Granny helped me in other ways too. For instance, he'd even get me extra bats. That may not seem like much but it's a big deal when you're in the minor leagues. He taught me the same way he taught Mike Schmidt, the best power hitter the Phillies ever had and probably the best-hitting third baseman ever to play the game. Soon I was hitting homers and Neal and Shoemaker weren't teasing me as much as they had the year before.

And soon pitchers were throwing at me. One night we were playing Asheville, North Carolina, a Ranger farm team, and I hit a home run first time up. Next at bat the guy hit me in the shoulder. That was enough for me and I charged the mound, just like I would have in the Dominican. Soon both teams were on the field knocking heads. No one got hurt, but that was the first pro baseball fight I ever had. I don't remember the guy's name, but I guess he can say he once hit George Bell with a pitch, his only claim to fame.

Spartanburg was my best year, my only full year in the Phillies organization really. I probably played against more future pros when I was in Helena, but the competition in Class A was tougher. We played a split-season schedule. Halfway through the season all the teams started fresh with 0-0 records. At the end the first-half winner would play the second-half winner in the playoffs. It was supposed to help attendance, but we didn't draw many people during regular play. We finished in fifth place over the first half with a 33-37 record, but in the second half we were 40-29 and in first. Over the course of the season I hit 22 homers, drove in 102 runs and batted .305. The 102 RBIs led the league and I also led the league in triples with 15, which showed I could run a bit back then, and I made the Western Carolinas League all-star team as the right fielder. In the playoffs we lost to Greenwood, three games to one. I hit two homers, but the Braves team had too much pitching.

After the season the Phillies sent me to instructional league in Clearwater again. Then I went home and began playing with Escogido Lions of the Dominican League. I'd been home only about four days after instructional ball and for the first time everything seemed easy even though it was a tough league. We had a good team, including Joaquin Andujar, who was then pitching for the Houston Astros. Our manager was Julian Javier, who had played second base for St. Louis when they won the World Series. I remember seeing his World Series ring and thinking, "Some day, some day."

One night in the dressing room after Escogido had just beaten Licey, Joaquin Andujar called me over to meet this tall gringo with a beard. Joaquin said, "I want you to meet David Hendricks. This is one Yankee I trust. I think you should trust him too." A lot of North Americans, some Dominicans as well, say Joaquin is *muy malo*, a bad guy. But I know he's honest. I wondered about him, though, when he introduced me to this stranger. I was sitting down and I remember thinking, "Who is this great big guy? What's he going to do?" I was worried he might be trying to hijack me when I went to North America. Joaquin explained that David was his agent, but I didn't even know what an agent did back then. I'd just heard the high draft picks say, "Well, I'm phoning my agent about this."

David's Spanish was okay, but he was kind of shy. It was his first time in the Dominican — maybe he was even scared a little bit. He didn't want to make his first impression a bad one. When he asked me if I'd like him and his brother to look after my future contracts, I didn't give him an answer, but said I'd get back to him in a few days.

Afterwards, Joaquin and I went out for a few beers and he did a real selling job on me. He explained how, the winter before, he had switched agents and hired the Hendricks firm on a Friday, and then won his arbitration case four days later. He was sold on the Hendricks brothers. I also knew that Alfredo Griffin was one of their clients, and so was Damaso Garcia, a young second baseman who played for Licey and had just been traded by the Yankees to the Blue Jays. Alfredo had introduced me to Damo a few weeks before and we'd hit it off right away.

The next day, back in San Pedro, I talked to Alfredo and he told me how David had flown down to see several of his clients, including Juan Bernhardt. Juan played a couple of years in Seattle but in '79 he played only one game before being sent to the minors. It impressed me that the Hendricks brothers had time for all their clients, not just the big stars. A couple of days later we played Licey again in Santo Domingo and I talked to Damo after the game. Like Alfredo, Damo said he was happy with everything the Hendrickses had done for him. David came around again that night. When I was sitting in the clubhouse taking off my socks I heard, "*Que pasa*, George?" I recognized David's voice. We talked and I said I'd like to go with him. So David said he, or one of his brothers, would come to see me during spring training.

In late January, Maria told me she was expecting a baby and wanted to get married right away. She was worried about what people would say. I told her I wasn't ready. You can't live for what people are going to say about you — they're going to say it anyway. If we got married before I went away, two months later the "talkers" would notice Maria was pregnant. Then they would say the only reason we had married was because she was having a child. At that time I didn't have marriage in my head at all, but I told her we'd get married in a year. I was only 19.

During my first year of winter ball, the 1979-80 season, I hit .290 with one homer and 16 RBIs for Escogido, so I figured I was ready to make another jump up the Phillies' ladder.

Late in spring training I got the chance to meet Randy and Alan for the first time when they came to Clearwater for a visit. Randy was a sharp dresser and a sharp talker, while Alan was quiet. We went out for dinner, told some stories and had a few laughs. Right from that first moment I felt those guys were treating me well, but there wasn't much for them to do that first year — there wasn't any contract to negotiate. The Phillies told me what I was earning, and that was that. As it turned out, however, from that day on the Hendricks family was part of the Bell family. At least twice a year since I signed with them, one of the three brothers has visited the Dominican. We've become very close. I was lucky: not only did I get the best agents, I got good friends.

My second spring with the Phillies was different. Managers and coaches from the other teams in the farm system were coming around the batting cage for a look when it was my turn to hit. After the All-Star season at Spartanburg I was considered a legitimate prospect. Some of the first-year kids said, "You mean you've got an agent?" I wasn't a new face on the block any more.

The second day there I looked up Granny Hamner, who was on another field. He said he'd be working with my group in the afternoon. That was good news. When I was in the cage later I smelled cigarette smoke and heard, "Eleven-for-eleven, eleven-for-eleven. You listened to me. Now why don't you tell these other kids to start listening to me too?" Hamner was joking about our visit in Spartanburg when the other teams hadn't been able to get me out for four games. Then we got to work and he told me the same things over and over.

I had a good spring again and the Phillies decided I had progressed enough to be sent to the Reading Phillies who played in the Eastern League Double A. Same for Ryne Sandberg. So we were a notch up from Spartanburg — two actually, because the Peninsula Phillies team in the Carolinas League was considered one level above Spartanburg. Some guys get stuck spending two years in Class A. I was ready for a big year, but somebody had other ideas.

My season at Reading was a rough one and a short one. I was in the Opening Day lineup as the right fielder and played every day — until April 24. On that day the Philadelphia Phillies came to town for an exhibition game. It's the same now when the Jays go to Syracuse: the major-leaguers don't want to play and all the minor-leaguers want to impress the people with the big club. Who knows when you'll ever get to face a major-league pitcher again? Tug McGraw, who led the Phillies to the World Series that year, was pitching when I came to the plate. I was looking for a fastball, but he threw me an offspeed pitch and I swung so hard I injured a disk in my back. I was told I'd need surgery, but I didn't want that.

Ron Clark, our manager, now a coach with the White Sox, talked to our trainer and decided I shouldn't play. They rested me for over a month. The only thing I could do was catch the ball and throw, so I helped out in the bullpen. I couldn't take batting practice. Watching and not playing was boring — I actually cried some nights, out of frustration. At the time I didn't know if I would ever play baseball again. One game when I was hurt I was sitting in the bullpen watching us play Bristol, a Red Sox farm team. The Bristol players started a fight over a beanball, just like in my dad's factory league. I came jogging in from the bullpen to help separate some players — but with my injury I wasn't going to do any swinging. As the fight went on, I saw Steve Crawford, a Bristol pitcher, hitting Jesus Hernaiz, our coach. That was too much for me, so I jumped into the air to hit him. Crawford was six-foot-five. But I popped him pretty good and then the two of us went at it. That was my second fight in pro baseball.

I wasn't playing, but I was travelling with the team. So I saw the parks and the players who would later make it to the bigs. One park I particularly remember was the old War Memorial Stadium in Buffalo where they filmed the movie *The Natural*. Right field was so short — about 260 feet — that during batting practice a pitcher used to stand about 30 rows up in the seats with a big bucket to collect all the balls from the left-handed hitters. The Holyoke team had a new manager that year, and his first time in Buffalo he didn't have anyone up there to get the balls. The local kids grabbed them all, and the second night he didn't have enough baseballs for his team to take batting practice.

Late in June, when I hadn't played in a game in two months, Ron Clark used me once as a pinch runner. Well, I re-injured myself in a collision at home, so they put me back on the disabled list. I waited and waited but my back didn't get much better. Later in the summer the Phillies sent me home. That suited me just fine since I didn't want an operation.

Although I hit .309 during that 1980 season, I played only 22 games and had 55 at bats. I felt my season was wasted. We finished second with a 78-61 record, only a game out of first place, but I was at home by then.

Soon after I got home I went to see my old friend Quiqui Ascebevo, the Phillies scout who signed me. I explained about my back and asked his advice. He took me into Santo Domingo to a doctor who gave me a cortisone shot. That helped and gradually my back got better.

That fall, on November 12, Maria went into labour. The baby was a healthy boy. We named him Christopher. Maria wanted to get married, but I told her not yet. I rented a house and moved out of my parents' home. Maria, Christopher and I lived together. My dad, whose father and mother never married, and my mom were over all the time. They didn't care we weren't married. They looked at Maria and me and saw we were happy. They were glad to have their first grandson. They used to come over around 11 in the morning and take Chrisopher back to their house to play with him and show him off. They spent a lot of time with him and still do.

In 1980-81 my Dominican League contract belonged to Escogido in Santo Domingo. But the Phillies told me not to play in any games. I couldn't take batting practice and I couldn't play in the morning games. I told them I was healthy but they were trying to sneak me through the December major-league draft unprotected. They didn't want any scouts seeing that my swing was back. The orders from the Philadelphia front office were simple: "Nada in November." In spite of that, Quiqui told me to go ahead and play in the morning games. Gradually my swing was solid: I was back to where I was in Spartanburg. One week I played five games straight in right field and I guess that's when the scouts saw me.

Each fall, clubs file their 40-man winter rosters. These are the only players they are allowed to protect. Teams who come in under the limit are allowed to select unprotected players from any other team's minor-league rosters to fill to the 40-man ceiling. (Players with fewer than three years' professional experience don't have to be protected.) However, the drafted player must spend the first year with his new team at the major-league level or else be offered back to his old team for half the purchase price.

Following the 1980 season the Blue Jays had few qualms about carrying an unproductive youngster with a bright future. They were a last-place team going nowhere, top-heavy with unproductive veterans. Besides, Vice President Pat Gillick had already enjoyed some success in this area when he snatched Willie Upshaw from the Yankee organization. By 1980 it was clear Upshaw was the Jays' first baseman of the future.

Late in 1980 the Blue Jays executives got together for one of their endless series of organizational meetings. Vice President Al LaMacchia, who signed the likes of Dave Stieb, Dale Murphy, Jamie Easterly, Bruce Benedict and a slender San Antonio slugger named Clarence (Cito) Gaston, insisted the Jays take Bell at the upcoming winter meetings in Dallas. A big question remained: was he healthy? LaMacchia prevailed, and that December, when the Blue Jays' turn came in the ballroom at Loew's Anatole Hotel, Bell was selected fourth overall in the major-league draft. This minor transaction on a Monday morning in Dallas attracted little attention at the time: last-place club adds minor-leaguer coming off injury-plagued year. Big deal! "Jays (Yawn) make deals" read a Toronto Sun headline detailing the acquisition of catcher Dan Whitmer and outfielder George Bell.

When I heard the news I was in the dressing room in San Pedro where we were playing that day — December 8, 1980. It takes me a while to remember what I hit that year — .247 with two homers, 10 RBIS — but I'll never forget that date. Suddenly I was surrounded by Dominican sportswriters who told me I had been drafted by the Blue Jays. I didn't really know what that meant. They explained that I would be on the major-league team the next season.

On the day I was drafted I took the word both ways: as good news and bad news. The good news was that I knew that if I did all right in spring training I would stay in the majors for the '81 season. It was also good news that I was going to be with my old friend Alfredo Griffin, and with Damo Garcia, a player I was getting to know. I'd

also be in the same organization as Tony Fernandez, who signed with
the Blue Jays a year after I did. At the same time I was sad when I
thought about all the friends I had made in my three years with the
Phillies.

When I think back to my very first professional year in Helena,
Montana, in 1978, I am always amazed at how successful so many of
those players have been. Besides me, there was second baseman Ryne
Sandberg who went on to star with the Cubs; centre fielder Bobby
Dernier who made it with the Phils, went to the Cubs along with
Sandberg and then ended up back with the Phils; and catcher Ed
Hearn who was traded to the Mets and then went on to Kansas City.
That's an unusually high number of guys who made it all the way
from the Pioneer League, especially when you consider the odds
against a player making the major leagues.

Looking back, I can see that the move to Toronto, to a young
team on the way up, was for the best. If I had stayed with the Phillies I
might even be out of baseball now. Who knows? Back then the
Phillies were one of the most active clubs signing players on the free-
agent market. A lot of guys on their minor-league teams didn't have a
chance of making it. We've won our division twice since '85 and the
Phillies haven't won once.

3

Rookie

"He's standing in the corner of the dugout, Billy Martin was cussin' him and he was mocking Billy right back. I looked at the kid and thought, 'Hey, that's the guy I saw in the shopping centre mall with the black eye the day before, that's George Bell'."
— *Former Yankee captain Willie Randolph,*
remembering when he first noticed George Bell
late in the '83 season

IT ISN'T MORE THAN A FEW MILES FROM THE CLEARwater home of the Phillies' minor-leaguers to Grant Field in Dunedin where the Blue Jays train, but to me, in the spring of 1981, it was a whole new world. I recall flying from Santo Domingo to Miami with Alfredo Griffin and Damaso Garcia. In Miami we hooked up with Otto Velez and flew to Tampa. Alfredo was in his third year with the Blue Jays, Damo was starting his second and Otto was in his fifth, so they knew their way around. From Tampa we drove over to Dunedin. On Highway 19 we passed the Carpenter Complex where the Phillies' prospects train. It seemed strange to drive right on by but this spring I was headed to the big leagues. In Clearwater, I'd catch a glimpse of a big-leaguer only if he came around to get some extra hitting. You never bumped into one when you were on the field we called Vietnam. The Blue Jays might have been the worst team in baseball but they were definitely big league.

When we got to Dunedin we checked in at the Ramada Inn where most of the Blue Jay players and staff stayed in those days. Now many of the baseball people either rent or own condominiums in the area but back then not too many could afford them. Maybe it's the memory of those first few days that keeps me coming back to that Ramada Inn every year, even though I now can afford a condo. I know how scared and nervous I was in 1981. As a veteran I like to sit around in the lobby and talk with the young guys, mostly the Dominican kids who are experiencing those same feelings. It's important to have somebody to set you straight, tell you how to act.

John Mayberry, the Blue Jay captain and top home-run hitter who played first base most of the time, was probably the nicest of any of the new people I met that spring. Big John showed me the ropes. He'd say, "Bell, you're not in the minors now. Bell, you've got to do things right." He'd tell me how important it was to show up on time. He pointed out when I was doing something wrong, when I was getting a swelled head. I admit my head was pretty large my first year but I always listened to whatever Big John said.

As young and inexperienced as I was then, it was easy to tell the veterans from the rookies, even on a team with few established stars. You could tell the big-leaguers just by the way they carried themselves, the way they'd get all over each other, rib each other with no mercy. The rookies, me included, didn't say too much and just tried not to make any embarrassing mistakes.

Lloyd Moseby, who had played against me for Medicine Hat in 1978 when I broke in with Helena, was in camp but he had already played a full year in the majors. On most teams he'd probably have spent another year in the minors, but in Toronto they figured he could learn on the job since the team wasn't going anywhere. Jesse Barfield was there too. Jesse had played at Knoxville Double A the year before, so he was a longshot to make the club. The three of us weren't close that spring. We were all outfielders looking for jobs, so we had the same goals, but you don't share your fears with people who might have the same fears. We had a few guys over 30 years of age: Mayberry, infielder Ken Macha, outfielder Rick Bosetti, pitchers Mike Barlow and Mike Willis, and Otto Velez, the designated hitter. So there were these older guys and the young guys who were green like Lloyd, Damo Garcia, Willie Upshaw and myself. Watching Willie you could tell for sure he was going to be a major-leaguer and not just for a season or two. He was awesome, smooth around the base, and at the plate he could pull the ball to right field.

We started taking batting practice against our own pitchers and this was tough. Outside of that exhibition game in Reading, when I faced a couple of Phillie pitchers — and got hurt — this was the first time I had ever faced a major-league pitcher. Jim Clancy was the first Blue Jay pitcher I hit against and I was impressed. Jim was a big, tall right-hander whose ball moved pretty good. After practice I told Alfredo what I thought and he said, "He's not even in shape yet, wait another week." But the guy who gave me the most trouble was Mike Barlow, another tall righty who threw hard. I mean he used to eat my hands — he was always jamming me with inside pitches. I'd hit the ball about two inches above where I was holding the bat and some- times I could still feel the tingles and shivers up to my elbows the next morning. At that time I weighed about 176 so I wasn't used to hard fastballs, inside. But if you're going to make it in the big leagues you have to learn to handle that inside pitch.

Bob Bailor, who played a lot in 1980, had been traded to the Mets in the off-season but there were plenty of outfielders in camp and there was plenty of competition for jobs. In addition to the young guys, there were veterans Barry Bonnell, Rick Bosetti and Al Woods. Apart from Jesse and myself, they had all played in 1980, so I had my work cut out for me. I had a pretty good spring. Pat Gillick and Bobby Mattick, the manager, told me there wasn't any pressure on me and they were going to keep me with the team. Jesse Barfield was sent down to Knoxville, but I knew he'd be back soon.

After six weeks in Dunedin, we flew from Tampa to Detroit to start the season and then we went home to open against the New York Yankees. I was excited when I walked into Exhibition Stadium that first day. There were numbers over the lockers that matched the uniform numbers and there was my number 11 hanging beside number four — Alfredo Griffin's.

After I left the clubhouse, I took one look at Exhibition Stadium and shook my head. Alfredo and Damo had tried to explain to me what it looked like, but somehow this wasn't what I thought a major- league park should look like. It was a strange-looking place. I had been in a lot of ballparks, but I had never seen a ballpark like this. It was like one day someone walked into the football stadium and said, "Hey! Let's build a baseball stadium over in the corner there." I had some good experiences at Exhibition Stadium, but the first time I saw it I just shook my head. The truth is, though, I wouldn't have cared if we played our games on a sandlot. I was in the big leagues: big-league travel, big-league money. And the only buses we rode were from the airport to the posh hotels where we stayed.

In those days, the Blue Jays were tight financially and to save money they flew mostly commercial flights. When we did charter, as often as not it was a prop plane. If that happened today, the players would be all over the front office. But at the time it was exciting. Still, those commercial flights could be a pain in the butt. Almost every time the pilot would come on and say, "We'd like to welcome the Toronto Blue Jays aboard." Then, for the rest of the flight, the other passengers would be asking for autographs, first for themselves, then for a friend and then for a friend of a friend. Some guys complained but I didn't mind. Nobody knew George Bell from George Burns in those days.

There were so many things I was impressed with that first year: little things like all the new balls we had for each game. The balls we used in batting practice in the majors were better than the balls we used during games in the minors. There were four or five clubhouse kids in every park who would get you anything you wanted — sanitary hose, pine tar, a new bat. Then there were big things like the airplanes, free membership in a fitness club, food in the clubhouse after games, and free stuff that companies would give us: shoes, bats and gloves. At that time the ball club gave us $42.50 a day for meal money. In Reading the year before, I got nine dollars.

April 9 was my first major-league game. I pinch ran for John Mayberry in the eighth and finished up in left field as manager Bobby Mattick made a switch. In our eleventh game of the season, April 21, I had my first major-league at bat and grounded out. But the next day, Mattick put me in the starting lineup and I hit a double into the corner of Exhibition Stadium against Milwaukee's Mike Caldwell. The pitch was a low slider. I've hit quite a few since then but that's one I won't forget. May 2 we were at Memorial Stadium in Baltimore when I hit my first major-league home run. Lefty Scotty MacGregor threw me a fastball and I smacked it over the left-field wall. I knew the moment the ball left the bat that it had a chance. When I got to the dugout Big John Mayberry said, "That was the first." And I said, "Big John, I know it was my first. I'm not stupid." And Big John said, "No, Bell, that was the first, the first of many you're going to hit for this team." I have a lot of souvenirs at home, but I don't have the ball from either my first hit or my first homer. I don't care. What's important is the pride I felt when Big John said those words to me.

If Big John showed me how to act as a rookie, it was Alfredo Griffin who explained the game: this guy was a fastball pitcher, this pitcher never throws a fastball when he's behind in the count, certain umpires have big strike zones and I should do whatMattick told me. I learned a lot about the major leagues from Alfredo, including how to take care of my money. Alfredo taught me that the more I earned, the more I had to be careful. I couldn't buy something in every store we passed when we were out of town. A lot of players were like that. For instance, Jesse Barfield was always buying those tiny portable TVs to watch on the plane.

Alfredo was like a big brother when I arrived in Toronto with the Blue Jays. On of the things I appreciate about Alfredo is that he's a clear thinker. Even when I'm wrong and I try to prove to him that I'm right, Alfredo is still with me. A few times I've proved he was wrong, but we never get mad at each other.

In May I played a lot in left field and had a five-game hitting streak. I had never played in left field before and I found it more difficult than right. In right you usually have a better angle on the ball because not too many left-handed hitters have power to left field. I always found there were more right-handed hitters with power to right field.

In my first days with the Jays some opposition players really stood out for me. I particularly remember watching Rickey Henderson, Dwayne Murphy and Tony Armas, the Oakland A's outfielders. I used to be envious of those guys; they were the best. You name it, they could do it: hit, run, hit for power, throw and field. When we went to Texas in June, I saw Al Oliver for the first time. The way he hit the ball was special. He'd always been kind of a hero to me and he was still playing with Texas when I broke in. That's when I saw what type of hitter he really was — line drive, line drive, line drive all the time. The next year he went over to the Montreal Expos and won the batting championship.

Two months into the season, even though the team was on a pace to lose more games than ever in its history, the novelty of playing in the big leagues hadn't worn off for me. Things were going along all right but I kept hearing guys talking about whether we would strike or wouldn't strike. On June 11 at Exhibition Stadium, Alfredo Griffin called me over after Kansas City beat us 10-5 and told me that all the major-league players were going on strike unless an agreement was reached by midnight. During the game, when the Royals were scoring runs, the Toronto fans were chanting "Strike! Strike!" They had seen enough of us.

A few days after the agreement between the owners and the Players Association was reached, the Blue Jays got together at Exhibition Stadium for several days of workouts. That's when I had my first fight with Jimy Williams, the third-base coach at the time. Even that far back Jimy and I had a lot of problems not too many people knew about.

As third-base coach, part of Jimy's job was to hit ground balls to the outfielders so that we could make throws to the bases. One day, before play resumed, Al Woods, Barry Bonnell and I were in left field at Exhibition Stadium working out, fielding ground balls and making our throws. Any time Jimy hit a ball down the left-field line, a long way from where we were standing, neither Al nor Barry would make a move to go after it. They wanted George the rookie to chase the ball. They were both in their fifth year in the majors and they figured they'd let me do all the work. I told them we should be taking turns getting the damn ball, the way it was done on any other team I'd been with. They ignored me. Jimy hit another towards the line and I ran for it. Then another. Then another. I was running all over the field while the other guys took it easy.

Finally I'd had enough. The next time Jimy hit one down the line, neither Al nor Barry went after it and they looked at me as usual, but I didn't go after the ball. When I stopped, Jimy got angry. He thought rookies were supposed to take crap like that. He glared at me and yelled something I couldn't hear. Then he walked back to home plate and that was the end of outfield practice. He started hitting ground balls to the infielders.

One impression which hit me right away my first year was how strange the fans can be. They were treating me well, but they were booing my friend Alfredo. Danny Ainge was with the team that year. Ainge was a baseball player back then and now he's a basketball player with the Sacramento Kings. He made $200 000, which was a lot back then. He never hit the ball, but the fans never booed him. Alfredo Griffin was a much better ballplayer for the Blue Jays, yet Toronto fans booed Alfredo a lot in '81 because he wasn't doing well at the plate.

In '79 Alfredo had been the first American League Rookie of the Year the Blue Jays ever had. That year he hit .287, then .254 and in '81 he was struggling in the .220s. Still he was making all the plays in the field. Despite all that, despite all he had done for the organization, the fans were booing him. I think the colour of his skin had something to do with it. Otherwise how can you explain that some of the fans would get on Alfredo but they would leave Ainge alone? Alfredo finished with a .209 batting average. In August, Ainge quit baseball and went to play for the Boston Celtics.

September 3 was a special night, though no one knew it at the time. We were in Chicago to play the White Sox. The club had called up Jesse Barfield when the rosters expanded. That night I started in left, Lloyd Moseby in centre and Jesse in right. That was the first time the three of us had started a game together. We were all going to turn 22 that fall — three birthdays within two weeks.

I had hit .310 in August and I had homers off Geoff Zahn of the Angels and Chicago's Britt Burns, but I didn't get a lot of starts after Jesse arrived. Mattick called me in and said that from now on I was his number-one designated hitter. That got me down. I had gone from being a right fielder to a left fielder and now I was a DH. Although my normal position was right field, the whole organization thought Jesse would be a better player than I was. And though I was Mattick's "number one DH" I wasn't playing every game. They were platooning me.

I remember one game against the A's in Oakland — one of my starts as the designated hitter — I was batting ninth. Anyway we scored a lot of runs in the first inning and knocked out their left-handed starter. In the second inning when it came to my turn at bat, they had a right-hander on the mound. What did Mattick do? He sent up Al Woods to pinch-hit for me. I was in the game, but never had an at bat. I was pretty upset. Even more so when we lost.

In that same series against the A's I had problems with another team for the first time in the majors. Looking back, it seems funny to me, but it didn't at the time. Billy Martin was managing Oakland then. We were leading 1-0 in the fifth inning when Jim Clancy gave up a single to centre fielder Tony Armas, and then third baseman Wayne Gross walked. A guy named Keith Drumright, who played second base, hit what looked like a routine double-play ball. Garth Iorg fielded it, tagged Gross and was set to throw to first for the double play, but Gross really hammered Garth. He nearly knocked the little Monster onto the outfield grass. (Somebody had nicknamed Garth "Monster" because the name Garth Iorg sounded like a monster's name.) We only got one out and the batter was safe. A lot of our guys, especially Alfredo, thought interference should have been called, but the umpires disagreed.

Mike Heath, the Oakland catcher, was next up and he hit one of those little rollers to short. A routine play for Alfredo, but the ball took a tricky hop on the grass and he couldn't come up with it. The A's scored a run and the scorer gave Alfredo an error. Then Dave McKay squeezed in another run which put Heath on second base. That's when we tried to work a pick-off play on Heath as he led off second, and that's when the trouble began. Heath had a fair-sized lead, so Alfredo cut in behind him and Clancy turned and threw to the bag. Alfredo slapped the tag onHeath, who had beaten the throw, but Heath thought the tag was too hard. Heath told Alfredo not to slap the tag on him like that again. Next pitch Alfredo put on the same play and the same thing happened. He tagged him just as hard. You could see Heath was angry, Alfredo too — I have seldom seen Alfredo so mad. They started arguing and Heath tried to lift Alfredo up to throw him down on the ground.

When this happened, Alfredo gave him a combination, a one-two, right in the face. Bam, bam! Just like Roberto Duran. Then Heath went after Alfredo, and that was enough for me. You don't do that to my best friend. No way. When that happened I was already out of the dugout. I wasn't playing, so I ran onto the field and threw a punch at Heath, who was now just one of several guys in a big pile between third base and the pitching mound. When the umpires separated the players, everyone was screaming insults. The brawl ended with a lot of threats. Somebody had bumped Jesse Barfield and, even though the fight was over, he was one of the guys who wanted to fight again. Here was Jesse, who seldom even raised his voice, yelling at one of the Oakland players.

The next thing I heard was Billy Martin hollering at Jesse, but what he was yelling was funny. Martin was screaming at Jesse as loud as he could: "Hey, Bell, you no-good, cocky Puerto Rican, you better straighten out your act if you plan on staying in the big leagues. If you don't I'll come over there and clean your clock myself. Don't think I'm kidding." I couldn't help but laugh. This was unbelievable. It was almost like watching are play on the TV. Here was this old guy so angry at me he's threatening to punch my lights out — except he was yelling at the wrong guy. He didn't know who I was. I was standing 10 feet away and I could hear every word he was yelling at Jesse. When everyone began to return to their positions and to the dugouts, I walked over to Martin and said, "I'm George Bell, No. 11. I'm not Puerto Rican. I'm Dominican. Remember my number because I'm going to be in the big leagues for a while." Later, when Martin managed the Yankees he knew the difference between Jesse Barfield and me.

I finished the year with a .233 batting average. I had five homers and 12 runs batted in, which was okay for only 163 at bats in 60 games. Because of the strike we played a split season, just like in Spartanburg in 1979. Our overall record was 37-69, but we were last in both halves. Outside of rookie league, this was the first losing ball club I'd ever played on. That's counting winter ball too.

When I went home people told me I should be pleased with my first year, but I was discouraged. It was obvious they thought a lot more of Jesse Barfield than they did of me. I think they thought he was about three or four steps ahead of me. We were the two rookies who played the most that year, so the comparison was easy. After he was called up, Jesse started almost every game. He had 95 at bats in September alone, while I had only 68 more than that in four months. I was thinking about quitting baseball and getting another job. But the longer I was home, the more I cooled out. Randy Hendricks told me things would work out. Alfredo said the same.

In November, Maria and I were married. I knew Maria was going to be good for me. We didn't really have a big wedding, just our families, including my three brothers, my sister, my mom and dad. Maria had her mother and father there and her first cousin, Rafael Ramirez, who first introduced us and who was now playing with the Atlanta Braves. I didn't want to get married until January, after our Dominican League season was over, but Maria wanted to marry sooner so we had a big fight. It wasn't our first and it certainly wasn't our last. I didn't know who to talk to for advice, but eventually I had a long talk with an old high school friend, Hireberto Rodriguez. He's a lawyer in San Pedro and he said, "You're going to get married anyway, right? Move it up a couple of months, make her happy." Then I went home and told Maria we'd get married the nineteenth. She was pleased, but she wasn't crying or anything. I mean we had been going out for a couple of years. So we pushed ahead our plans. By then Christopher was almost 11 months old.

That winter I played ball again with Escogido. Felipe Alou, who used to play with the San Francisco Giants, was the manager. Escogido was based in Santo Domingo, the capital, so since I was from San Pedro that meant that every time I played in my home town I was booed. They would really get on me, calling me a traitor for playing for another city. It's always that way in the Dominican. The Escogido team owned my contract, so there wasn't anything I could do.

It would be like a hockey player who grew up in Toronto coming into Maple Leaf Gardens playing for the Montreal Canadiens.

I batted .318 with a home run and eight runs batted in. We won the league championship and went to the Caribbean World Series, but they dropped me from the roster when they picked up other players to play against the champions from Mexico, Venezuela and Puerto Rico.

The spring of '82 was the dawn of a new era in the sleepy Florida town that bills itself as "Delightfully Different Dunedin." Former manager Bobby Mattick would look after the minor-league system, while Bobby Cox was the new man who would guide the Jays on the field.

Cox was the key to Phase III for the Toronto team. Roy Hartsfield had looked after the expansion castoffs during Phase I, the first three years (109-, 102- and 107-loss seasons). Bobby Mattick had shepherded the team through Phase II in '80 (67-95) and the '81 strike season (37-69) as prospects emerged onto the Toronto scene. Now it was up to Cox, who had been fired in Atlanta, to take the Jays to the next two levels: contenders and division winners.

Where Hartsfield and Mattick had from day one set an avuncular tone in the clubhouse — caretakers for the motley collection of maybes and neverweres — Cox made no bones about his attitude. He expected victories. There would be no more indulgent pats on the back after a loss. In Cox's vocabulary, "nice try" did not exist. The change in atmosphere was evident from the very first day of the season but Bell would not be a part of it.

My second spring with the Blue Jays I hit the ball pretty good, but it didn't matter. In my four years of pro ball, I had really played only one full season as an everyday player, at Spartanburg, so they decided to send me down to Syracuse. I thought I played well enough to stay with the team and I was pretty upset when Bobby Cox gave me the news. Just as I had figured in the fall, Jesse Barfield made the Opening Day roster with the Blue Jays. They thought more of him than of me. Again I felt like I wanted to go home, and again Randy

Hendricks talked to me and said, "Come on. You have to go out there and play hard."

When I went to the minor-league camp, Jim Beauchamp, who used to play outfield for the Braves, was the Syracuse manager. The two of us didn't get off to a very good start. One day we were playing the Reds' Triple A farm team at Al Lopez Field in Tampa. The pitcher threw me a high pitch, inside. I started to swing, tried to hold up and as I did I took my eye off the ball. I felt the ball hit my bat, but I thought I had fouled the pitch back into the screen. Since I had pulled my head off the pitch, I had no idea where the ball went. In fact, it hit the fat of the bat and dribbled back to the pitcher. I didn't run at all. First thing I knew, they were firing the ball around the infield after the out.

By this time Beauchamp was yelling at me from the third-base coach's box for not running out the ball. He yelled at me all the way back to the dugout and at the end of the inning he came into the dugout and started cussing me. If there was one thing he could do well, it was cuss. I yelled back. I told him I would have run if I had known where the ball was. That was the first time I'd ever had a real blow-up with a manager. After the game we rode the bus back to Englebert Complex in Dunedin. When I was at my locker, one of the clubhouse kids told me to report to the office where all the coaches dressed. I didn't know what to expect. Was this going to be Round Two? Instead, Beauchamp said he was sorry for blowing up. I explained again that I would have run but I had taken my head off the pitch and lost sight of the ball. He apologized, so I said I was sorry too. He knew he was wrong and I knew I was wrong. People might think I never say I'm sorry, but I do apologize. Saying sorry is a chance to show people how you feel inside. A lot of people know they're wrong but won't admit it. After that, Beauchamp and I didn't have any problems. A few days later we flew north to Syracuse to start the International League season.

When we got to Syracuse Jim Beauchamp called me in and told me I had a pretty good chance to be a big-league player someday. Not that year. That season was like a repeat of Reading when I hurt my back, or maybe worse because I thought I was a lot closer to making the majors than I was. Guys have probably had worse seasons than I had at Syracuse, but I can't think of many. I mean some guys get hurt once and are done for the season. I didn't lose the whole year, but I was hurt three times and had to go on the disabled list each time.

I played about 15 games to start the season and felt terrible. The weather was awful, colder than Toronto, or even Helena. I knew I had a problem, but I didn't know what it was. I thought I was cold all the time from the damp, rainy weather, but I had picked up mononucleosis. They placed me on the disabled list April 20.

I was back in the lineup in May, but on June 8 I was down again. I took a hard swing at an inside pitch, and as I did, my left knee locked and I went down in a heap. They operated on my knee and the operation went well but I was on the disabled list until June 30. I had been swinging the bat okay in workouts and now I was ready to make the best of what was left of the season.

Eight days after returning I was on the DL again. My comeback had lasted one plate appearance. We were playing the Columbus Yankees when the pitcher, Lynn McGlothen, who later had some good years with the Cubs, hit me on purpose. The poor guy was killed in a car accident a few years later, but at the time I was mad enough to go after him with a bat. The only reason I didn't charge the mound is half my face had been caved in. The ball hit me in the lip below the nose, and my jaw was fractured. McGlothen told a couple of American players, who told me later, that he was throwing at me because he thought I was cocky.

I didn't think I was cocky then and I don't think I am now. But if cocky is trying to do your job and help your team win, maybe I am. I try to do my job 100 percent of the time whenever I'm at bat but pitchers don't like that. When a pitcher sees a guy drive one of his pitches down the left-field line with the bases loaded, he doesn't like that guy at all. I had never hit a home run off McGlothen, but I'd had a base hit up the middle to score a run in '81 and knock him out of the game when he was pitching for the Chicago White Sox. Some of our guys told me he never liked me after that. Obviously he remembered.

I saw a lot of good ballplayers that season — I can't say I played against them, but I saw them — and the one I remember most is Don

Mattingly. Mattingly was playing for Columbus and you could tell he was going to be good. He was playing some in the outfield and some at first, but first base was his position. He was hitting line drives off the walls. He wasn't a big home-run hitter yet, but he hit the heck out of Syracuse pitching, just like he does against the Blue Jays today.

My happiest day in Syracuse came June 14 when Maria had Georgie, our second son. This time I was in the delivery room when Maria was giving birth. Since Georgie was born in Syracuse I guess he could become an American citizen, but I hope he'll grow up to be a Dominican like me. Because of the injuries and because we had something new, something special to show my dad and mom, we were in a rush to get home. Now Maria and I had two sons, just like my dad and mom when they started their family.

I had played in only 37 games and finished the year hitting only .200 with three homers and 19 RBIs. I had as many homers as I did turns on the disabled list. Once again I thought I was finished with baseball. The only good news was that I was able to spend a lot of time playing with the two children and more time with Maria than in other years because the injuries kept me from playing winter ball.

In spring training at the Jays' camp in Dunedin in March 1983 there was as much competition as in 1981 and 1982. Besides Jesse Barfield, Lloyd Moseby, myself, Barry Bonnell and Mitch Webster, there were two new outfielders, Dave Collins and Hosken Powell. I figured whoever had the most hits would play and I had a pretty good spring, but they sent Webster and me down again. That year Lloyd played every day in centre, Collins split time with Jesse in right, and Bonnell started in left. Powell was used as a reserve outfielder and pinch-hitter.

This time, I wasn't upset. I wasn't happy, but I knew that with all my injuries the year before I had to prove myself all over again. First thing Jim Beauchamp did when we got to Syracuse was call me into the office. He said, "I want you to play hard because you're one guy here with the tools to go up to Toronto and help out the big team. You have to be ready because the first chance they get they'll call you up." As much as I wanted his words to come true, I didn't have a very good April or May. I was still recovering, getting back in shape.

A lot of guys might have been playing well for the Chiefs, including a young lefty named Jimmy Key, a control pitcher, who could zip a fastball inside when he needed to. But I wasn't. Near the end of May I was hitting only about .225 with four homers when the Blue Jays sent Epy Guerrero to see me. Epy and I had a long talk. He said the Blue Jays were worried about the way I was playing and they wanted him to find out what my problem was. I told him I didn't have any problem. I just wasn't hitting very well. Epy told me I had to work harder and become more serious. He said to treat the start of June like the start of the season.

Right after that, I got hot as a pistol. I had a great month, hitting 10 homers, driving in 21 runs, batting .303 and being named the player of the month. It's hard to explain, but the little pep talk I received from Epy made a big difference. The right man said the right words at the right time. Now I figured the call would come soon, and it did: we were in Rochester July 11 and Jim Beauchamp called me in. "Hope you're ready, because you're going up to the big club," he told me. To make room for me the Blue Jays wanted to send down Hosken Powell, but he wouldn't report to Triple A so they had to place him on waivers and they lost him to another team. It wasn't until about three years later that Epy told me that if I hadn't picked up my average they were going to demote me to Knoxville Double A. That would have been the end; I would have quit for sure. That's how close I came.

So, instead of being out of baseball I was back in Toronto. Only this was a better ball club than in 1981. I remember that first year you could look around the clubhouse and see only three real pitchers: Dave Stieb, Jim Clancy and Luis Leal. Now we had Doyle Alexander, Jim Acker, and a hard-throwing right-hander named Jim Gott. Most of the older guys were gone, and the green guys had changed colours: they'd become veterans. The team was more mature. Jesse was on his way to 27 homers, the same as Willie Upshaw, who also wound up with 104 RBIS. Ernie Whitt and Buck Martinez were a strong platoon behind the plate. And Bobby Cox was in charge.

My first game was in Kansas City the next night. Vida Blue was pitching and I remember Lloyd saying that Blue had three World Series rings from when he played with Oakland in 1972-74. First time up I hit a double off the top of the left-field fence. Later I hit another one to almost the exact same spot — except it was about 10 feet higher — for a home run. That was a good way to start. I wanted to do well right away to show Coxie he could have confidence in me. I knew some guys came up, went two or three games without a hit, then started to press and the next thing they knew they had a giant-sized 0-for-20-something streak going. In the same game Barry Bonnell, Buck Martinez and Dave Collins all homered and we beat the Royals 9-6.

When I first came up from Syracuse one guy really gave me a hard time: Cliff Johnson. He tried to train me the way he was, but nobody can do that to me. I'm not going to sit there and listen to bull. Johnson used to call me stupid, tell me I was an idiot. If I'd had three hits he'd give me hell for popping up in my last at bat.

One of his favourite tricks was to come up and punch me in the shoulder, hard. He thought that was funny. I quit doing that back in high school. Another thing he really thought funny was to hit you hard in the shin, right on the bone, with a bat. Once I hit him back just as hard and he got pissed off. He would sneak up by the batting cage while you were working on your swing or paying attention so that you didn't miss your turn, and hit you. But I didn't let him get to me. It was fun just being on the team. We were playing well under Coxie, we had a respectable record and for the first time we had a shot to win it all.

On August 23 we beat the first-place Orioles 9-3 and we were only a game and a half behind. The next day we were leading into the ninth but our bullpen couldn't hold them off and they tied the score 3-3. The only good thing for us was that Joe Altobelli, who was managing the Orioles, had pinch hit for both of his catchers, Rick Dempsey and Joe Nolan, so he had to use little Lenny Sakata, an infielder, behind the plate. Sakata looked funny wearing Dempsey's equipment, which came up past his knees. Even some of the Oriole guys were laughing when Sakata went out to talk to his pitcher, big Tim Stoddard, at the beginning of the tenth.

First up for us was Cliff Johnson, who homered off Stoddard to put us ahead 4-3. Then Barry Bonnell singled and Dave Collins came to the plate. Now Altobelli brought in Tippy Martinez, a left-hander. Bonnell took a bit of a lead, Martinez threw over to first baseman Eddie Murray and picked him off, just like that. But Collins walked to bring up Willie Upshaw. So it was one out and a man on first. John Sullivan, our first-base coach, called Collins over and told him to be careful, not to take too big a lead. But Collins was really pumped up, figuring he could steal the base easy, and Martinez went and picked him off too. Well, now they're laughing so hard in the Oriole dugout that they were almost falling off the bench. But Willie singled and Coxie was yelling from the dugout, "Stay on the damn bag." Where I was sitting on the bench you could hear Sully shouting at Willie not to take too big a lead. Martinez came set, paused and fired to first, picking off Willie too! I couldn't believe it. I'd never seen that before, not even in my dad's factory league. Our guys were itching to run so much they couldn't hold close enough.

Still, we were up a run when Joey McLaughlin came on to try to save the game in the bottom of the tenth. But Joey gave up a homer to Cal Ripken that tied the score and then he walked Eddie Murray and John Shelby, so Coxie went to Randy Moffitt. Then little Lenny Sakata hit a three-run homer and it was all over. We weren't laughing at him now. What a night! There have been dropped fly balls and booted ground balls, but I think that was one of the most embarrassing moments in the history of the Blue Jays.

It was also the first of three straight losses in 10 innings, the next night in Baltimore and the game after that in Detroit. And we never recovered. Like all first-timers we learned we had to pay our dues. In early September we were well back of the Orioles and on September 21 we were eliminated.

In 1983, we just didn't have the bullpen that other teams did. Joey McLaughlin was a pitcher with good stuff, but he was different with the game on the line. I don't know why. Some guys, like Tom

Henke, really get into it when it counts: they get better. With McLaughlin though, you never knew what was going to happen. Usually he was wild: walk, wild pitch and then he would be hurt bad by one base hit.

I finished the year batting .268 with two homers and 17 RBIs in 39 games. I thought I might win a regular job in1984. I'd gone back to Syracuse, stayed injury-free like they wanted, and hit the ball.

When I went home for winter ball I was traded from Escogido to the La Romana Azucareos, about 45 minutes east of San Pedro. That meant I was booed in Santo Domingo, where I used to play for Escogido, and San Pedro, my home town too. So getting booed is definitely nothing new for me and I had my best year of winter ball ever. I batted .316 with 10 homers and 40 RBIs. The 10 homers tied the league record for the three-month Dominican League season. The only other hitter to have 10 homers was Winston Llenas, later a coach with the Jays. We won the league and went to the Caribbean World Series in Puerto Rico and I hit .450 with three homers. After that season of winter ball I told my Maria she wouldn't be having any more babies in Syracuse.

The 1983 season, Bobby Cox's second as manager, marked the first time in franchise history that the team had finished with a winning record (15 games over .500). In the process the Toronto ball club with the birds on their caps became the media darlings of North America. Who were these guys anyway? A converted outfielder, Dave Stieb, went 17-12 on the mound; a player scooped from the major-league draft, Willie Upshaw, drove in 104 runs.

Right from the start the Blue Jays accelerated the building of their talent pool by digging in deep into the Caribbean, signing one Dominican prospect after another and continuing to place an emphasis on the major-league draft each December. In addition to Bell and Upshaw, by 1983 this had brought the organization keepers like Jim Gott (December, '81), Jim Acker ('82) and Kelly Gruber ('83). Meanwhile the Seattle Mariners, Toronto's expansion cousins, stuck with the amateur draft, selecting collegians and high-schoolers each June and January, and waiting patiently. They are still waiting,

*having never posted a winning record. In this their fourteenth season
of operation, the Mariners have had three different owners, six
general managers and 10 dugout generals.*

*By the end of 1983 the Blue Jays' two-pronged strategy was
finally beginning to pay off as Willie Upshaw had now supplanted
veteran John Mayberry at first base. George Bell was clearly going
places with his quick bat. And a young shortstop named Tony
Fernandez was pushing at his countryman Alfredo Griffin. The
glaring weakness was the lack of a stopper. While Joey McLaughlin
struggled, Randy Moffitt, a journeyman reliever, brother of tennis
star Billie Jean King, led the club with 10 saves.*

*After failing to land an established closer at the winter meetings
in Nashville, on January 10, they settled on free agent Dennis Lamp
for $3 million over five years. In the second half of 1983 Lamp had
saved 15 games for the White Sox. With the Jays' biggest hole
supposedly patched, off-season pundits immediately began selecting
the Blue Jays as the team to beat in 1984 in the American League East.*

I hit .448 in Dunedin in 1984. Before we left Coxie explained the
way things were going to be in the outfield: Lloyd Moseby would be
in centre and I would play every day with Jesse Barfield and Dave
Collins platooning. Except it wasn't an ordinary platoon. When
Jesse played I would start in left field, but when Collins played I
would be in right. Jesse had more experience but he had been batting
against left-handers only. So for the first time since Spartanburg I was
back at my old spot in right field — at least some of the time. Rick
Leach, who'd been brought up from Syracuse, was the extra
outfielder.

When Coxie was managing, everything was glorious. Under
Coxie I changed from a kid to a grown man. He could communicate
with everyone. He showed the players respect and demanded the
same. He showed confidence in me and he also disciplined me. I used
to be crazy in the dugout sometimes after I would strike out or hit a
line drive real hard and the shortstop would make a hell of a play.
Coxie would calm me down. "Next time you do that, Georgie, I'm
fining you $100," he would say the following day during batting

practice. But he'd wait until there wasn't anyone else around before he said anything.

No, I didn't have any trouble with Coxie, but I knew I was going to have trouble with Jimy Williams again and I did. Jimy and I hadn't had any arguments since '81 — of course I had been in Syracuse for most of the time. Things went along okay for the first couple of months of the season. Then one night in June, at Exhibition Stadium, I was in right field taking outfield practice. As usual Jimy was using his fungo bat, hitting the balls to all the outfielders one by one. No problem until he started hitting every ball down the right-field line to me. When I was in left, I didn't mind him hitting the ball down the line. In fact, I liked having the ball hit there since otherwise the throw to second was too easy. But Jimy was hitting two-hoppers down the right-field line when it was time to throw to third base. Now right field to third base compared to left field to second or third is a much longer, more difficult throw. No one's going to make a good throw on a ball like that. Even Jesse with that rocket arm of his had trouble throwing people out at third on balls along the right-field line. So the more Jimy hit the ball down the line, the more annoyed I got.

Finally I got tired of running all the way over to the line and making such a long throw, so I let one of the balls he hit go all the way to the wall. When Jimy saw that, he just stopped hitting to me. From then on, he just hit balls to left and centre. Fine, I said to myself, if he's not going to hit me any balls there isn't any reason for me to stand around. So I walked in from right field. Then all hell broke loose.

When we got inside the clubhouse, Jimy went crazy. He was like a madman. He said, "You have to get to that ball, go chase it down. If you don't make the original play, run out to the wall and get the ball." He was screaming at me in front of all the other players. Jimy kicked the cart we put the dirty uniforms in and knocked it over. He screamed, so I screamed back, "I don't care what you say, Jimy," and I started cussing him in Spanish *"No joda! Cono!"* Then he called me a "No-good, lazy fucker." I walked away and players just shook their heads. I stayed away from him for a few days. Coxie never mentioned a word to me, although, being the manager, he knew what had happened. You can't keep many secrets in a clubhouse. But that was the way Coxie was, he knew enough to leave me alone.

That spring we were playing pretty good, but not as good as the Tigers' who started 35-5. When we finally met Detroit for the first time — on June 4, the start of a four-game series — we had a 34-15 record and were only three and a half games out of first place. The game was on ABC's Monday Night Baseball, one of the few times the Blue Jays had been on coast-to-coast in the United States. Howard Cosell was there, but he spent all his time talking to Detroit manager Sparky Anderson. Willie hit a homer in the second and I hit a two-run homer in the seventh to put us up 3-0. Then, in the bottom of the seventh, everything came apart. Dave Stieb hit Chet Lemon with a pitch, Dave Bergman got a single and Howard Johnson hit a three-run homer to tie the game. Jimmy Key, who was a rookie reliever that year, pitched out of a jam in the ninth to get us to extra innings, then found himself in his own jam in the bottom of the tenth.

So Coxie brought in Roy Lee Jackson to face Dave Bergman, and it was one of the best at bats I've ever seen. The Tigers had two on and two out. A single would win it for the Tigers. Jackson threw the first two pitches for strikes. One more and then we were going to the eleventh inning. Bergman fouled off the next four pitches. Then Roy Lee missed with three straight pitches to make the count 3-2. Bergman fouled off two more. At this point he stepped out and, out of the side of his mouth, said to our catcher, Buck Martinez, "Is there a curfew on this game?" Bergman fouled off the next pitch. Then, on Roy Lee's thirteenth pitch, he hit a three-run homer to right. It was a long walk in from the outfield.

We won the next two games, lost on Thursday and left Detroit just as we came in — three and a half games back. But we never got close again.

For me the 1984 season was as memorable for things that happened off the field as on. Late in the year Cliff Johnson was quoted in a newspaper saying that the Blue Jays were being run like a country club, that we weren't dedicated enough and that we didn't have enough mental toughness. The story came out when we were in Minneapolis. Coxie cancelled batting practice that day and called a team meeting.

I couldn't believe it when Coxie started to chew out Cliff in front of everyone. I'd never seen him do this before. At first, Cliff sort of denied saying what he was quoted as saying, and then Coxie hit him with the clincher. "Cliff, were you out late the other night?" The answer was yes. "Dedication?" screamed Coxie, slapping the back of one hand into the open palm of his other hand for emphasis as if he was arguing with an umpire. "You want to talk dedication, Cliff? Who was the guy to miss the workout in Oakland after the All-Star break?" Cliff didn't say a word. Everybody in the room, including Coxie, knew the answer. "You call that dedication?" Coxie shouted. "I don't want any more of this, UNDERSTAND?"

That incident wasn't typical of Coxie's style, confronting a player in front of the rest of the team. That Cliff was one of the senior players didn't matter to Coxie. He'd stepped over the line. He had insulted the manager and the whole team. Cliff was always saying, "The Yankees wouldn't do things this way." Well, Cliff forgot Coxie was once a Yankee too. Unlike some managers, though, Coxie got out all of his built-up emotions and then forgot about the incident. He wasn't the type of guy to hold a grudge. And he didn't treat Cliff any different afterwards.

The only other time I remember Coxie ripping anyone in front of the whole team was earlier that same year with Dave Collins. Collins had gone in as a pinch-runner and didn't hustle so Coxie was upset.

Late in the year I had a long talk with Cecil Cooper, a .300-plus hitter for Milwaukee. I asked him why I had so many problems bringing guys home with men on base. Cecil said there were two things I had to do: concentrate on one particular pitch and show the pitcher I was not too anxious to hit the ball. Let him pitch around you if he wants, he told me, but when you see your pitch, you take a cut at it. After that I became a better situation hitter. I was still a free swinger but now I had a new approach. I concentrated more and it paid off. In pressure situations I was now more likely to hit the ball in the alley or out of the park.

When the 1984 season ended we were 15 games back of Detroit. We had come close but the Tigers were just too strong. In my first full year as an everyday player I played 159 games and batted .292, with 26 homers and 87 runs batted in. I won the Labatt's "Blue" Player of the Year. But in a few days the same sportswriters voted Dave Collins as the Blue Jay player of the year. Collins had a good year, hitting .308 and stealing 60 bases, but he had only two homers and drove in 44 runs.

I heard about this during the off season when I was at home in San Pedro. Some writer — I forget his name — phoned me in the Dominican and asked if I was upset. I said no. He said, "Are you sure?" I said I was sure. So then he asked, "Why do you think Collins won and you didn't?" and I said, "Maybe because I never spoke to you guys." So then the big story was that I was upset at Collins, angry because I didn't win. That was the reason I stopped talking to newspapermen. But I never talked to them anyway — not even in the Dominican. I'd never sit with the media and talk with them the way Jesse Barfield, Ernie Whitt or Collins would. Why talk? They see the game. They're going to write what they see anyway. Two guys I always got along well with and who always treated me fair were Garth Woolsey of the *Toronto Star* and Ken Fidlin of the *Toronto Sun.*

That year my winter-league contract had been traded again, this time to the Licey Tigers, who were based in the capital, Santo Domingo. That meant I was booed in La Romana, where I had played the year before, in my home town of San Pedro and also in Santo Domingo by the Escogido fans. It didn't hurt my play. I batted .295 with five homers and 27 RBIS and we won the Dominican League. Then, at the Caribbean World Series in Mexico, I hit over .400 and we won the whole thing.

As the winter season ended I started thinking about our team for 1985. With Dave Collins gone to Oakland I'd be the everyday left fielder in 1985, Lloyd would be in centre and Jesse would be the everyday right fielder after three years of platooning. My good friend

Alfredo Griffin had been traded to Oakland along with Dave Collins for reliever Bill Caudill, but I knew Tony Fernandez could do the job, taking over for Alfredo. And now we had two ace relievers in Caudill and Gary Lavelle, who'd also been acquired in the off-season. Rance Mulliniks always says, "It doesn't matter how good a team you have for the first seven innings of a game. If you don't have a reliever who can close it out, your team isn't worth a damn." Everyone said Caudill would give us the one piece of the puzzle that was missing. He had saved 86 games in the previous three years.

Mostly though I was thinking about playing without Alfredo. We talked a couple of days after he was traded. He was in real pain. I told him that I felt bad for him, but that he had to go and do well for Oakland. I knew we would remain close even though we would soon be wearing different uniforms. That's the way it is in baseball — you have to get used to losing your best friends.

4

The First Championship

"You know when I came over here in 1982 Pat Gillick told me our outfield would be Jesse Barfield, Lloyd Moseby and George Bell someday. But Barfield wasn't ready, Lloyd struggled and George needed time in the minors. It ended up just like Pat Gillick said."
— *Former Blue Jays manager Bobby Cox*
March 20, 1985

YOU HEAR ABOUT GUYS BEING "GOOD IN THE CLUB-house" but I never really knew what that meant until I met Bill Caudill. I could see that Caudill was a great guy in the locker room long before I considered him one of my friends. He always knew the proper thing to say to a guy who was down and the right thing to say if someone got too smartass. If a guy left a lot of runners on base and had a bad night at the plate, Bill would walk past his locker when no one else was around and whisper, "Tomorrow, tomorrow. I can feel you're going to bust out tomorrow." But if a guy got too smart, Bill always knew how to put him in his place. We'd never had a guy with the Blue Jays as quick as Caudill was.

Caudill had quite a sense of humour. Tony Kubek, the former Yankee shortstop, used to broadcast our games. Once during 1985 spring training, Bill snuck up behind him and soaked him with a bucket of ice-cold water while Tony was doing a TV interview. Tony had said something about Caudill on the air which Caudill hadn't liked. Kubek was soaked from head to toe, but he laughed it off. Kubek could dish it out, but he could take it too.

Garth Iorg, who platooned at third base with Rance Mulliniks, was also a practical joker. Garth was always putting shaving cream in someone's shoes, crawling underneath the card table to set someone's shoe laces on fire or hiding a guy's shoe on getaway day when we didn't have much time.

But Caudill took things a full step further. He'd plan for days. Take what he did to John McLaren, our third-base coach. McLaren is good at throwing batting practice and almost as good at needling people. Freddie McGriff and Cecil Fielder, two good-looking young hitters on the Jays in '86, were a couple of his favourites. He liked to tease them about what they wore to the park. McLaren dresses like he just stepped out of a men's fashion magazine — *GQ* or something.

Anyway, one day we were on the coast playing the California Angels and Caudill came in wearing a new pair of pointed cowboy boots made of alligator skin. Right away McLaren started teasing him about wearing what was left of an endangered species, about the colour of his pants clashing with his boots and saying that the gator's brother was going to show up some night in the hotel, looking for revenge. He kept it up for quite a while, but Bill didn't say a word. He just smiled.

On getaway day a couple of days later, a Sunday afternoon, Caudill snuck up the runway into the clubhouse during the game, took a pair of scissors and cut McLaren's pants off at the knee. After the game everyone was packing and changing at his own locker, but with one eye on McLaren waiting to see his reaction.McLaren came out of the shower, wearing a towel, and started to brush his hair. A few guys were already giggling as he reached for his pants, which Caudill had folded neatly on the hanger in his locker — just the way McLaren would have folded them. Well, John's face turned white as he unfolded his pressed slacks to find a sloppy pair of cut-off shorts. The whole locker room broke up.

There wasn't anything McLaren could do because we were leaving for the plane soon and everyone's suitcases had gone on ahead on the equipment truck. His only solution was to tape the cut-off portion of his pants back on, and that's the way he walked onto the plane. Of course, as soon as we were on the plane everyone went up to ask him where he had bought the "trend-setting" pants. It must have been a long trip home for McLaren, but he took the joke well and the next day Caudill gave him $100 to buy a new pair of slacks.

Caudill wasn't just an asset in the clubhouse, he was an asset on the mound as well, at least when the season began. We opened in Kansas City and got beat by Buddy Black 1-0, but then we came back with 1-0 and 4-3 wins in the next two games — both in 10 innings — and both times Caudill picked up the win. Everything was happening like everyone said it would. In the second win I threw out Willie Wilson at the plate, singled and tripled even though I was limping. On March 26, during spring training, I'd hurt my left knee running up an embankment at Holman Stadium at Vero Beach trying to catch a fly ball hit by Pedro Guerrero of the Dodgers. That was the knee they had taken some cartilage out of years ago when I played for Reading. Before the season started they had to drain my knee of fluid.

Even though I was playing hurt, our bullpen was healthy. When you have a weak bullpen, there is a feeling on the bench and in the field that grows and grows in the late innings when you're ahead. Everybody's thinking: what's going to happen tonight? And sure enough there's a walk, a base hit, another hit and the other guys have tied it up. It affects us in the field, too. I bet if you looked at the stats of teams with bad bullpens you'd find more errors than for teams that have guys coming in throwing strikes. When a pitcher is throwing strikes everyone is into the game. That's how we felt at the beginning of 1985. I can't say we started the season feeling like a bunch of supermen but we knew we had offence, starting pitching and defence, and now we thought we finally had a bullpen to slam the door in the other team's face.

Caudill saved a lot of games for us early in April and May. Even though we got him in a trade for Alfredo, my best friend on the team, the first thing I knew Caudill was one of my closest friends. He finished April with three wins and five saves, but he had two losses and a 6.28 ERA, which he wasn't happy about. He kept telling us he would do better. I'd never seen Bobby Cox so happy. He would still take losses hard but he was more composed than in other seasons. He knew if we got blown out one night, we were going to come right back and win the next close one. We were four games up at the end of May.

The 1985 season was our best year on the field, in the clubhouse and in the dugout. We had a lot of guys pulling together, the right way, under Coxie. A lot of managers get advice from coaches or the front office, but no one told Bobby Cox what to do during the game, on the field or in his office before the game. Coxie would give a player an opportunity to play. If the guy did the job, he left him out there and let him play regularly. If a guy didn't do what he was supposed to — hustle, produce, try to move a runner over — then he was on the bench. Sounds easy, but Coxie took the time to explain what was expected right from the start so there weren't any "What's going on here anyway?" questions.

When a team is going well it is easier for the manager to look like a genius. I remember once Coxie brought in Jim Acker with the bases loaded, to face Boston's Jim Rice and Dwight Evans. Acker, who was only in his second year and wasn't used to pitching in such situations, pitched out of the jam. Maybe Coxie was lucky, or maybe he knew something no one else did, but in 1985 he made a lot of right decisions.

In June we started a 10-game road trip by winning two of three at Yankee Stadium, so on June 12 we were six games ahead. I always enjoy playing against the Yankees because of Don Mattingly. Whenever I get a base hit against the Yankees and I'm standing on first, Mattingly will comment. He might say, "You looked fooled on that and you still hit it." Usually when he said that he was right. Once in a while when we're standing around the batting cage before a game, we'll talk hitting and certain pitchers. I really respect Mattingly's ability. In my opinion he is the toughest out in the league when the game is on the line. He's a competitive guy, plays hard and won't take crap from anyone.

The next stop was Boston. Bruce Kison started the first game. In one at bat Damo Garcia must have fouled off eight or nine pitches, and one of them must have been over a foot outside. All the foul balls were pissing Kison off. Finally Damo singled. Kison stood on the mound and swore at him. A pitcher tries to throw as few pitches as possible and a hitter will do anything to stay alive with two strikes, so Damo was just doing his job, but Kison took it personally. In the end, we lost the game 8-7 but Kison didn't get the win.

The Boston organization's approach to the game is different from that of other teams: it's almost like they don't want to have any Puerto Rican, Dominican or black players. Jim Rice, Oil Can Boyd and Mike Easler were there in 1985, but over the years they haven't had many Latins or blacks. Now, in 1990, they have Ellis Burks; my pal Tony Pena, who signed as a free agent; Luis Rivera; and Carlos Quintana. Tony is from the Dominican, Rivera is Puerto Rican and Quintana is from Venezuela. Maybe they're changing, but I wonder. It was the same with their minor-league clubs. I've never gotten along well with the Red Sox, going all the way back to '80 when I was with Reading and Steve Crawford and I got into that fight. He was with the Bristol Red Sox that year and so was their second baseman in 1985 — Marty Barrett.

Everyone in Boston knew the Red Sox pitchers tried to throw at me. Al Nipper was the worst — he was always knocking me down. So I was ready for trouble when Boston came to town for a four-game series starting Thursday, June 20. Only this time the trouble was Kison.

We won the first game 6-5 and the bad feelings between our teams got worse. On the first pitch of the game Doyle Alexander hit their lead-off man Steve Lyons. Later their starter, Bob Ojeda, hit Damo Garcia. Then Friday night the Red Sox started ragging me. It began in the second inning when I had a pitch I felt I could hit, and just missed, popping it up. I was angry at myself for missing the pitch, so I slammed the bat down in front of the plate and began to run to first in case someone dropped the ball. As I ran along the first-base line, pitcher Mark Clear, Steve Lyons and Bruce Kison screamed insults at me from the Boston dugout. Kison was yelling that he was going to hit me the next time he pitched. After that every time I was at the plate the three of them yelled at me. Since I bat from the right side, I could see into their dugout easily, so I knew who they were. They could yell all they wanted because we beat them 7-2 and I knocked in a run.

The next day, Saturday, the game was in the afternoon. When I was in right field chasing down balls during our warm-up, it started again. This time two of their pitchers, Bob Stanley and Mark Clear, were down the right-field line in foul territory yelling and hooting at me — they wanted to fight right there. But I was getting ready to play a ballgame, so I walked over close to the line and said, "I don't want to fight with you guys. I only want to tell you guys to leave me alone. Let me play my game and quit bothering me." They started laughing at me, but I just headed over towards centre field. In the game they beat us 5-3.

By Sunday the guys on both teams were really angry and now it was Kison's turn to start. It didn't take long for the game to turn nasty. In the second inning Kison threw a pitch at Ernie Whitt's head. Ernie just managed to get out of the way. That upset the whole team. Then in the fourth, with us ahead 2-0, Kison hit me in the middle of the back with a fastball. With all that had gone on the past few days I didn't have to be a detective to know it was intentional. I'd had enough and I charged the mound. When I got there I did something I've been criticized for — I aimed a karate kick at Kison. It hit him in the glove and stomach. I went to karate school for a couple of years in the Dominican so I knew a little about how to defend myself. If someone was going to get hurt it wasn't going to be me. Then I swung at their catcher, Rich Gedman, who had been chasing me and had caught up just as I kicked Kison. Gedman made the mistake of taking off his mask.

By this time, John Sullivan, our first-base coach, was on the scene. He tackled Kison, who was trying to get me when I went after Gedman. Both benches emptied, and there was a lot of pushing and a lot of angry words. The next thing I knew Jim Rice of the Red Sox had lifted me off the ground and was dragging me towards our dugout. I respect Rice a lot because I know he has gone through the same kind of crap with pitchers throwing at him over the years. He calmed me down and walked me all the way back to our dugout. All the time Bob Stanley was screaming at me, "Now we *are* going to start throwing at you."

John Sullivan was on the ground. The scariest place to be is at the bottom of a pileup. First baseman Bill Buckner kicked Sully in the face. When the fight was finally over and the players were back in the dugouts, the umpires kicked me out of the game.

My karate kick had been playing tough, but there's no excuse for what Buckner did — kicking a man in the face while he was lying on the ground. After the game Buckner said, "Sure I kicked him. This is war and the man went after my pitcher." Well, the war was between Kison and George Bell, not Sully and Buckner, but then he probably thinks that was the manly thing to do — a guy 35 years old kicking a man 45 years of age who's lying in the dirt. Sully's ear was cut and his face was burned from being pushed along the artificial turf.

Kison stayed in the game, but not for long. I'd fought back at him one way, and two innings later, with the score 2-0 and the bases loaded, Ernie fought back another way — with his bat. When Kison delivered the pitch Ernie was waiting for, he went down on one knee, like he usually does when he goes after a ball low and inside. He tomahawked the ball to right field, a line drive. Ernie was past first before he saw the ball had cleared the fence. After that I've never seen a noisier home-run trot. He yelled at Kison all the way around the bases, calling him every name he could think of. Ernie was so fired up we were worried about giving him high fives when he reached the dugout. Ernie knows about goals and stats, but he was so into that game he didn't even know he'd hit his first grand slam until Jesse Barfield told him later in the inning. After the game, the writers asked Ernie what he was saying and he said, "Nothing you could print." Needless to say, that game only made the feeling between the two clubs worse.

That wasn't the only time the Blue Jays and Kison had words. Later, when Kison was with the Angels, Lloyd Moseby got a big hit off him. As Lloyd was running to first, Kison stood on the mound screaming like a little kid at Lloyd, "Dickhead, dickhead." No, I'm not apologizing for charging the mound to fight Kison and standing up for my team. If I brought one thing to the Blue Jays when I started playing every day it was the realization that we couldn't be pushed around. I wasn't going to take any bull from the other teams. And what Kison did was bush-league bull.

A lot of pitchers try to intimidate me, but they should know by now they can't. I've been hit so many times that I've gotten used to it. It won't work. And I'm not afraid to go out there and kick somebody's ass. In the same way I give a pitcher respect when he deserves it, when he goes out there and strikes me out with the bases loaded. I don't scream at pitchers when that happens. I drop my hands and go back to the dugout. I'd look like a fool if I screamed at a guy just for doing his job. When a guy like Mike Boddicker strikes me out by changing speeds on me, I don't get mad at him. All I can do is smile as I'm walking back to the dugout. I've been batting against Boddicker since the minors. He got me out when he was at Rochester and when he was with Baltimore. Now he's with Boston and still striking me out. Some nights after he's fanned me Boddicker will smile back or nod. It's like he knows I respect him and he respects me.

There are a lot of successful pitchers who never throw at players. Roger Clemens, for instance, is one of the best in the game, yet he never throws at me. In fact you seldom see the best pitchers hit batters because they know how to pitch. Oh, once in a while, if a guy is getting roughed up or if the other pitcher has hit one of his guys, somebody like Clemens might brush you back, but the good pitchers never ever try to hit you in the head.

I just don't respect those pitchers who are trying to hit me. You have some hitters who play a whole season's games and never get hit with a pitch. So why was George Bell hit with a pitch eight times in 1985 — twice as often as anyone else on the team — and knocked another 10 or 15 times? George Brett, Don Mattingly, Mark McGwire and Jose Canseco don't get thrown at as much as I do.

The best thing about 1985 was the way Jesse, Lloyd and I came together, the year we all turned 26. We were all on the way up and this was the first time we were playing every day in the combination that would last a little more than four years. It soon paid off. Before long we communicated so well when we were on the field that we always seemed to know what the others were doing out there.

For example, when two of us were going for a ball in the gap, we didn't even have to look at each other. Lloyd caught everything he could get to, but if there was a ball in between, he'd try for it low and I'd reach high. That way, if we collided, one glove didn't knock the ball out of the other. Sometimes when we were in the locker room we only had to look at each other and we knew what was going on right away. I mean we could communicate without even speaking. After a game Lloyd might raise his eyebrows, make a funny face and we'd laugh — we'd know he was referring to a fly ball he had misjudged off the bat in the second inning and just barely caught. Jesse might blink his eyes and we knew he was thinking about a ball that he'd lost sight of in the sun and just saw at the last second — Exhibition Stadium was tough on the right fielder. Maybe I'd nod my head over my left shoulder and they knew I had had some real loud fans behind me in left. That's how close we were that season. We concentrated on the game and we were in tune.

The three of us often talked about how to play the hitters: this way when Dave Stieb was pitching, that way when Jim Clancy was pitching. Guys from other teams would come into Exhibition Stadium and they'd have their meetings to go over our team and the scouting report would read: "On a ball hit to right field be careful trying to score from second, because Jesse Barfield is going to throw you out. Be careful if you hit the ball in the gap on a hit-and-run because Lloyd Moseby is going to run down the ball. And on a ball to left don't try for home, because George Bell is going to throw you out." We heard that from a few guys, friends who played for other teams. So that was on our minds — the scouting report for their baserunners.

The first time I ever heard the term "The Best Outfield in Baseball" was in 1981, my rookie season. People were referring to Oakland's Rickey Henderson, Dwayne Murphy and Tony Armas. Now I was hearing it again about Lloyd, Jesse and me. That just made us want to do better. I had 13 assists that year, though I also had 11 errors.

We were in Oakland July 4 when the American League informed me I had to sit out the suspension for kicking Kison in the stomach. Since I couldn't even be in the dugout, I spent the game in the press box. That was an eye-opener. I sat with the Toronto sportswriters, Larry Millson from the *Globe and Mail*, Garth Woolsey from the *Toronto Star* and Ken Fidlin of the *Toronto Sun*. I always thought everyone just sat up there and ate hot dogs, but those guys were either on the telephones or writing the whole game. They were so busy I wound up having to go get them coffee. Some of the Oakland guys worked hard too, but the radio reporters spent most of the time laughing, telling jokes and doing impressions of Howard Cosell. They might as well have been sleeping. Then they'd come into the clubhouse after the game with serious faces, asking the players what happened.

On July 10, just before the All-Star break, we were in Seattle and I saw one of the greatest plays ever. The game was scoreless and Phil Bradley was on second base when Gorman Thomas singled to right field off Tom Filer, who'd just been called up from Syracuse. Jesse Barfield fielded the ball and it beat Bradley home. Buck Martinez caught the ball and turned to make the tag. Bradley kept coming like the football player he used to be, and lowered his shoulder. Buck, tough as nails as always, held onto the ball and Bradley was out, but the ligaments in Buck's ankle were ripped and his leg was twisted under him when he fell.

With Buck lying on the field in pain, everyone began converging on home plate, but time hadn't been called yet, and Thomas, who had gone to second on the throw home, was now starting for third. To my amazement Buck was still into the game. He looked up to see Thomas heading for third, raised himself up and tried to throw Thomas out. The ball slipped out of his hand and came out to me in shallow left. So now Thomas, who had started all of this with an ordinary single to right, took off for home. I threw home, and Buck, who had almost passed out by now, caught the throw and tagged Thomas just as he was going to step onto the plate. Thomas wasn't sliding — he didn't expect a throw home. Heck, no one had even expected a throw to third. So Thomas was out 9-2-7-2 on one of the rarest double plays ever. But Buck was out too — out for the season. I helped the others carry him off the field on a stretcher and went to visit him in the hospital that night after the game.

When Seattle came back to Toronto July 22-23 after the All-Star break, Bill Caudill had his twelfth and thirteenth saves. They'd been a long time coming, his first in 32 days, but they gave him the Blue Jay record for most saves in a season. He looked good in those two games. Then he pitched twice more in the next four days and did all right, but I guess the ball club wasn't happy with his fastball; he was 4-4 with a 3.08 earned run average. On July 28, they called up Tom Henke from Syracuse.

Had Bill lost his job? We'd soon see. Henke had looked good in the spring but some of the guys said he hadn't done well when he'd had his chance with Texas. We were in Baltimore for a four-game series. Coxie ran him out there the first night and he got the win as we beat the Orioles 4-3 in 10 innings. He looked awesome — talk about a hard thrower! Henke threw two scoreless innings and struck out two. Two nights later he got the win again. In the two games he had pitched three innings and hadn't allowed a base hit.

This was the year I really developed into a hitter. Coxie had me hitting third, so I was often batting with men on base, and a lot of guys were helping me. First there was Cito Gaston, our hitting coach, who had joined in 1982 while I was in Syracuse. He always had time and he spoke to me in his low, quiet voice. In the dugout he'd needle me when I missed pitches I should have been able to handle and he'd tell me what he would have done with that pitch when he was playing. When people find out he hit 29 homers for San Diego in 1970 they know they're talking to a teacher who actually played the game. Players from other teams also helped me learn, hitters I admired like Don Mattingly, Cecil Cooper and Don Baylor.

Mattingly and I talked only about hitting, but Baylor and I talked about getting hit. Baylor was with the Yankees that year. I'm still trying to figure out why he allowed himself to get hit by pitches so often. He gave pitchers a good target, by standing close to the plate with those big arms of his over the strike zone. He was tough. I respected him as a player. He told me he didn't mind taking a pitch in the side or in the arm.

When August began we were still in first place but the news-paper writers were all over Damo Garcia. They said he didn't walk enough and they kept advising Coxie he shouldn't be our leadoff hitter. But Coxie stood up for his guys. He told Damo, "You are the king, you're the king no matter what happens. I don't care what the fans say, what the writers write, or what the people say on radio or television. I don't care. You are going to be my leadoff hitter for the season." That's the way Coxie was.

Coxie was good for me too. I was still young and sometimes I'd overreact, throwing my helmet when I'd struck out — that kind of thing. Coxie said that was bush. Once he fined me $500, but not for throwing my helmet. I hit a hard line drive, but as I started running I saw it was right at the third baseman and I stopped. Then the ball went off the third baseman's glove and rolled a few feet away. I was halfway to first and tried to start running again but I was too late. He threw me out. Coxie fined me for not running hard all the way. I don't think I would have beaten the throw, but Coxie was right. Just like he was right chewing out Dave Collins in 1984 for not hustling. Coxie made me promise never to do it again and at the end of the season he gave me my money back, but he said I had to keep my promise.

Coxie was something. If I had played 15 or 16 games in a row and we had a day game after a night game, Bobby would come over to me right after the game and say, "Georgie, go home and relax, have a few *cervezas*, tomorrow you get a day off."

In late August, we were in first place by five games when we went to Comiskey Park in Chicago for a three-game series. Com-iskey is one of my favourite stadiums for hitting and I had just received a new shipment of bats. It turned out they had a lot of pop in them. In the first game of the series, August 23, I homered against Dave Wehrmeister. The ball went onto the roof in left field, over 450 feet away from home plate. The next day I hit a ball into the centre-field bleachers; they measured that one at 484 feet. It turned out I was only the sixth guy in 75 years to hit one that far. Lloyd said, "Hey, Bell, you keep hitting them that far and they'll move you up to the next league." So on Sunday I hit another one onto the roof in left field. This one was against lefty Floyd Bannister. After the game the reporters told me that in the history of Comiskey there have been a total of only 43 roofshots and I was the first one to do it twice in one series. Only Jimmy Foxx and Ted Williams ever hit more than one each.

Before the trading deadline on August 29 we traded three minor leaguers to get Cliff Johnson back from Texas because Pat Gillick and Coxie weren't happy with Jeff Burroughs. I wasn't too thrilled about having Cliff back in our clubhouse. He could hit but he was a bad influence. Soon after he was back he said to me, "Bell, don't think you're going to steal my job as the DH," and I said, "I don't want to be a DH, Cliff. That's a job for lazy people like you." Cliff didn't like that too much — he's a bully and expects to get things his way. Some of the things he did around the clubhouse were just plain stupid. He'd bring the bat boys into the clubhouse and start wrestling, throwing them around — this 230-pound guy wrestling with 15-year-olds. This was his idea of fun.

Tom Henke continued to pitch like a veteran and we were still in first place at the beginning of September. That meant Bill Caudill was sitting on the bench. Bill may have moaned in the papers about not getting the chance to pitch, but he was an upbeat guy in the clubhouse. He hadn't turned out to be the bullpen saviour everyone had predicted but he had saved a lot of games for us earlier and without him we probably wouldn't have been in first place. He never said much about his arm, but I wouldn't be a bit surprised if he had hurt it early in spring training and tried to pitch through it. He wasn't the type to ask to go on the disabled list. Caudill was mostly a fastball, curveball pitcher. His breaking ball stayed flat and was easy to hit, so if the fastball wasn't there you could see that he would be in trouble.

Late in the year my dad came to see me play. That was the first time he'd ever seen me play in a Blue Jay uniform. He enjoyed the game, but after the game he gave me hell for swinging at bad pitches. All my brothers — Jose, Rolando, even Tito, who is now with the Orioles' organization — phone me up after they see the Jays on TV. It's always the same: "Do this" or "Why did you do that?" Soon as I get home the phone is ringing and one of my brothers is on the phone ripping my butt if I strike out or pop up.

Twenty years from now fans will look back at the raw numbers and marvel. The Blue Jays spent 150 days of the 172-day season in first place in the American League East. But this was far from being a cakewalk like it was for the Detroit Tigers in 1984, with manager Sparky Anderson sitting, feet up, his club running on cruise control. The Jays actually staggered to the finish line as all of Toronto, even the odd closet Blue Jay fan in Montreal, most of Canada and sailors at sea held their breath and hoped.

On September 25 and 26 the Jays lost the final two games of their home stand to Boston and then headed to Milwaukee five and a half games up. When they beat the Brewers 13-5 on September 29 they completed a three-game sweep for their ninety-eighth win of the season to stay five and a half games ahead with only six games to play. A piece of cake, not too difficult a hill to climb, and all that. But for these first-timers it suddenly became a mountain, as the Yankees continued to race down the stretch. The Jays were swept in a three-game series in Detroit, losing 6-1, 4-2 and being shut out 2-0 on October 3 in the series finale. Now they were only three games in front. Was this a full-blown September swoon, just what the long-suffering Jay fans secretly expected? In Toronto, the whole city was into it. In the endless banter between anchor persons on TV, the noun "Blue Jays" had been replaced by such terms as "our team" and "we," as in "Can we do it?"

Now it came down to the final three games of the 1985 season against — who else? — the Yankees from New York City, New York, a city so big they had to name it twice, to paraphrase philosopher and football player Big Daddy Liscomb. The Yankees needed three straight wins to force a tie, which would in turn force a playoff on Monday. If not, the Blue Jays would win their first division title. Would the Jays stumble and bumble into second place? Had they come this far to fall just short?

Jimmy Key started for us against Ed Whitson on Friday night and I've never seen the fans so into a game before. There were 47 686 spectators and not one of them was quiet. They cheered as soon as the anthems were over and they cheered every strike Jimmy threw. This wasn't your average Friday night crowd, at least not in left field. Often there are drunks out there booing and yelling at me, but not this time. A friend of mine from Toronto once told me a lot of people in Ontario grew up hating the Yankees because they won so often. These people must all have been at the park that night cheering for us.

The Yankees went ahead in the fifth when Willie Randolph singled, Bobby Meacham doubled and then Rickey Henderson singled, scoring two runs. But we weren't worried, we had lots of time left and, sure enough, in the bottom half of the inning we scored two gift runs. Ernie Whitt was on with a walk, and Damo singled. After a wild pitch Lloyd hit a ball to third baseman Andre Robertson, and he threw it away. So now we were tied 2-2. It stayed that way until the bottom of the eighth.

Lloyd walked and Coxie, who never liked to bunt, had Garth Iorg sacrifice Lloyd to second. Then Lloyd scored on Cliff Johnson's single to give us a 3-2 lead. That was when it started to rain, but the umpires weren't going to call it, not a game that could decide the season. The way I figured it, we had a lead and an advantage — let it rain on their bats. When Coxie brought on Tom Henke for the top of the ninth, I didn't think we could lose. Henk, who started the season facing the Columbus Yankees, looked strong against the New York Yankees that night. He got the first hitter, Mike Pagliarulo, to pop up and the crowd roared. Now we had two outs to go. Next was Willie Randolph. The fans were on their feet cheering every strike. It was as if we were at Yankee Stadium on a sunny fourth of July with Ron Guidry in his prime striking out 18 guys. When Guidry was pitching, as soon as he got to two strikes on a hitter all the fans would stand and clap, wanting strike three. The rain wasn't bothering us or the crowd. The fans were doing Yankee Stadium one better — they were cheering every pitch.

Henke struck out Randolph and we were only one out away. All that stood between us and the AL East title was Butch Wynegar, one of their catchers. Wynegar was hitting .221, with only four homers all year, the last one in June. This was it, we could all feel it. Henke threw strike one and the place went berserk. I looked over at Lloyd in centre and he was dancing like he does when it's really, really cold. Now the guards were getting ready to stop people from running onto the field. "One more, one more," I thought to myself, but if Wynegar was going to hit it, I wanted him to hit it to me. Henk went right after him — he wasn't going to waste a pitch. Wynegar swung and the ball sliced through the rain towards right field. The ball carried and carried and went through the rain for a home run. Tie game! It was his first homer since June. We'd have to win in the bottom of the ninth.

The place went from being as noisy as an airport at five in the afternoon to as quiet as an airport at four in the morning. From all the way out in left field I could hear guys swearing in our dugout. Poor Henk was a little bit shook up and he gave up a single to Bobby Meacham. Then he walked Rickey Henderson. All this happened before the players and the fans had stopped shaking their heads. We were stunned, in shock. Now it was Don Mattingly's turn. Instead of being an out away from winning, we were a base hit away from losing and Mattingly was the guy who could do it.

Coxie brought in lefty Steve Davis to face Mattingly. Davis got Mattingly to pop up to shallow centre and Lloyd ran in to make what looked like a routine catch, but the ball hit off his glove and fell to the ground. I couldn't believe it. If you hit Lloyd a ball like that a thousand times, he'd catch it a thousand times. No one in the stadium could believe it. Now the stadium was even quieter than when Wynegar homered. There was Meacham running around third to score and suddenly we were down 4-3. Dennis Lamp got us out of the inning, but we couldn't score against Dave Righetti in the bottom of the ninth. Game over. Now we had lost four in a row and we were still one win away from the AL East Championship.

When the game was over, Jesse told Henke not to feel bad, he'd save the clincher for us the next day. Later Lloyd said, "I just missed it, it wasn't the first error I've ever made and it won't be the last." He didn't blame the rain, he didn't make any excuses. I was told later that not only was the champagne on ice but it had been brought into the locker room before Wynegar hit his homer. A friend of mine who has an ulcer told me that when Wynegar hit the ball it was as if someone had kicked him in the stomach. Jesse described it best. He said it was like watching a horror movie. Maybe the most surprised of all was Wynegar. He wasn't trying for a homer against Henk, he just wanted to get on base. He later said he just didn't want to be on the field while we were celebrating.

We all got to the park early the next day. Our team felt just the opposite of Wynegar: we all wanted to be on the field when the celebrations started and *everyone* wanted to catch the ball for the final out. We weren't done — we were determined. Not many of our guys had won anything before. The odds were in our favour. We had Doyle Alexander pitching and he was always tough against the Yankees. He wanted to get back at them for releasing him, saying he was washed up. And we all knew we had to win because on Sunday, the final day of the season, the Yankees were going to come back with Phil Niekro, who was going for his three-hundredth career victory.

We wanted to start quickly and erase any doubts from the night before. In the first inning it was obvious everyone was swinging for the fence, we were so pumped up. Cito Gaston kept telling us on the bench just to go for a base hit, not to worry about the homers, not to try to do too much. Cito was talking, but the guys weren't listening. In the bottom of the second, Ernie Whitt homered off right-hander Joe Cowley to put us ahead 1-0. Then with one out in the third, Lloyd came all the way back from being so down the night before, like I knew he would. He homered to right and we were up 2-0. Next at bat was Willie Upshaw and Willie homered too, to make it 3-0. At this point Billy Martin took out Cowley and brought in Bob Shirley. Al Oliver hit a double, Garth Iorg singled and I hit a fly ball off Rich Bordi, deep enough for Oliver to score. We were up by four. We were on our way.

In the fourth, Ken Griffey doubled off Doyle but then Willie Upshaw made a great play at first, diving to steal an extra-base hit away from Mattingly. Griffey went to third on the play and then scored on a single by Dave Winfield to make it 4-1, but Willie's play had kept the Yankees from having a big inning. That was the play of the game, no question.

We got back the Yankee run in our half of the inning when Tony Fernandez doubled and then scored on a single by Damo Garcia. Through the eighth, Doyle put up zeros, scattering four singles and a double. Nine outs to go, then six — we were counting them down. Now to the top of the ninth with Doyle still pitching — three outs to go. The place was going bananas; the fans were on their feet cheering. This time there wasn't going to be any game-tying homer.

First up was Don Mattingly. Mattingly scares me any time during a game but especially during the late innings. I moved back a few extra steps; I didn't want a double over my head. As far as I was concerned he could have a bloop single to left if he wanted it. But Mattingly grounded to Willie Upshaw for the first out. Dave Winfield was next and he popped up. Now the people in the left-field seats were singing, dancing and hugging. Some people were even crying. Then Ron Hassey hit a routine fly towards me in left field. I came in, caught the ball and sank to my knees. I squeezed it so hard I could feel the stitches of the ball through my glove. I'm sure the crowd was cheering but I don't remember. All I knew was I had that ball in the glove and we had finally won. Then I raised both arms towards the heavens. I'm a religious man, not a fanatic, but I was saying: "Thank you" to the Man upstairs.

I was still kneeling when Tony Fernandez reached me. Now I could hear the crowd. Tony and I exchanged high fives. We both hugged and I asked him what he thought was going on in San Pedro right then. We ran into the infield together. What a sight! The fans in the stands were jumping up and down. Our dugout was emptying and for a second or two I could see Damo grabbing Doyle, and Willie coming in to bear hug the two of them: an American, a Latin and a black. It was wonderful. And then all you could see were guys bumping into one another and hats flying off.

I've played ball so long, that I have many good memories and many bad ones. It's difficult to pick the best, but I think when I'm telling my grandchildren about all the thrills I had in baseball, this will be the one I'll tell them first — catching the ball for the final out of the 1985 regular season. I don't have the ball from my first hit in 1981, but I have that 1985 ball in my trophy case in San Pedro. The memories of the whole day — the game, the clubhouse, the party afterwards — will stay with me as long as I live.

I wish I had pictures of the scenes in the clubhouse. Everyone was out of control. It was the first time most of us had won anything but we were quickly learning how to celebrate with champagne, reporters, and TV lights. Talk about sights: Cito Gaston, with tears in his eyes, was lifting Kenny Carson off the ground. Kenny had been the Blue Jay trainer since the team started and Cito was yelling, "We finally made it! We finally made it!" It was one of the few times I've ever heard Cito raise his voice. And Cito deserved so much credit, not just for the outfield, but all the hitters. Cito and Carson were like little kids. Jesse Barfield and my pal Sully were hugging and crying. Dennis Lamp, who had an 11-0 record as a set-up man after struggling the year before as a short reliever, was squirting shaving cream on everything that moved.

The only guy I felt sorry for was Buck Martinez, who had broken his leg in Seattle. Buck was in uniform and soaked in champagne but he wasn't going to be able to play in the postseason because of the injury, which was too bad. We were playing his old team.

When the celebrations were going strong, Willie Randolph, the Yankee second baseman, came into the clubhouse and congratulated all of us. That showed a lot of class. The first guy he went to see was Damo, whose locker was beside mine.

Bill Caudill told everyone to shut up for a second. With Caudill you never knew what was coming next, but he took a champagne bottle, hoisted it and said, "Let's drink a toast to Pudge." That was Caudill's nickname for relief pitcher Gary Lavelle who wasn't there that final weekend because he'd gone to California to have his elbow examined.

About an hour into the celebrations just as things were beginning to calm down a little, the doors opened and in rushed all the wives of the players. By now most of the champagne was gone, so we were spritzing each other with beer. It was difficult to tell whether someone had tears of happiness or just beer running down his cheeks. I know with Paul Beeston, our vice president, it was champagne because I had really soaked him. Beeston and I have always gotten along pretty well. He smokes cigars, I smoke cigars. He teases me, I tease him. He doesn't wear socks, I wear socks. He's down to earth and not a stuffed shirt like you might think big-shot bosses are. When we won I was very happy for him and for Gillick too. I soaked them both.

I remember asking Pedro Guerrero when he came home after the Los Angeles Dodgers won the World Series, what it felt like to win. He said, "It's an impossible feeling to describe. Phone me after you win something and tell me if *you* can describe it." It felt great. I guess that's why in those TV interviews in the dressing room after a World Series or a Super Bowl the word almost everyone uses is "Great." "I feel great." I was so happy for Coxie and Cito and for the fans of Toronto who had seen so many losses. Pedro was right: the feeling is impossible to describe.

The Blue Jays — led by an outfield of Lloyd Moseby (.259 batting average, 18 homers and 70 RBIs), Jesse Barfield (.289, 27, 84) and George Bell (.275, 28, 95) — with dues paid in full during the regular season, were now set to play a best-of-seven series under the microscope of the North American media. Postseason play was a whole new ballgame and the Jays were rookies. By contrast, their opponents, the Kansas City Royals, had played in October five times, only once reaching the World Series, but losing to the Phillies in '80. So postseason experience was on the side of the Royals, managed by that unflappable gentleman, Dick Howser. So were the past-performance charts. Kansas City had won seven of 12 meetings with the Blue Jays during the regular season. Nevertheless after the first two games in Toronto it looked as if all the regular-season records could be thrown out the window.

In Game One, Dave Stieb pitched a five-hitter and the Jays scored twice in the second and three more times in the third to beat Charlie Leibrandt 6-1. In the second game the Jays were down 3-0 early after Willie Wilson homered off Jimmy Key. But by the sixth inning the teams were tied. In the eighth George Bell hit a sacrifice fly to put Toronto ahead 4-3. Kansas City tied the score in the ninth and went ahead in the top of the tenth 5-4. But in the bottom of the tenth, veteran Al Oliver had a two-out, two-run single off Dan Quisenberry to give the Jays a 6-5 victory. The doubters were beginning to sing a different song.

I was upset with what Jimy Williams said after the second win. During the game Jimy was coaching third. Both Tony Fernandez and I came around third to score and both times Jimy threw up his hands for us to stop. I don't know about Tony, whether he had his head down or not, but I saw Jimy all the way and he gave me the sign too late. If I had stopped, they would have thrown me out sliding back into third. After the game I heard a reporter ask Jimy about Tony and myself not stopping and Jimy said, "Guess I'll have to get some Dominican stop signs." Everyone was excited, we'd made a great comeback, we were up 2-0 and Jimy had to say something dumb like that.

We were worried most about George Brett getting untracked. In our team meeting before the playoffs Coxie had told our pitchers he didn't want Brett beating us, no matter what. "Walk him if necessary, but don't, don't ever give him any good pitches," Coxie said. Kansas City didn't have a whole lot of offence besides Brett and our strategy worked for the first two games. But in the third game, in Kansas City, Brett hit two home runs off Doyle Alexander and helped start the winning rally by blooping a single into shallow centre off Jim Clancy in the eighth. The Royals won 6-5 even though we had a 5-2 lead early in the game.

The next day Stieb pitched another great game but we were losing 1-0 until the ninth. Again, Oliver delivered for us, this time a pinch-hit double to bring home two runs. Then Henke closed the door and we were up 3-1. One win was all we needed to be in the World Series.

The feeling on the bench was different before Game Five in Kansas City. We weren't really cocky, but we were inexperienced. We had to win only one, so the feeling was: "So what if we don't win?" That was wrong and we lost our concentration. In the fourth inning the Royals were ahead by two runs when I led off with a single. Then Cliff Johnson hit a single to left, so I headed for third. I thought I beat the throw from Lonnie Smith but umpire Dale Ford called me out. It was a bad call. Everybody knew I was safe: Coxie said I was safe; people who saw the replays said I was safe. And that wasn't the first bad call in the playoffs. Another ump had made a mistake in the second game when Willie Upshaw hit the ball right in front of home plate — the ball went foul and the umpire called it fair. Willie was so sure it was a foul ball he didn't even run. And in the third game Lloyd had made a great shoestring catch in centre field that was ruled a trap, not a catch. Now there was the bad call on me at third. By this time I was fed up. In the end the Royals beat us 2-0.

In the locker room after the game I turned to Lloyd Moseby, who had his locker beside me, and said that I thought the umpires were anti-Dominican, even anti-Canadian. They didn't want a Canadian team in the World Series. What I said was meant just for Lloyd. I meant it half-jokingly, half-seriously. However, one reporter heard what I said and the next thing I knew about 25 reporters were gathered around my locker asking me to "expound" and "explain." I was still mad, so I talked. I pointed out that every TV station I saw in the U.S. was saying that a Canadian team being involved in the World Series would be bad for the ratings. Instead of two markets, they would have only one for their commercials. It might have sounded like sour grapes, but if I feel something I say it. Sometimes I regret it later.

Looking back I don't know if the anti-Dominican and anti-Canadian charges were accurate, but I felt that way at the time. I still think for a Canadian club to make the World Series is going to be tough. You could see that during the 1985 playoffs.

Anyway we came back to Toronto and lost the sixth game, when Brett hit another homer off Doyle to break a tie. Now the pressure was really on. We didn't want to be known as a team that blew it.

The seventh and deciding game at Exhibition Stadium had Bret Saberhagen against Dave Stieb — their ace against our ace. In the sixth inning we were leading 2-1 when the Royals broke the game open. As usual, Brett got it started. He walked with one out and then Stieb hit Hal McRae. With two men on Stieb retired Pat Sheridan, who had homered earlier. Now he was facing Steve Balboni who strikes out a lot, so it looked like Stieb might get out of the jam. Instead he turned up the heat, walking Balboni to load the bases. If I had been managing, as soon as Stieb went to two balls on Balboni I would have taken him out and brought in Clancy. That's one of the few times all year I disagreed with Coxie.

Next Stieb faced Jim Sundberg, their catcher. Sundberg was a lot like Butch Wynegar, having hit .245 and driven in only 35 runs during the season. With two balls, no strikes, Stieb fell behind in the count. Since Stieb didn't want to walk a run in, he threw a "here hit-it" fastball down the middle. I relaxed when I saw the ball off Sundberg's bat. It looked like an easy fly ball to right. I thought, almost everyone thought, that Jesse Barfield would make the catch easily. But at that time of night the ball was carrying pretty good and it hit off the top of the fence for a three-run triple. That was the ball game and the season.

Coming into the locker room that night knowing there wasn't any more baseball to play, that our season had ended when it shouldn't have, was one of the lowest points in my life. We'd come so close. Who knew when we'd get the same chance again? Twelve days before we had all been laughing, drinking and slapping each other on the back when we beat the Yankees. Winning sure beats losing. I'm certain if we're ever up 3-1 again we won't blow it. We learned a lot from the experience.

It's easy to blame someone else when you lose — the umpires, the way Coxie managed (he took a lot of heat for putting Clancy in the bullpen and going with three starters instead of four) but neither of these was the main reason we lost. The bottom line was the Blue Jays. We blew it! We stopped hitting, we left too many men on base. I think we became overconfident. I don't mean one or two guys, but the whole team, myself included — we were up 3-1 with the final two games in our park and we thought we had it made. I hit .321 in

the playoffs and had nine hits, the most on the team, but I drove in
only one run.

In St. Louis on October 21, the day before game three of the 1985
World Series, the Atlanta Braves staged a press conference. In September Braves owner Ted Turner had tried to hire away Blue Jays
manager Bobby Cox, but the Blue Jays had refused Cox permission
to talk. Now, with the Jays' season over, he was allowed to negotiate
— and he had. The press conference was to announce his hiring as
Atlanta's new general manager. When the news reached the Dominican it was not welcomed by at least one resident of San Pedro de
Macoris. But Bell refused to show his disappointment. When asked
by a reporter for a reaction, all he said was, "It's no big deal." Events
would prove otherwise.

As thoughts turned to the approaching 1986 season, Bell was
thinking about his new contract. With three years and 84 days of
service — three years are needed — he was eligible for salary arbitration. And he was in a good bargaining position. In 1985, while
earning $370 000, he'd batted .275 with career highs in home runs
(28), runs batted in (95), and stolen bases (21). Not bad for a former
Dominican factory-league bat boy. The Hendrickses had in mind a
substantial raise for their client, but as the February 1986 hearing date
approached the two sides were still far apart.

The Jays had offered Bell a one-year contract worth $560 000.
Bell and Hendricks had requested $850 000. They were also looking
for a multi-year deal but the Blue Jays weren't interested. Unless a
last-minute agreement was reached both sides were heading into the
hearing room in Chicago.

The salary arbitration process works like this: first, the player's
agent presents all the facts that show why he thinks his client
deserves the amount requested. Then the team defends their figure.
This is a situation almost guaranteed to create bad blood between
team and player. No one wants to sit in a room while some high-
priced lawyer rhymes off every negative stat he can muster, stopping
just short of saying, "In conclusion, sir, this man seated right here
before you today may possibly be the worst ball player in the game."

A couple of days after the initial presentation, both sides rebut the other's case-in-chief, and then give a final summation. The arbitrator announces his decision within one or two days. But he doesn't pick a number out of midair. He carefully considers the presentations and decides on one side or the other. There is no middle ground. And in arbitration the figure is always for a one-year contract without any incentive clauses.

I had no idea what was involved. This was my first arbitration hearing. When you went to Helena, Montana, they didn't have salary arbitration. They just told you when to be there and how much you would be paid. I knew arbitration wasn't going to be much fun. Damo Garcia told me that. The year before he had been upset over all the negative things the Blue Jays had said about him in the hearing room. And Damo had won his case.

A couple of days before the hearing I flew from Santo Domingo to Chicago. Travelling with me was Epy Guerrero, by now a good friend. This was Pat Gillick's idea: Epy's job was to talk to me on the plane, to try to convince me to sign for what the Blue Jays wanted. Some say Epy looks like Manuel Noriega with his slumped-over shoulders and sad, tired eyes. The eyes may be sad but they are sharp when it comes to finding a ball player. Anyway, this trip was really a good joke, something we still kid about years later.

We flew from Santo Domingo to Miami and we didn't have a single drink, but on the Miami to Chicago flight we began downing a few rums. I made sure Epy drank more than I did. By the time we landed, Epy was drunk and he'd never had a chance to talk about my contract. I still tease him about that: "When are we going to talk about my '86 contract?" I ask him. But it wouldn't have mattered if Epy had pressed me because I left all that to Randy.

The weather was cold in Chicago and there was snow on the ground outside the Hyatt Hotel where we were staying. I'd seen snow only a couple of times before. A few years before, when I played in Triple A, we were snowed out in Syracuse and we flew to Toronto for some games at Exhibition Stadium while the Jays were on the road.

We all met at eight o'clock that night in Randy Hendricks' suite. I walked into the room — a two-storey suite with a spiral staircase, beds upstairs and a meeting room on the lower level — and I couldn't believe what was going on. The room was full of smoke from Beeston's big cigar. Randy, David and Alan Hendricks were arguing with Beeston and Gillick. No, arguing is not the best word — they were screaming at each other. Epy and I were completely lost.

They made a fuss when I came in and said they were glad to see me, but after that I might as well have been watching TV in another room. They were comparing the contracts of players with similar years of service. Randy got them going when he said, "George is the best player you've ever had; it's right there if you guys would just look at the numbers." Beeston wouldn't admit it. Gillick wasn't agreeing either. I understand in his job he can't be friends with everyone.

I probably have a better relationship with Beeston than with Gillick but I understand that's the way negotiating contracts has to be. Gillick feels he has to be the tough guy to show the players he's the boss. His style is to go eye-to-eye with the players and the agents. That's okay with me. Gillick and I get along; the only thing is, he never looks me straight in the eye.

That night in Chicago I just sat and watched the two sides go at it. We were there four hours and I don't think I said a thing. During all this talking and shouting we were drinking Coca-Cola, which was a good thing, because at one point I thought they were all going to get into a fistfight. Eventually Randy became so angry when they laughed at one of his suggestions for a long-term deal — three years for $2.9 million — that he took off and walked up the staircase and said he wasn't coming back. David and I have fun, but Randy is too serious. Randy is business, business, business. He's a lawyer and graduated at the top of his class. Sometimes you have to relax.

But I know Randy respects Beeston and Gillick. And Gillick and Beeston respect Randy, David and Alan. Although someone may raise his voice, we still get things done, mainly because just at the time everyone is getting angry, someone always makes a joke, puts some humour into the conversation. That night there weren't many jokes and when we finally went to bed we didn't have an agreement. I didn't sleep too well even though both Randy and David said not to worry.

The next morning after another bargaining session we eventually agreed on a one-year contract worth $725 000 with some incentives. The base was a little bit more than the mid-point — $705 000 — of the two offers. So everything was fine. I was happy with a raise of $355 000, almost double my 1985 salary. We had asked for a three-year deal which would have carried me from 1986 to 1988 so I would have been a free agent in '89, but the Blue Jays didn't want that. We were looking for a $900 000 base, so if I made all the incentives it would have come out to just under $3 million altogether but we never got the long-term contract done. David said not to worry, the long-term contract would come. David, who first brought me into the Hendricks team back in Santo Domingo, said the Blue Jays had made a mistake. They could have tied me up for three years at less money than they'd have to pay later. I wasn't sure, but as it turned out David was right.

5

Most Valuable Player

"I hear he has a bad shoulder. I wouldn't doubt he damaged it carrying his team."
— *Sparky Anderson, Detroit Tigers manager, on George Bell, late September '87*

THE 1986 SEASON, JIMY'S FIRST AS MANAGER, WAS disappointing. Our starting pitching seemed to fall apart: Jimmy Key didn't win his first game until May 9, and Dave Stieb finished the year with only his second losing record — for the first time since he'd been a Blue Jay he won fewer than eight games. He lost his first five decisions and didn't get a win until May 30 by which time we were 11 games out.

I think Stieb realized in 1986 he was human. In a way when he's out on the mound he's like me at the plate. He doesn't like to lose and I admire that in him, but when I first joined the Jays he was real cocky. We almost hooked up in fights a couple of times. If I — or someone else in the outfield — made an error, Stieb would start popping off. I don't chew out other players on the field or yell at pitchers when they give up home runs in a close game, but then that was Stieb's style.

The worst incident came one afternoon in May when we were playing in Cleveland. Brett Butler, now with the San Francisco Giants, was the leadoff hitter and he hit Stieb's first pitch of the game over Lloyd Moseby's head in centre field. I mean he hit a bullet and

Lloyd didn't have a chance — Willie Mays wouldn'thave caught that ball. So Stieb started staring at Lloyd and walking around the mound, shaking his head from side to side and slamming the resin bag on the back of the mound. Finally he faced the next batter.

At the end of the inning we came into the dugout and right away Stieb started screaming at Lloyd, "Don't be afraid to get a jump on the ball." Then he said Lloyd wasn't trying. By now Lloyd was ready to shake him, pop him one in the face — I'm talking about killing him. I've never seen Lloyd so angry. I got over there fast, broke up the fight and said, "Come on, guys, things like that can happen. Let's leave it until after the game."

Later in the season during a night game at Exhibition Stadium, the same thing happened to me. Lloyd missed a catch-up against the fence, Jesse threw a ball away and I made a terrible throw from left. In the dugout, Stieb started screaming at me so I told him, "Strike them out if you're that good." After the game Stieb told all the reporters, "We've got some guys out there who can't even play defence." When we saw this in the papers the next day we were all pretty upset. After another game he was interviewed on TV and he said, "All you had to do is show the highlights. Don't show the pitcher. Everybody will know Dave Stieb was pitching because everybody played so terrible."

That's stupid and babyish, but I don't blame him, as much as I blame the Blue Jays. The people who run the Jays minor-league organization were responsible for those things happening with Stieb because right from the beginning they spoiled him. You can't say it was this guy's fault or that guy's fault or Stieb's fault. It was the whole organization's fault — whoever was in charge in the minors and whoever brought him to the big leagues. They told Stieb that he was the best, that he was everything.

All in all 1986 was not Stieb's year. He was 7-12 with a 4.74 ERA. We're good friends now, but that year Stieb was something else.

But what I'm going to remember most about the 1986 season was how Jimy treated my friend Damo Garcia. When we were at Dunedin in 1986, Jimy's first spring as manager, a lot of things began to go wrong. Some things weren't Jimy's fault. Like Gary Lavelle and

Tom Filer, who had gone 7-0 for us the year before, going down with arm injuries, and Doyle Alexander requesting a trade. But the first thing Jimy and Pat Gillick decided was to move Damo to ninth in the batting order and put Lloyd in the leadoff spot. What was Jimy trying to prove by that? Damo was good enough to be Coxie's leadoff man. I know people said Damo didn't walk enough, but I think the real reason was Jimy wanted to prove it was *his* team. During the '85 season Damo hit into a double play only 12 times because he was too fast. He led the team in hits in '85 with 169. That means he was on base 184 times. Yet they make a big fuss when Wade Boggs or Pete Rose get 200 hits.

Damo and Jimy started fighting in spring training when Jimy made the lineup change and this went on for the whole year. Damo went to the press and said things he wasn't supposed to say — he knocked the club, said he wanted to be traded, claimed it was Pat Gillick, not Jimy, had changed his batting order. He said too much; he should have kept those thoughts to himself.

In Seattle, on our first trip to the coast, Damo was down in the dumps because of the way Jimy was treating him. He didn't like hitting ninth — he thought it was an insult. So Cliff Johnson started calling Damo "Happy" or "Mr. Happy." Cliff had been messing with Damo since Damo was a rookie with the Yankees in 1979. Cliff was always punching him and Damo always told him not to, but like a little kid Cliff wouldn't stop. When Cliff called Damo "Mr. Happy" Damo would call Cliff "Mule Face" and Cliff didn't like that.

On May 14 we were in Oakland. Stieb was pitching and the game was tied 3-3 in the seventh inning when Ricky Peters hit a ground ball between first and second. The ball went off Damo's glove, Jerry Willard scored and the A's were ahead. Then Jose Canseco, Dave Kingman and Mike Davis all hit homers off Stieb — he lost it quickly — and we got beat 9-4. Now we were six games below .500. After the game Damo was upset and so was Jimy. Jimy said Stieb lost his concentration because of Damo's error — like it was Damo's fault for the three homers. Damo was so angry he went into the bathroom, put his uniform top, his sweatshirt and hat on the floor, poured alcohol on them and lit a match.

That got Jimy even more upset. He kept saying you had to respect the uniform you wear. Damo respected the uniform; he just didn't respect Jimy. I have no idea why Damo burned his uniform. Only Damo knows, or maybe Jimy knows.

Meanwhile Cliff and Damo's relationship was going from bad to worse. At Exhibition Stadium August 5, before a game against Kansas City, Cliff was on the disabled list. Since he was injured, he didn't have a regular turn in the cage during batting practice. If he wanted to hit he should have been hitting before the regulars started. But he kept sneaking into the cage, taking time away from the other hitters. You learn in Class A you're not supposed to do that. First Damo told Cliff to get out of the cage. "Try and move me if you can, Mr. Happy," was Cliff's comeback. "Get out now, Mule Face!" shouted Damo. So Cliff came out, but he came out to fight Damo. Damo shoved Cliff, then they started throwing punches. Jimy and Sully grabbed Cliff and Tony Fernandez grabbed Damo and took him into the clubhouse. But when Damo came out Cliff started again. "Well, here comes Mr. Happy now," he yelled with his big voice. All that did was make Damo want to fight him all over. Cliff should have been picking on someone his own size.

At least it was a pretty good year for "The Best Outfield in Baseball." Coming up to the All-Star break, we all had a shot at making the All-Star team. Jesse was hitting .299, with 21 homers and 65 RBIs. I was hitting .307 with 16 homers and 62 RBIs and Lloyd was hitting .278 with 13 homers and 49 RBIs. We were all way down in the voting, but AL manager Dick Howser of the Royals selected Jesse and Lloyd among the extra players. Ernie said the reason I wasn't chosen was "because you kicked the Royals' butts every time we play them." I figured he didn't pick me because of one time when I hit second baseman Frank White, breaking up a double play in 1985. I was upset because there wasn't any comparison between Lloyd's numbers and mine. Someone in the front office told me that Howser had made a mistake picking Lloyd instead of me. Like Billy Martin in 1981, he got George Bell mixed up with another outfielder. But then

I found out how sick Howser was. The All-Star game in Houston was the last ballgame he ever managed because he had a brain tumour. Howser was a class guy when he managed against us, especially in the playoffs in '85.

When we started play after the break, we were ten and a half games out. We got beat 1-0 in 15 innings in Oakland on July 27. Our season was getting pretty frustrating. In the seventh inning I got kicked out by plate ump Al Clark after I slammed my bat on the plate. I was so mad I kept arguing with Clark and I wound up touching his chest, so the league fined me $250 and suspended me for two games.

On August 23 things started to look up for a while. We beat the Twins 7-4 to start a nine-game winning streak that cut Boston's lead down to three and a half by August 30. But they were playing us tough. The last four days of the streak when we won, so did Boston. Then we lost seven of the next nine and suddenly we were nine games behind. On September 28 Oil Can Boyd beat us 12-3 to clinch the American League East. So we were there when the Boston players were jumping and dancing around the field. We finished in fourth, nine and a half games out. Lloyd had a good year, batting .253 with 21 homers and 86 RBIS. Jesse led the league with 40 homers while hitting .289 and driving in 108 runs — the same number as me. I hit .309 and had 31 homers.

Two weeks later I was home sitting on the front porch rocking the newest addition to our family, Kevin. Kevie was born September 10, the same birth date as Roger Maris. Now Maria and I had three boys.

Other than Jimy's hiring as manager, the off-season was pretty quiet until February 2 when Damo phoned to tell me he had been traded to Atlanta for right-handed pitcher Craig McMurtry. I told him he'd probably be happier away from Jimy and back with Coxie, but was sad we wouldn't be playing together. I not only lost a good friend, but I moved into the spot Damo had occupied in Jimy's mind. That wasn't where I wanted to be.

After a season that saw the Blue Jays win 15 fewer games than in 1985 and finish fourth in their division, the Jays were a changed team when they came to Dunedin to start the 1987 season. Cliff Johnson was gone, as well as Garcia. Bill Caudill would be released at the end of spring training. Everyone wondered if things would be easier in Williams' second year as manager.

At second base, Mike Sharperson, Nelson Liriano, Garth Iorg and Santiago Garcia were bidding to replace Damo. The Jays thought the pitching was solid with a rotation anchored by Dave Stieb, Jimmy Key, Jim Clancy, and newly arrived Joe Johnson. John Cerutti and Jose Nunez would share the fifth spot. And Mark Eichhorn, who had a great year in 1986, was the set-up man for closer Tom Henke.

Spring training hadn't started well for me. Jimy fined me $1000 because I refused to weigh in. I told him, "I don't have to weigh in because I don't have that clause in my contract. I'll weigh in if I want to." I refused, so he fined me. But the team looked good. We thought we had a chance of winning the division even though we had five rookies on the Opening Day roster, the most since the Jays' first year of operation. But we didn't start the season that well. After 19 games we had 11 wins and eight losses and were in third place, six games back of the Milwaukee Brewers.

On April 29, three weeks into the 1987 season, we had a night game at Exhibition Stadium against the Minnesota Twins. We hadn't had a losing series against them in Toronto since 1981. And Mike Smithson was pitching against us; we always hit well against him. As always for a night game, I arrived at Exhibition Stadium around 3:30 in the afternoon.

I went to the clubhouse, got undressed, put my underwear and socks on and sat down to play some cards with Jimmy Key, Rick Leach and Jim Clancy. During the game Leach walked over and checked the lineup card taped on the wall near the entrance. He yelled over, "Hey, Bell, I'm in left and you're DH-ing." I thought he was joking. I had no reason to think I wouldn't be starting in left field as usual. He walked over to the table and I could see he was serious.

I looked at the lineup and instead of seeing the number 7 for left field beside my name, saw that Jimy had written: DH. I turned on

Leach and told him, "You're not taking my job." I was steamed and I stayed steamed. Apart from Cliff Johnson in 1985 trying to be funny and saying I was going to be the DH some day, this was the first time the idea had ever been mentioned. Jimy had just put up the lineup like he would for any other normal game. I had a right to be upset. Coxie would never have done something like that behind my back.

I went out of the clubhouse, down the long hall into Jimy's office and said, "I'm not your DH." I told him I wanted to have a meeting after batting practice. "I want you, me, Beeston and Gillick there too." Jimy said he would see what he could do. I could tell he was annoyed, but he said he would try to arrange it.

Batting practice didn't go too well; I was so angry I couldn't hit the ball. At one point I broke a bat and on my way to the dugout threw it up into the empty seats. Jimy saw this but he didn't say anything.

When the team came into the clubhouse after batting practice, Jimy and I went into Gillick's office. I started out by saying I thought Jimy should have asked me about being the DH. And then I told him right to his face I wasn't going to be the DH. He got mad. You could see his neck muscles bulging. Then I asked Gillick, "How come I'm DH-ing when I have the chance to be in left field?" Jimy answered, "We're giving you a rest. You don't have to play the outfield, but you're still in the lineup as the DH." That was bullshit. It was the first month of the season, we had just come home from Chicago, and had had an off day. I didn't need a day off. "No way I'm going to be the DH," I told him. After that Jimy did most of the talking but he didn't say much. Eventually I left. When I got back to the clubhouse the lineup had been taken down. About 6:30 John McLaren, our third-base coach, put up a new one. I was back in left field, Fred McGriff was the DH and Leach wasn't playing.

About 20 minutes before we were supposed to go out, Jimy came in and spoke to the whole team. Everyone was there except Jim Clancy, who had gone down to the bullpen to warm up. Jimy ripped me in front of everyone. "Let's get one thing straight around here," he said. "I'm running this team, not George Bell." Then he looked at me and said, "You're a goddamn shit disturber. From now on you play where and when I tell you." I just repeated what I'd told him in Gillick's office, that he had no right to make me DH.

The next day was an off day and no one was writing about our win over the Twins (we beat them 8-1 to be five and a half games behind the Brewers). Every newspaper and TV station in Toronto was on my case. They said I shouldn't be in the starting lineup against the Texas Rangers that night. Or if I was, it should be as DH, just to show Jimy was the boss. All three papers had stories saying that Jimy should bench me. Don Cherry, the hockey guy with the sharp clothes, even got into it. He said he would have made me climb into the seats for the broken bat I'd thrown up there the night before and then the two of us would fight it out behind closed doors. That was where the DH business ended, or seemed to. I played in left that night against the Texas Rangers and we won.

But Jimy stayed angry. He almost ignored me, and when he did talk to me he didn't talk properly. When you talk properly to a person you tell him right to his face what's going on. You can't believe in a person who tells you only half of what's on his mind and the rest he tells to somebody else, like the press or Pat Gillick. That was the way Jimy always treated me. Only now we hardly talked at all.

"Fine," I thought to myself, "I don't care. The only thing I'm going to do is go out there, do my job and go home. I'll come back the next day and I'll do my job again." That's when I decided I would show the Jays and Jimy that I could still play, that I wasn't a DH. I'd let my bat talk for me.

In May I really took off at the plate. I batted .352, with 11 homers and 31 RBIs and we made a bit of a move. On May 9, we were in Arlington Stadium in Texas, which is one of my favourite places for hitting in. And this turned out to be one of my best games ever. We won 15-5 as Dave Stieb, who'd got off to a slow start again, got his first win, and I drove in seven runs with a two-run homer, a solo homer, a bases-loaded triple and a groundout. That was my third straight, three-hit game and the seven RBIs were the high for the season. When I get on a streak I just can't wait until we go through the batting order again for another turn at the plate.

There was another memorable thing about that game: Cito Gaston got mad. It happened when Ranger right-hander Mike Loynd hit Lloyd Moseby on purpose with a pitch. Lloyd charged the mound and Cito ran like a bolt from the dugout. He ran so hard sticking up for one of his guys that he pulled a hamstring. A lot of guys who know Cito Gaston think he's mild-mannered and soft-spoken, as he is. What they don't know is what a temper he has.

The reason I play so well in Arlington is it's probably the best-kept infield and outfield in the league. The hitting background in centre makes it easy to see the ball. And the weather is close to what I'm used to: always warm so you never have to worry about getting loose. I like Anaheim too, where the Angels play. The Royals' Stadium in Kansas City is okay and I don't mind Yankee Stadium. Maybe it's the background or maybe I'm more relaxed there. I don't really have the answer — the air, the atmosphere. I do know that I'm more relaxed playing on the road.

By the end of May, Milwaukee had fallen out of second, losing 12 straight, and we had taken their place, two games behind the Yankees. Then, early in June we went into New York. Plenty of guys don't like New York — Tom Henke for one. He's from Missouri and hates concrete about as much as he likes hunting and fishing. When he shows at the park someone is sure to ask him, "How'd the house hunting go?" or say, "I saw a nice inexpensive place you can buy in Manhattan with a fair-sized back yard for the kids." Ha! He hardly even goes out of the hotel when we're there. He still pitches well — Henk pitches well everywhere.

I don't mind the city at all. I seem to hit the ball well and I get a chance to see my brother, Jose, who drives a cab in Manhattan. I wanted to buy him a taxi permit a couple of years ago but the medallion alone cost $160 000 U.S. That's a lot of money and Jose understood. Since Rolando moved to New York last May, I'm thinking about getting the two of them set up with a corner grocery store.

So I don't mind New York, but that's only if we go in and we're out of there right away. But I wouldn't want to play for a New York team, no thank you. On my next contract, whether it is with the Blue

Jays or someone else, I think I'll ask for a no-trade clause to block a trade to the Yankees, the Mets, Cleveland and the Dodgers. Most players would agree with me about Cleveland, but most free agents want to play in New York or Los Angeles.

In our league, Cleveland is without a doubt the worst city to visit: it has the worst ballpark and the stadium has the smallest clubhouse. I'd never want to play for the Dodgers because they had an opportunity to have the whole Bell family playing in their organization. They signed all three of my brothers and they tried to sign me too. Instead, they released Jose and Rolando and traded Juan to the Orioles. The Yankees have a great franchise and Don Mattingly is one of my favourite players, but I don't know if I could play for George Steinbrenner. In the Dominican we have a saying that if two men have the same first name the chances are they won't get along. Steinbrenner isn't cheap. He looks after his players when the subject is money, but I don't think he really treats his players fairly. I'm sure we'd fight.

Anyway, the first game of that June series, with Dave Stieb pitching like his old self, we beat Rick Rhoden 11-0. That put us in first. Everyone said Rhoden cheated by scuffing the balls, but I don't really mind if the guy scuffs the ball because I look for only one thing — the ball. I'd be more mad at the pitcher for throwing at the batter than for doctoring the ball in some way. The guy who throws at batters is dangerous.

In the next two games John Cerutti and Jimmy Key beat the Yankees and we swept the series, so now we were two and a half games in front. The Yankees and the Blue Jays have had a strange relationship the past few years. We always seem to beat them in New York and then they come to Toronto and beat us — all the time. So it wasn't much of a surprise when, at the end of the month, the Yankees came into Exhibition Stadium and swept a three-game series to knock us out of first place. At the beginning of July we were three games behind the first-place Yanks.

At the time of the 1987 balloting, no Blue Jay had ever been voted to the annual All-Star game between the best from the American

League and the best from the National League, but each year at least one Jay had been selected by the AL manager. (Rules stipulate all clubs must have a representative on the All-Star team.) On June 11 when the commissioner's office released the first set of votes, George Bell found himself sitting in eighth place behind Rickey Henderson, Dave Winfield, Kirby Puckett, Bo Jackson, Jim Rice, Jesse Barfield and Rob Deer. Bell had 154 499 votes, fewer than half of Henderson's total. The three top vote getters would be the starting outfield.

With the release of this first set of numbers, a gigantic furor arose in Toronto. It was as if the whole city had been insulted. Big Brother to the south was not giving a Canadian team any respect. More likely George Bell was low because the Blue Jays had been home for exactly two of the first 16 days of voting, but that fact was lost amidst the cries of outrage.

Tub-thumping continued as newspapers pushed "Vote George," commercials were aired and planes pulling messages "VOTE FOR GEORGE" circled Exhibition Stadium. By July 1, with only a week remaining, Bell had 661 384 votes, second only to Rickey Henderson; Kirby Puckett was third; and Dave Winfield was fourth, only 86 351 votes behind. Bell had a .294 average with 28 homers and 73 RBIS — good year for some — and there was almost half a season to play.

On July 8, I was standing at my locker talking to Manny Lee. We were playing the Rangers that night at Exhibition Stadium. It had been on the radio that the final All-Star vote totals would be announced at six o'clock. I knew I had a shot, but other years I thought I was going to be selected and I wasn't. About 5:30 there were already a few reporters hanging around waiting for the results, just in case.

A few minutes before six, Howard Starkman, our public relations man, came in and walked over to me. "Congratulations, George. You're going. The first Blue Jay ever voted to the starting lineup." There are always people with big ears in any clubhouse, but as soon as Howard shook my hand everyone knew. Plenty of guys came over and congratulated me, but the first guy I made an effort to go over and shake hands with was John Sullivan, our coach. Sully and

I have always been pals. He was the guy who fed me the good pitches every day in batting practice to get me going. He'll throw batting practice no matter how bad his arm hurts.

I was walking back to my locker from shaking hands with Sully when John Cerutti said, "So, George, are you going?" I said: "Ah, I might go home for the three days." Everyone hadn't stopped laughing when Rick Leach yelled, "You better go after all the money you invested for those planes carrying 'Vote for George' banners." Everyone really laughed then.

Being elected was one of my best thrills in baseball. I don't know if the fans realize how important it is to the players when they vote for us. The next day AL manager John McNamara added Tony Fernandez, who was batting .310, and Tom Henke, who was 0-4, but had 14 saves.

On July 12, the day before the All-Star break, we were playing Kansas City at Exhibition Stadium. That was when I had a chance to say thank you to the fans. In the first inning a plane circled the park with a banner reading "THANKS FOR YOUR SUPPORT FANS — GEORGE BELL." The fans cheered me and, if I could have taken my glove off, I would have waved to them. After the game reporters asked me questions about how much it cost. "No comment" was my answer. I didn't want to spoil my image. Mike Firestone, a buddy of Jay Vice President Paul Beeston, had suggested the idea. Firestone thought it would be a nice gesture on my part and I agreed.

Walking into the dressing room in Oakland on Monday, July 13, for the All-Star game workout was something I'll remember forever. Like the sign outside said, these were all-stars. The best. Mark McGwire of Oakland, Don Mattingly of the Yankees, Wade Boggs of Boston, Mark Langston of Seattle, Bret Saberhagen of Kansas City, Cal Ripken of Baltimore, Dan Plesac of Milwaukee, Jack Morris of Detroit and many others.

We took batting practice first, before the National League, and I made a point of finding Ryne Sandberg of the Chicago Cubs who was on the NL team. I hadn't seen him, or his wife, Cindy, since 1981 when he was still in Clearwater and I was in my first year with the Blue Jays. Ryne said he was surprised how much my English had improved. We joked about those early years in the minors, all the way back to Helena, Montana. We wondered what had happened to all the guys we had played with and what they were doing now. We talked about that outfielder named Will Cumer, from the Bahamas, the carbon copy of Boston's Jim Rice. I told Ryne we'd meet again some day in the World Series. If I had to compare Ryne to someone on our team it would be to Tom Henke. They have the same sort of temperament. What Henke says, he means. If he's mad, you know it. And like Henke, Sandberg would laugh and make jokes in the clubhouse.

The game took place on a Tuesday night with a 5:30 start on the coast, so it would be prime time back east. That meant we were going to be hitting into the setting sun for the first few innings. John McNamara had me in left field, batting fourth in the lineup behind centre fielder Rickey Henderson, first baseman Don Mattingly and third baseman Wade Boggs.

In the first inning, with a man on base, against Houston's Mike Scott I hit a fly ball which Ozzie Smith of St. Louis caught in shallow centre field. My friend Joaquin Andujar, who was playing for Oakland that year, had told me to expect Scott to throw his split-fingered pitch, but he fooled me with a change-up. I'd never faced Scott before. A lot of guys on the bench were complaining about how difficult it was to pick up the ball in the bright sunshine, but what really surprised me was the amount of intensity in our dugout. Everyone wanted to show that the American League was the best, especially after Tim Raines of the Expos had said on TV that they couldn't lose a second straight year to that "bunch of guys from a Triple A league."

The game was scoreless in the fourth when I came up again, this time against Rick Sutcliffe of the Cubs. I'd faced him before when he pitched for Cleveland and I knew he had a good breaking ball. But he fooled me on a fastball. I started to swing, tried to hold up but made contact. The ball hit the bag at first and Will Clark of the Giants fielded it for the second out. I figured that might be it. Since the day before most of the guys had been saying that it was a long way to come for only a couple of swings. We had Kirby Puckett of Minnesota and Dwight Evans of Boston on the bench, but McNamara kept me in there.

The next pitcher I faced was Orel Hershiser of the Dodgers. I'd batted against him in the Dominican. Three at bats and three different pitchers — I'm glad it's not like that during the season. Hershiser was with Licey when I was with La Romana, but when I faced him in the sixth it was a bit different: millions of people were watching, and we had nothing but zeros on the scoreboard. I pulled a pitch to third, hit it pretty good, but Tim Wallach of the Expos fielded the ball and made the throw to first. That was all for me.

On and on it went as one zero after another went up on the scoreboard. Finally, in the eleventh, Larry Parrish came in to pinch-hit for Henk, who had pitched two and two-thirds scoreless innings. Parrish got a single and advanced to third. Then, with two out, it was up to Tony Fernandez to face Lee Smith of the Cubs. At this point Henk turned to Alan Trammell in the dugout and said, "Tram, I went the whole first half of the season without a win and now I'm going to be the winning pitcher in the All-Star game. How 'bout that?" But Smith struck Tony out.

In the top of the thirteenth we were still tied at zero when Ozzie Virgil of the Phils and Hubie Brooks of the Expos each hit singles off Oakland reliever Jay Howell. Then, with two out, Raines hit a triple and drove in two runs. We couldn't score against Sid Fernandez of the Mets, in the bottom of the thirteenth, so that was it. We were 2-0 losers.

In the clubhouse afterwards we saw Raines interviewed on TV as the player of the game, and he said, "The National League has proved once again their league is better." Not by much! They didn't score a run for 12 innings either. The two teams had only 14 hits in 13 innings, so not many guys were hitting even after the sun went down.

After the All-Star break, play resumed in Minnesota and the Blue Jays won nine of the next 15 match-ups. All that did was reduce the deficit to two and a half games. As the second half got underway, George

*Bell had 28 homers and the talk began, as it does each mid-season, of
assaulting the home-run records of Roger Maris and Babe Ruth.*

*But after hitting 11 out of the park in May and June, Bell had
only five home runs in July, and he entered August with 32. On the
first of the month the Jays were in second, two and a half games
behind the Yankees.*

On August 7, we beat Cleveland 15-1 to knock the Yankees out of
top spot and moved into first place for the first time since June. In that
game I hit my thirty-fourth homer, which gave me the most ever for
a Dominican player, including my friend Pedro Guerrero, who hit 33
for the Dodgers in 1984. After Cleveland we went on to Boston for a
three-game series. I hate playing left field in Boston. I didn't mind
the place back in 1984 when I was playing in right field, but when
you are in left field with that Green Monster behind you, it's almost
like you're in a cage and you don't have anywhere to run after the
ball. Left field at Fenway becomes a reaction position, a lot like third
base. The ball is on you in a hurry, or it's over your head and off the
wall and coming back at you. You're so close — 315 feet — that even
left-handed hitters can go the other way and bounce the ball off the
wall.

Throughout the whole month we were in and out of first place
and ended August a game behind the Detroit Tigers. They'd lost 11 of
their first 30 games and now they were on a roll. As much as my
numbers improved Cito was always pushing me to do better. One
time he called me aside and told me I had a real shot at winning the
Most Valuable Player award. He said, "You know that's the biggest
honour in baseball you can get," but I remember telling him, "If I
win but we don't win our division, it won't be worth much." Then
we went back to talking about hitting. It paid off. August was a better
month than July — I drove in more runs, had a .321 batting average,
nine homers and 28 RBIS. I now had 41 homers and 122 RBIS.

Maybe because I was doing so well I seemed to be more of a
target for pitchers than ever. On September 7 in Milwaukee in the
first inning, Bill Wegman hit me on purpose right on the nose. There
was blood all over the place and I had to come out of the game.

Tommy Craig, our trainer told me it was broken. John Cerutti, who was pitching for us, wouldn't retaliate. I was upset and complained to Ernie Whitt. Ernie said he knew it was intentional and twice he asked Cerutti to pitch high and inside to Paul Molitor, one of the Brewers' best players. Both times Cerutti refused. I told Ernie that was chicken-shit, but Ernie said not to worry. That was just one example of how our pitchers didn't protect me that year. I was hit seven times in 1987. I don't think one of our pitchers ever let the other team know they'd have to pay for this. I played the next day.

Of course you can't put all the blame on the pitchers. Jimy Williams didn't want them to retaliate. He was afraid that during a fight somebody would get hurt — but I was already hurt: my nose was flattened. Not fighting back was just one of the many mistakes we made that year, some because of inexperience, some because of a lack of guts. I was prepared to fight anybody on the field to stick up for my team. Sometimes it seemed like I was the only one on the Blue Jays who would start a fight with the other team.

In New York on September 11 we moved into first place when we beat the Yankees 6-5 in 10 innings. We were going good now. On September 14 we played the first of a three-game series at Exhibition Stadium against the Orioles who were headed to a 100-loss season. But like the saying goes, anyone with a bat is dangerous. Well, we had the bats. That night we pounded out 10 homers to go into the record books in an 18-3 victory. It was the most home runs ever by one team in a single game. Ernie had three, Rance and myself had two each, with Lloyd Moseby, Fred McGriff and Rob Ducey hitting a homer each. During the game guys were joking, asking each other what they had had for breakfast. The baseballs looked like beachballs that night and they were flying like Frisbees. I was happy to have hit one in that game because later Cito Gaston had the six of us pose with bats; he has the picture hanging in his office. I would have paid to be in a picture Cito thought enough of to hang in his office. We swept the Orioles to stay tied for first with the Tigers.

On September 21 we went to Memorial Stadium in Baltimore and won three close games. That was one of my best series of the year. The first night, with one out in the ninth, I singled against Mike

Boddicker to bring Lloyd home and we won 2-1. The second game we were tied 3-3 in the eighth and I singled Lloyd home again; we eventually won 8-4. The third night I hit a two-run homer off John Habyan in the fifth and we won 5-1 to stay half a game in front.

I enjoy batting in those situations. I try to prepare myself for late-inning at bats with men on base and the game on the line. To me it's the best part of the game. You have a chance to be a hero by getting on base to tie the game or by keeping the rally going. I'm a better hitter in those situations because I've learned to be more selective late in the game and make the pitcher throw strikes.

The long-distance, 162-game schedule was now down to a 100-metre sprint. When the final dash began in Toronto, September 24, with Detroit in town for a four-game series, the Jays led the Tigers by half a game. It was the first time in 74 days that the American League East rivals would be knocking heads. Everyone from your favourite bartender and barber to TV talking head and newspaper columnist said this series might decide the AL East division. It should have. And the first game, September 24, is etched in the minds of Blue Jay fans as indelibly as the names Jim Sundberg and Butch Wynegar.

The game was scoreless in the third inning when Mike Flanagan, the veteran left-hander we'd acquired in August to help us in the stretch drive, faced Jack Morris. The game was beginning to look like a pitcher's duel. Bill Madlock was on first base with one out when Kirk Gibson grounded to second baseman Nelson Liriano and Nellie threw to Tony Fernandez to try to start the double play. Tony came across the bag, threw to first and then jumped high into the air with Madlock barrelling in on him. Madlock didn't pay any attention to the bag at all. His slide caught Tony's legs. Tony did a flip in midair and landed on the metal frame for the cut-out portion of the artificial turf. Madlock not only broke up the double play, he broke Tony's right elbow.

The next day a reporter asked Madlock if he was going to phone Tony in the hospital to see how he was and Madlock said, "Call him? What for? I'm not the Welcome Wagon. That's the way we play in the National League." He'd played with the Cubs and the Pirates and I think he'd made Tony his target — it was that simple. Tony is too nice. I kept telling him he had to throw the ball low at the guys' heads when they were coming into second on a double play — then they'd slide before they got near the base. But Tony didn't listen to me. There are lot of guys who will hurt you if you let them.

With Tony out for the season, Manny Lee took over at shortstop. We won that night 4-3 to move in front of the Tigers by a game and a half. Ernie Whitt scored the winning run on a wild pitch in the eighth inning, about the same time Tony was at Mount Sinai Hospital having his elbow operated on.

We won the next two games to move ahead by three and a half games. We'd won three straight without Tony, and winning seemed a sure thing. But now in the final game of the series we had to face our old amigo Doyle Alexander who is always tough late in the season. After moving to Detroit from Atlanta for the stretch drive, Doyle won his first eight starts.

That Sunday afternoon we had Jim Clancy pitching against Doyle. Fans were holding up hundreds of cardboard signs given out before the game reading "FOIL DOYLE." We scored a run in the first inning when Nelson Liriano singled, stole second, and I knocked him in with a single to left. That was it until the ninth when Tom Henke came into protect our 1-0 lead. We figured Henke was about to get his thirty-fifth save. Instead Kirk Gibson hit a 1-1 fastball over the right-field fence to tie the game.

In the top of the twelfth the score was tied 2-2 when Gibson came up again with a man on second. Jose Nunez was pitching for us now and Gibson blooped a single into shallow centre field, putting the Tigers ahead to stay. When people think of Gibson they think of his dramatic home run for the Dodgers off Dennis Eckersley in the first game of the '88 World Series, but his hits against us that day were just as important for the Tigers.

After the game when we filed into the clubhouse, most of the guys were pretty down. We had been three outs away from being in the lead by four and a half games with only six to play. We should have won the Sunday game and everyone knew it. So we were all sitting there in the locker room moping when Rance Mulliniks, who is always quick with a line, looked up and said, "C'mon, guys, we beat them three out of four and if you don't like three out of four you don't like big tits!" That broke the mood and people began to lighten up. The writers were already in the clubhouse, so Rance's quote turned up in the three Toronto papers. The *Toronto Sun* ran it just like Rance said, word for word. The *Star* quoted Rance saying: ". . . if you don't like three out of four, then you don't understand." According to the *Globe and Mail* Rance said, ". . . if you don't like three out of four then you don't like ice cream."

The night after our marathon loss to Detroit, Milwaukee came into Exhibition Stadium. They were nine games behind and out of contention; that meant they were loose, with nothing to lose. We didn't hit a lick the first night. We were thinking that our offence wasn't the same without Tony. We lost all three games and we lost Ernie Whitt who went after Molitor with a roll block, trying to break up the double play. He cracked two ribs and was gone for the season. I realize now what Ernie had meant when he told me in Milwaukee not to worry after John Cerutti refused to retaliate when I was hit on the nose.

We were still a game ahead in the standings on October 1 when we got on the plane to fly from Toronto to Windsor for our season-ending, three-game series against Detroit. I don't believe in omens, but we had a bad one soon after takeoff. A Canada goose flew into one of the engines on our Canadian Airlines DC-9 and some of the guys said they could see flames five or six rows back of the engine. I was sitting with Juan Beniquez and when this happened he was so nervous he was shaking. He wasn't the only one.

We had to return to Toronto right away for an emergency landing to have the engine looked at. A lot of guys now didn't want to fly to Windsor. We must have had about 15 players who wanted to rent cars and drive down. But Jimy Williams took charge of the situation and said no. There was a lot of grumbling, but after about a three-hour wait we all went back onto our charter for Detroit. When we were getting on the plane, I asked the stewardess if the meal was cooked goose, but not a lot of guys laughed.

When we left Toronto our lead was a game and a half, but by the time we got to Detroit it was down to a game — the Tigers had beaten the Orioles that night. I heard Sparky Anderson, the Tigers manager, saying on the radio he had decided I wasn't going to beat him with a big hit or a homer so he'd told his pitchers not to give me anything good to hit, nothing at all in the strike zone. That was the same strategy we had tried with George Brett in the 1985 playoffs. With Ernie and Tony out of the lineup it wasn't a surprise.

The situation was simple. We had to win one game to ensure at least a tie — two wins and we'd win the division. Some guys were nervous, worried about choking, and almost everyone badly wanted to win. But we also had a few guys — I'm not mentioning any names — who didn't really care. They were disappointed because of their individual years. They just wanted to go home. But I thought if we made the playoffs we were in good shape for the World Series. Minnesota had already clinched the AL West and we had beaten Minnesota nines time out of 12. It wasn't going to be easy, but it was one of the best chances we'll ever have to go all the way.

Friday night we lost a close one as Doyle Alexander, again pitching tough in a tough situation, beat us 4-3. But we made two errors. Take away the two unearned runs we would have won. Little Manny Lee hit a three-run homer for us, but that was all we could do against Doyle. (After the game Doyle said that he had come to the park wearing the same yellow sweater that he wore on the second-last day of the season in 1985 when he held off the Yankees to help us clinch the AL East.) So we were tied for first with identical 96-64 records. We had to win at least one game to force a one-game playoff.

On Saturday Mike Flanagan pitched one of the best games I've ever seen and Jack Morris was almost as good. There always seemed to be runners on base, but Flanny kept us in the game. From the fifth inning on, with the score tied 2-2, Jimy always had someone warming up — one hit and Flanagan would have been gone. But he just kept pitching through 12 innings. Neither team could break the tie. Finally, when Jimy told Flanagan he wasn't going out for the thirteenth, Flanagan sat down on the bench and said, "Sorry I couldn't hold 'em, guys." That was typical. He always had his sense of humour. They talk about guys in the old days pitching great games, guys like Juan Marichal, Sandy Koufax, Tom Seaver and Bob Gibson going 12 or 13 innings. To me, Flanagan's game ranked with the best of them.

In the thirteenth, Jimy sent out our left-hander, Jeff Musselman, to take over. Next thing we knew there were two men on and our old friend Kirk Gibson was at the plate. Musselman pitched him carefully; he walked him to load the bases. Now Jimy brought in Mark Eichhorn to pitch to Alan Trammell. Trammell hit a shot that squirted by Manny at short, and the Tigers had won 3-2. Now they were in first place, and our backs were to the wall.

After the game some writers asked Jimy why he hadn't brought in Tom Henke and Jimy said he hadn't brought Henke into tied games all year and he wasn't going to start now. The next day in the paper a writer asked the question, "What about tied pennant races?" Jimy didn't have an answer for that one.

After that loss, everyone on the team was down, but I just kept saying we would have fun the next day and beat them in the playoff on Monday. We had an upbeat batting practice, but the wind was shifting, blowing in and then blowing out from one group of hitters to the next. Frank Tanana, who had beat us twice earlier in the season, was pitching for the Tigers and we didn't think he could beat us a third time.

The game started well but, in the second inning, when Jimmy Key jammed him with an inside pitch, Larry Herndon managed to lift a fly ball to left. As the ball left the bat I remember thinking, here's another out, but it just carried and carried. I probably could have reached that ball if I had stepped on the auxiliary scoreboard, but I never believed it would go that far. The ball landed in the fourth row of seats. Tigers 1, Jays 0.

Once through our order, twice through. Tanana was putting up one zero after another. So was Key. The tension was incredible. The "1" on the scoreboard was looking bigger and bigger. Nothing in the sixth, nothing in the seventh. Our season was slipping away. In the eighth, Lloyd Moseby led off with a single and stole second. Then it was my turn at the plate. I was trying to drive the ball somewhere, anywhere — just a lousy single to score a run and tie the game. Instead I hit a 1-0 offspeed pitch, a fly ball to straightaway centre.

Two more easy outs for Tanana and we were down to our last at bat. In the top of the ninth, Tanana quickly got rid of Cecil Fielder and Manny Lee. So the game and the season was down to Garth Iorg.

I remember the people at Tiger Stadium standing, clapping and stomping their feet as Iorg came up. I kept thinking this can't happen, this won't happen. But it did. Tanana threw him an outside pitch and Garth bounced the ball up the first base-line. Tanana ran over, picked up the ball and threw underhanded to first baseman Darryl Evans. Suddenly the Tigers were jumping up and down, hugging each other. I felt sick. This was the start of a celebration we were supposed to be enjoying. Instead, we were watching from the outside.

Long before Garth had come to the plate, a lot of the guys had headed up the runway to the clubhouse. It was too painful. But I stayed. I sat there on the top step of the dugout and after the third out I turned around, my back to the field, and put my head in my hands. I couldn't believe how close we had come. When a guy talks about pain in baseball, he is usually telling how he fouled a ball off his instep, the same place he'd taken a foul ball a few days before or maybe about a painful shoulder from running into the wall. But this pain was worse. This was pain of the heart. The division had been ours and we'd blown it. I don't know how long I sat there, but when I finally went into the clubhouse some of the guys had already showered. They wanted to get out of Detroit as fast as possible.

When we flew back to Toronto, I felt awful, the worst I'd ever felt after a game. I had let my teammates down by trying to do too much all by myself. What a terrible feeling! We'd all let the city down. I was 1-for-3 in the final game, but then we didn't have much offence. Before we went into our slide, a lot of people were telling me I was a sure thing to win the MVP award. Now those same people were saying Alan Trammell should be the winner. He had hit the ball better than I had on that final weekend and his team had won. To tell you the truth, I didn't give a damn about the MVP that final day. I didn't even know what Trammell had done at the plate. The MVP was for the fans and the sportswriters to worry about. I had only wanted us to win.

I had only two hits in my last 26 at bats, a terrible end to what had been a great year. My season had been something else, but we had come up short. Even though we didn't have our best offensive lineup on the field, there's no way we should have lost seven in a row, no way we should have lost three straight to Detroit. The injuries aren't an excuse. It was my fault I didn't hit. With Ernie, or another dangerous hitter behind me, I would have seen better pitches, more fastballs, but my job is to hit whatever they throw at me.

I knew we were a better ball club than Detroit. We had more talent, but we also made a lot more mistakes from start to finish that season. We won 96 games but we would have won 107 easily, without all the mistakes. We didn't move guys over with a man on second and none out so that all we would need was a fly ball to bring in a run. Time and again we got thrown out on the bases and made bad throws from the outfield. We bunted poorly. If you could have totalled the physical and mental mistakes each team made that year I'm sure we would have been the worst in the league. My 11 errors didn't help. Most of the time we sat around waiting for things to happen instead of making them happen. Too often we went up there like robots. Jimy has to take some of the blame — he had us sitting and waiting for the three-run homer — but it was a team thing.

The '87 season was the most emotional we'd ever been through as a team: up and down, up and down long before we got to Detroit. It was a frustrating year. We never really played at a consistent level like we did in '85.

I was still down when I headed home about five days after our terrible weekend in Detroit. Flying into Santo Domingo for what I expected to be a quiet off-season, I was really surprised when I cleared customs and saw about two thousand people at the airport waiting to welcome me home. Most of them were from the San Pedro area, but some were from the capital. Even though my team had lost they welcomed me back as a hero. They clapped, cheered and chanted: "George! MVP! George! MVP!" Plenty of my friends were there. The Dominican sportswriters presented me with a four-foot statue of me as our country's MVP. They'd even brought the town fire truck to lead the parade back to San Pedro.

This was still early October, long before they announced the MVP Trophy for the AL. Whether I ever won the MVP award didn't matter that night because the Dominican people and the Dominican writers told me that I was the MVP of all the Dominican players. That homecoming was one of the happiest in my life.

There were so many people in my house that night, we could hardly move. My dad and mom, my brothers, my sister, cousins, all my family were there. I've never seen Maria so happy, so proud. Epy Guerrero, our scout, was there along with Hireberto Rodriguez, who'd given me needed advice about getting married, and a whole bunch of school friends. We drank and talked and laughed late into the night.

George Bell's 1987 season — a .308 batting average, 47 homers and 134 runs batted in — was his best offensively, excluding his .309 batting average in 1986, a career year. Even the most distinguished players, those who have been models of consistency have one year more productive than usual, a career year. Bell's improvement wasn't a giant advance on previous years. He was well established as one of the most dangerous hitters in the majors.

In his three previous years Bell had averaged 28 homers and 96 RBIs while maintaining a batting average of .292. In 1987 he finished among the top 10 in most offensive categories in the AL. He was first in runs batted in (134), extra-base hits (83), and total bases (369). He was second in homers (47), behind Oakland's Mark McGwire, in runs scored (111), and in slugging percentage (.605). He was fifth in game-winning hits (16), sixth in hits (188), seventh in outfield assists (14) and twelfth with a .308 batting average. As in previous seasons, when the game was on the line, Bell was at his best. He batted .337 with runners in scoring position.

Only Don Mattingly, who drove in 145 runs for the New York Yankees in '85, and Andre Dawson, who knocked in 137 in '87 for the Cubs, drove in more runs in a single season. That's how good Bell's totals were compared to those of the other swingers in the swinging 'eighties. Where else did Bell's career year place him in baseball's voluminous record books? His 47 homers were the most ever by a Latin American player, besting the mark set by Orlando Cepeda of the San Francisco Giants in '61. Bell also equalled Minnesota slugger Harmon Killebrew's '62 record for most homers on the road — 28. Even with the poor finish he batted .294 in '87 against the Tigers. But was all this good enough to give him the Most Valuable Player award? Detroit's Alan Trammell had hit .343 with 28 homers and 105 RBIS — and his team had won.

While the Tigers were flying to Minnesota to open the AL Championship Series, 28 members of the Baseball Writers Association of America, two in each city, were mailing their ballots to BBWAA executive-secretary Jack Lang. On them the writers had marked in order of preference the 10 men they judged most deserving of the 1987 MVP award. A first-place vote was worth 14 points; second place, nine points; and on down to one for being tenth on a ballot. On November 17, the final tally was in: Bell had a total of 332 points, thanks to 16 first-place votes, while Trammell had 311 points and 12 first-place votes. Other honours followed: he was named AL Player of the Year by Baseball America; to the Sporting News AL All-Star team; he was the Blue Jays Player of the Year for the second season in succession and Sporting News Most Valuable Player in baseball in 1987.

I didn't hear about being named the MVP the usual way. I've heard stories where Jack Lang calls and identifies himself and the player says, "Soon as I heard, 'This is Jack Lang,' I knew I had won." Lang phoned me but I wasn't home. Instead it was Howie Starkman, our public relations man, who phoned later in the day to give me the news. Howie was my good-news man in 1987: he was the one who told me I had been voted to the All-Star game too.

That evening, I had a telephone interview with a lot of press people from Toronto who were gathered at Exhibition Stadium. As I was talking, many of my friends came to my house. They'd heard the news but they weren't sure it was for real. Gradually they realized it was true.

We had a huge celebration that night! Many *cervezas*. There weren't as many people as the night half the town showed up at the airport, but the news spread by word of mouth and by around 8:30 there was quite a crowd. I remember my dad giving me a big hug and saying, "You're the best." Everyone was happy — the papers, the writers and all the baseball fans in San Pedro were happy. That was one time when I drank rum. I don't usually drink hard stuff and I knew my head would hurt the next day, but I didn't care.

In the next few days a lot of people said I was lucky and Trammell should have won the award. And every time they mentioned that I won, they always added, "but he had a poor finish." They didn't have to tell me that. You're wrong if you think the awards eased the pain of losing I wanted to get on with '88 as soon as possible and forget about the final series with Detroit.

6

The DH Experiment

"Even thinking of making George Bell the designated hitter makes little sense to me. He's still a good outfielder. It's not like he has a busted up shoulder and can't throw the ball 20 feet. The guy can still play defence."
— *Whitey Herzog, manager of the St. Louis Cardinals,*
March 22, 1989

IN LATE 1987 MY CONTRACT TALKS WERE STALLED. For the first time in my career I thought I had a chance for a multi-year deal — we were looking for $6.6 million guaranteed for three years — and my agent, Randy Hendricks, assured me that our request was reasonable. But the Jays weren't buying. Pat Gillick and Paul Beeston wanted to talk about a one-year deal only. A one-year deal would mean I would be a free agent at the end of the 1988 season because I would then have six years service in the majors. In early December, at the winter meetings in Dallas, the Jays still hadn't moved, so Randy gave them an ultimatum: either they offered me a long-term deal or 1988 would be my last as a Jay. At the end of the year I'd become a free agent no matter how much the Blue Jays offered me.

On January 16, I worked a baseball-card show billed as an "MVP Show" in Arlington, Texas. Andre Dawson, the MVP in the National League, and I were the two headliners. We signed autographs and posed for pictures. Since I'm home for most of the off-season, I don't usually do card shows. I don't really enjoy them. When people pay to get in, they think they own you: "Do this! Sign here! Do that." I did one other show in New York, a year later, and those are the only two I've ever done. I don't mind talking to the little kids, but the adults can be a pain. They ask you to sign 10 of your cards. What do they want 10 for? So they can sell nine of them, that's why. It's the same at every hotel we stay in during the season.

Rather than flying home immediately after the card show, I went back to the Sheraton Hotel near Arlington Stadium where the team stays during the season, because we had a meeting scheduled with the Blue Jays. It was the first get-together since Randy had given them our ultimatum. It was quite a meeting. I thought we'd just be talking about my contract and money, but they wanted to talk about a lot more. On my side were Randy and David Hendricks. But the Blue Jays had brought a lot of people: Paul Beeston, Pat Gillick, Jimy Williams, Al LaMacchia, another Blue Jay vice president, and Gordon Lakey, one of our scouts. Al's best friend is Tommy Lasorda and he's one of the guys, along with Epy Guerrero, who suggested the Blue Jays draft me from the Phillies. He scouts the NL and Lakey scouts the AL.

At first there was a lot of good-natured talk about my contract, like any other time Beeston and the Hendrickses and I get together. Then Gillick announced they wanted me to DH some of the time in '88 and I agreed. DH-ing 10-to-15 games would be easier on my legs. Then Jimy got into it. "You're going to DH most of the games, George," he told me. I said: "Jimy, there's no way." In the four previous years in the majors I had missed only 18 games altogether and had never been on the disabled list, not once, even though my shoulders acted up once in a while. A total of 18 games in four years. That's less than one three-week stint on the disabled list. I'd need crutches before I'd go on the disabled list.

Then Jimy said all the coaches and scouts agreed with making me the designated hitter, but I knew it was his idea. He said that I was losing speed in the outfield and that Al LaMacchia agreed. I respect Al very much, but I looked Jimy right in the eye and said, "Fuck you. I haven't lost my speed. Lost speed? That's fucking baloney, Jimy." So Jimy backed off a bit. He said they were worried about how my knees would hold up. Also, they thought the kids — Sil Campusano

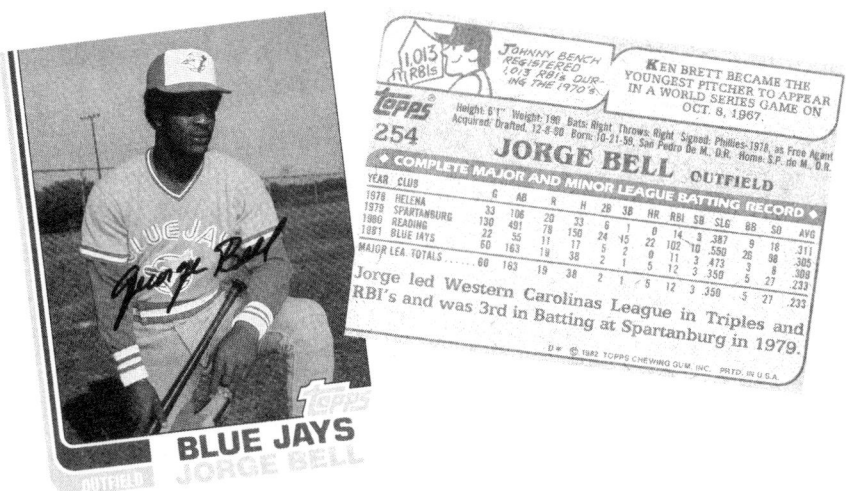

His Topps rookie card
read: "Jorge Bell" and
came out in 1982 after his
first year with the Jays. It
sells for $16.

As a lean, mean swinging
machine when he was
recalled from Syracuse in
July 1983.

He can be found in left field, at the plate and sometimes on the mound: taking a swing at Boston catcher Rich Gedman after he charged the mound to deliver a flying kick to Boston's Bruce Kison in 1985.

The Best Outfield in Baseball, some said, from left to right: George Bell, Lloyd Moseby and Jesse Barfield, in the dugout at Exhibition Stadium.

Old friends, good friends: Toronto's only Rookie of the Year, Alfredo Griffin, looks up at former teammate Damaso Garcia after being out at second in 1986.

FRED THORNHILL/TORONTO BLUE JAYS

Managers old and new. Above, manager Jimy Williams and ex-manager Bobby Cox who was at Exhibition Stadium for an old-timers game in 1986. Below: Cito Gaston, then the hitting coach, watches Jimy Williams' sleight of hand in 1988.

VERONICA MILNE/CANADA WIDE

Manager Cito Gaston has some words of advice at Tiger Stadium in 1989.

Frustration at the end of the final day of the 1987 season: the Jays lost seven straight to finish second.

Elation when negotiations ended: Jays vice president Pat Gillick sees if the hat fits after locking up Bell with a multi-year contract in February, 1988.

Papa Bell, with Georgie on his shoulders, holds Kevin in his arms, while Christopher stands on his own two feet, outside their San Pedro de Macoris home.

Masters of ceremonies at the first annual George Bell-Alfredo Griffin Celebrity Golf Tournement at Casa de Campo in the Dominican Republic, in 1987.

FRED THORNHILL/CANADA WIDE

There she goes! A game-winning grand slam off Mitch Williams of the Texas Rangers in September 1988.

and Rob Ducey — were ready. I know I can be erratic when it comes to throwing the ball, but I wasn't the worst when it came to cutting off balls that were going into the gap. And I didn't think Campy and Duce were ready to play in the big leagues.

After that quite a few people got into the argument. Randy stood up for me as always. Gillick argued the move would make the Blue Jays a better team. Finally I told them they could put up or shut up about the DH. "If you guys pay me the money I'm asking for, I'll DH for you." I upped my price to $7 million for three years, guaranteed. If I was going to lose money on my next contract because I was only a DH and not an outfielder, I wanted more on this contract. I doubted they would agree to this, but I hoped the demand would put an end to it. I was only fighting for my rights. I didn't yet have a contract for '88. What kind of a contract would I get next time around if at age 28 all I could do was be the DH? The DH position is a place for older, broken-down guys. Fred McGriff had been the DH against right-handers in 1987 but for him it was a temporary stop. The Jays wanted to keep me there until I was finished playing.

Jimy left that meeting in Arlington thinking I was going to be the DH, and I left the meeting thinking I'd DH maybe 15 games over the course of the season unless they paid what I had asked. I was determined not to DH unless they paid my price.

I flew to New York on February 16. The arbitration hearing was scheduled for the next day. When I checked into the Grand Hyatt it was late afternoon and I was tired, so I decided to take a nap. I was asleep when a couple of reporters from Toronto who I had seen in the lobby woke me up. Since I wasn't going to get any more sleep, I invited them up to my room. I told them I hoped we could get the contract signed in the morning and I asked them, "If you own a shoe company and one man makes a hundred pairs more than anyone else, why shouldn't he be paid more?" One asked me how I thought I compared with Don Mattingly, who had a contract similar to what we were shooting for. So I said, "Maybe I was lucky I hit 28 homers in 1985, lucky in '86 when I hit 31 and lucky last year. Maybe if I'm lucky enough I'll find a million dollars in the street tomorrow."

All three Hendricks brothers were at the Hyatt. So were Beeston, Gillick, and Gillick's assistant, Gordon Ash. Around 10:00 P.M. I found Randy and Paul Beeston in the second-floor cocktail lounge, the Sun Garden. Back and forth it went. One moment the Jays wouldn't give me a $50 000 bonus if I made the top five in the Most Valuable Player balloting, the next moment they would. Most of the talk was about the worth of the total package and how many years it would be spread over. About midnight everyone else showed up — they'd gone out to dinner — and Beeston said, "Who paid? I hope we didn't get stuck with the bill for dinner, too." I remember Gillick saying at one point that the ball club was worried about my shoulder or my knee. David's response was: "Pat, every year you keep saying that and every year George keeps getting better and better. When is your prediction going to come true?"

Randy and Pat and Paul were making notes on cocktail napkins and passing proposals and counterproposals back and forth over drinks. They were writing down numbers — million-dollar numbers — but they had to be careful where they printed. If the napkin was wet from a beer glass, then the pen wouldn't work. I've always thought that baseball is a business run so differently from most others. For example, I've seen a player get called into the manager's office after a game and told he's being sent down. The player is wearing a towel and the manager is naked after coming out of the showers. What other business is run like that?

Randy would say, "Hurry up, let's get this done. I have to get some sleep." Beeston would answer, "Why? I don't have to work tomorrow," and we'd laugh. Randy wanted to get to sleep. He had to be on his toes to present his case. After we'd been in the bar for a while Randy got angry — the Jays weren't compromising — so around 1:30 A.M. the two of us headed for the elevators. About an hour later Randy came down, gave another proposal to Beeston and Gillick and headed back to his room. When we went to bed their highest offer was $5.4 million over three years, but we wanted more.

After a few hours of sleep, Randy, David, Alan and I had eggs and coffee in the Hyatt coffee shop. Over breakfast Randy said that Gillick had phoned, woken him up and said, "Hello, Randal, maybe we should talk again." They were up to $5.6 million. David told me he figured we'd wind up with a total package of around $6 million. Then we all piled into a cab and went up to the American Arbitration Association building on 51st Street.

On the sixth floor, where the hearing was to take place, we met Beeston, Gillick and Ash in a empty room, the George Meany room. There was a table big enough for 20 or 30 people. The mahogany-panelled walls had probably heard a lot of disputes between unions and bosses. Beeston made a suggestion to David and me and all of a sudden Randy called the two of us out into the hallway. He was upset. "Look, you two, just shut up for 20 minutes, will you?" he told us. "You're going to ruin this deal." We'd been all set to take their offer.

By this time we were late for the scheduled start of the hearing. Now Beeston called Randy and me out into the hallway where Gillick was already waiting. Beeston offered $5.8 million. I looked at Randy and nodded, Beeston stuck out his hand and we shook — we had a deal. Then Randy and Beeston shook hands while I shook hands with Gillick. They had given in some and so had we. If they hadn't, we would have been headed for the other room, the one where the arbitrator was waiting.

With the deal sealed Gord Ash went around the corner and motioned to the press waiting down the hall, and in they came. This time all that the mahogany walls heard was Randy explaining the contract. We'd agreed to a package that called for two years plus an option year. The Blue Jays would pay me $5.8 million over three years if they picked up the option on the third year and $4 million guaranteed for the first two years if they didn't. That wasn't much different from what David had figured at breakfast, but it was about $800 000 less than the total package we'd been asking for.

My salary would be $1.9 million for '88, $1.9 million for '89 and $2 million in my option year of '90. That made me the ninth-highest-paid player in the game for 1988. I didn't get any signing bonus like some guys have been getting lately, but $200 000 of the final year was guaranteed. That meant I'd be paid that amount even if the Blue Jays didn't pick up my option. There was also a $50 000 bonus for making the All-Star team, the Silver Slugger (best offence at each position), or any of the MVP awards: regular season, the AL Championship Series or the World Series. So even if I didn't make any of the incentive clauses, and even if they didn't pick up my option, I was guaranteed $4 million over two years.

We were all in a pretty good mood. When the photographers were ready to take pictures of Gillick and me, Randy said, "Turn around in your chair, George, so they can get your good side." And my long-time pal David, of all people, said, "I was talking to one photographer in the hallway and he said, 'Taking George's picture is my toughest challenge since taking Cliff Johnson's picture.'" So Gillick and I were really laughing when the photos were taken.

That afternoon we all went out to eat and had a lot of laughs. The Hendrickses can always make Beeston laugh. Beeston says they have the market cornered when it comes to combining every human characteristic. Beeston can always make me laugh. I don't know many presidents of baseball teams, but they certainly can't all be like him. Earlier when Randy was going over the bonus package and we were arguing, Beeston looked very serious and said he wanted to add one more clause: "What about Comeback Player of the Year?" Since I was coming off an MVP year, we all laughed. I had no idea that these would be some of the last laughs I'd have with the Blue Jays for a long time.

All the time we talked in New York, my being the DH was never mentioned. Not once. Jimy wasn't there and we didn't bring this up because it wasn't our idea. Then when the Jays came up short with the money, I assumed that was it. So I left New York and headed for Santo Domingo expecting to be the regular left fielder and maybe the designated hitter in a few games. Soon the newspapers were referring to me as "The Two-Million-Dollar Man."

I was still at home in San Pedro five days later when the trouble began. The pitchers and catchers, who always report early, were already in Dunedin at training camp. Jimy was there and so were the reporters, and Jimy announced that I'd be the everyday DH in 1988. Under Jimy's plan, either Sil Campusano or Rob Ducey would win the job as the new, starting centre fielder come Opening Day and Lloyd Moseby would move to left field.

That day Larry Millson of the *Globe and Mail* phoned me to ask how I felt about being the new DH. I told him, "The Blue Jays are full of shit when they said they're trying to take care of my knees when I'm only 28 years old. I've played 631 games in the last four years." I was still in the Dominican for our Independence Day, February 27. I went to our national parade and then set off fire crackers with all the kids, just like my dad did with his children. In my baseball career, however, there wasn't a lot to celebrate; I knew I was in for a fight. For Jimy to discuss making me DH with the press first was the wrong way to deal with any player, whether he's the MVP or a rookie. Some of my friends said I shouldn't even show up at camp. I hadn't felt this low since 1982 at Syracuse when I had suffered one injury after another. To me it was a slap in the face. What would they have done if I had hit only 40 homers the year before instead of 47? Release me?

I flew into Tampa March 1, the day all the players had to report under the Players Association agreement. Dave Perkins of the *Toronto Star* met me at the airport and drove me over toDunedin. I told Perky, "We'll see who lasts longer with this organization, Jimy or me." I told him, "If the Jays want a DH, they should sign Cliff Johnson." I don't know whether the Blue Jays were worried about me coming to camp cocky. I know for sure, though, that not too many MVP winners came to camp and were told, "Sorry, you can't play your position anymore." I was hurt, insulted and angry. Maybe Jimy thought that he could make me do whatever he wanted because the Blue Jays were paying me a lot of money.

At the Englebert Complex the next day all the media asked me what I thought was going to happen. I said, "A bomb is going to explode." There were only a few fans around but they were yelling at me, telling me to do what I was told. I hadn't even made an error yet or struck out with a man on third. They didn't know the whole story.

Sometimes I think Jimy's main reason for coming to spring training was to kick my ass. When I was at home in San Pedro during the off-season I got a letter from Jimy saying I had to report to spring training weighing 195 pounds. The letter said it would be a $100 fine for each pound I was over. When I weighed in at 200 pounds I had to pay a $500 fine. That spring it was like Jimy was doing everything he could to get me. And the thing was, he got me.

I wasn't happy, but I kept my mouth shut after the first few days. I did what I was told. In spring training the players are divided into two groups for about the first 15 games or so. Every morning everyone works out. In the afternoon one of the two groups plays the game. The starting lineup is split evenly between the two teams because there is a rule for every spring game that at least four everyday starters have to start or else the fans complain. Jimy was playing me every other day like everyone else, but one game as the DH, the next one as the left fielder. That meant that out of every four days I was playing only one game in the outfield.

I was getting more and more upset. So was Lloyd. One day he told me, "I'll play anywhere, Egypt or Japan, but not left field." Lloyd said he'd been in centre field for eight years and wasn't about to move over to left close to the fans where they could throw rocks at him. And he also said if he was in left I might be one of the people throwing the rocks because he had taken my position. I wasn't angry with Lloyd. I sympathized with him and he felt for me. Willie Upshaw, Lloyd's best friend, didn't agree with what they were doing either. Jesse was the only one untouched by their changes, so Lloyd called him the "guarded one" and the "franchise." A season and a half before we'd been part of The Best Outfield in Baseball and now we had both lost our positions. Lloyd said moving him to left field was like ordering Tony Fernandez to take his Gold Glove and play first base.

Early on Jimy told Lloyd the change in outfield positions wasn't "etched in stone." Just like their plans for the rotation "weren't etched in stone." One morning early in spring training Lloyd came up to me in the clubhouse at Grant Field, real serious, and asked what I was doing after the game. Before I could answer he said we should go on an expedition for this stone where the Blue Jays had done all the writing, but hadn't got around to the "etching" yet. He figured it would have to be an awfully big rock. That was one day I had a laugh. I didn't have too many that spring.

Spring training is usually fun as well as work. You renew friendships, catch up on what everyone did over the winter, get yourself in shape and move at a relaxed pace. But the more I was the DH, the meaner I felt. I tried to get in condition. After practice I'd work out extra in the batting cage, but it's not the same as playing your position.

About the second week of spring training Jimy had me in his office for one of his talks, just the two of us. At this point I'd just about had it with being the DH, but I listened to what he had to say. He said he wanted me to be the DH so that I could get "700 quality at bats." He also said that if I was the DH I wouldn't miss any games. I looked it up, and no one in the history of the Blue Jays ever had 700 at bats. In '86, Tony Fernandez had 689 as the leadoff hitter and that's the most anyone had. What was I going to do, bat leadoff? Bat twice an inning? That 700 at bats was nonsense and I told him so. He said I had a chance for 60, maybe 70 homers if I was the DH. I had 610 at bats in '87 and hit 47 homers. What was I going to do? Hit 23 more home runs in 90 more at bats? What kind of math is that?

In our meeting I told Jimy all of this but he didn't like to be told he was wrong. That's the way Dominican people are; if we know we're right and you're wrong, we'll tell you right to your face. We aren't afraid because you're the manager or because you're the boss. If you don't admit it, that's your problem. Jimy was making a mistake moving me to the designated-hitter's spot: he was weakening our team and hurting my earning power. He wasn't used to having a player tell him he was wrong. Before I left his office I asked Jimy why he was trying to screw with my mind and ruin my career. I told him I was the only guy playing the game with a chance to win the MVP award twice in a row and I was halfway there. He looked at me and said, "I don't care about your career, I'm not concerned about you winning the MVP. I'm trying to win." So was I.

A few days later I looked up as I came walking back from batting practice and I heard this guy talking Spanish with a drawl. It was David Hendricks. He'd come to Dunedin to try to cheer me up. We stayed up until about two in the morning drinking rum, smoking cigars, talking over good times we'd had together and hoping things would soon get better. David left the next day and said, "We'll be laughing about this next time I see you because it will all be over. You'll be back in left." David also didn't think either Campy or Duce could win the job in centre. Most days I'd get some Kentucky Fried Chicken or some Chinese food and head back to the Ramada Inn. Until David showed up it seemed I was the only person in Dunedin who really cared about what I was going through. My dad knew I was right and he was very supportive. My mom was 100 percent behind me. She told me, "Hang in there. Don't let anybody put you down, and fight for what you think is right."

From the time Hurricane George blew in from the Caribbean amidst boos, catcalls and whispers from the Blue Jays' fans, he had been the centre of attention. Each day brought variations on the same questions from the media: "Have you accepted the role of DH?" "What's the big deal? You are still going to get your at bats," and "Do you think they are mistreating you?"

Never in the annals of baseball history had an MVP been treated in such a manner. Never mind that Bell put together back-to-back seasons with a .300 average, 30-plus homers and 100 or more RBIs. Bell was only the fifth player — Don Mattingly, Eddie Murray, Dale Murphy and Cecil Cooper were the others — to do so in successive years since '82. Over in the National League MVP Andre Dawson was welcomed to spring training like visiting royalty. The contrast was, to say the least, striking.

When Paul Beeston took the dais as an after-dinner speaker during the 1988-89 off season in Sudbury, he reflected the '88 season was lost in Florida — before the Blue Jays even began the 162-game schedule — because of the way the club handled the George Bell situation. This month-long period will not go into the Blue Jays' history books as the franchise's finest hour.

That St. Patrick's Day Thursday was a beautiful Florida spring day: bright sunshine, a gentle breeze off the water, a high sky with clouds. It was going to be easy for outfielders to catch flyballs. We were playing the Red Sox at Dunedin — at least the Blue Jays were. When

John McLaren, our third-base coach, put the lineup card on the wall I was the DH again. That's when I decided I couldn't take it anymore. This wasn't working out: DH one day, a day off, play left, another day off. At this rate I wasn't going to be ready for Opening Day. I decided to make a stand. I had told them no nicely, three or four times. I said to myself, "*No mas, no mas.*"

About two hours before the game I came in from batting practice and went over to talk to Cito Gaston, our batting coach. I knew I could trust Cito. I asked him if he would please tell Jimy I wasn't going to DH for him anymore, the experiment was over. Cito, a man I love like a brother, asked me if I was sure. I nodded yes. A few minutes later Cito came back to me and said, "Jimy isn't putting you in left field." I said, "Well, forget it, I'm not DH-ing anymore." If they wanted me out there they'd have to put me in left field.

I came out of the clubhouse and, instead of turning right and heading along the fence towards the dugout, I turned left and walked down the left-field line and sat on the tarpaulin in our bullpen. I looked up in the seats; a lot of the people were dressed in green because it was St. Patrick's Day. I just sat there. I don't think any of our guys knew I'd told Cito I wouldn't DH. I knew Cito wouldn't tell them. From my seat on the tarp I watched Mike Flanagan get the Red Sox out in the top of the first. I stayed where I was as Nelson Liriano swung his bat in the on-deck circle. I was due up fourth. I watched Steve Curry, who was pitching for the Red Sox, make his warm-up pitches and I thought back to when the two of us had been together eight seasons before at Reading Double A. Now we were back on the same ball field, but I wouldn't be hitting against him. Nellie led off with a ground ball to third base, but Randy Kutcher made an error. Then Curry walked Lloyd. Up came Rance Mulliniks, which meant I was supposed to be on deck. Rance flew out to right field.

Then over the loudspeaker at Grant Field came the voice of announcer Gerry MacDonald: "Now batting for the Blue Jays . . . number 11 . . . the designated hitter . . . George Bell." The fans were booing by the time he said my number, never mind my name. Others were laughing when he said designated hitter. I didn't budge. It was Jimy's move and he didn't wait long. Rance wasn't even back in the dugout when Willie Upshaw came out to pinch-hit in my spot. He was taking his practice swings when out bounced Jimy. He came stomping down the left-field line towards me with his hand down the front of his pants like he always did when he was walking to the mound to make a pitching change or whenever he was upset.

Once Jimy was past third base he signalled for me to come into his office inside the clubhouse. As I walked up the alleyway leading to the clubhouse entrance the fans in the left field bleachers were yelling — some at me and some at Jimy. Not many were on my side, although I don't know if everyone really knew what was going on. When we got inside Jimy's office, he acted like he was going to whip my ass. Jimy didn't say much. All he did was scream in my face, "This is my team. You're not running it, you're not ruining it either. I tell you where to play and when. I'M THE MANAGER!" When he was finished I yelled back at him, "Soon as you find someone to replace me in left you can take me out of there. If not, tell Gillick he can trade me. Because if you don't do one or the other you have to put me out there. I'm good enough to play for *your team*." It wasn't ever really his team — it was Toronto's team.

If Jimy thought I was going to be scared and do whatever he said, he was wrong. Some people think you're always supposed to do what the boss, or the manager, says. What if a manager says to run into the wall to catch a ball when we're winning 10-1? Get hurt banging into a wall at full speed when you're ahead by that much? Forget it!

After Jimy was finished screaming, he fined me $1000 for refusing to be the designated hitter and told me I'd be suspended if I ever refused to bat again. Then he headed back to the field and I went out into the clubhouse. I was sitting in front of my locker, with my head down, when the photographers and writers started to come in one-by-one. In spring training, the media is allowed to come into the clubhouse any time they want during the games. That day there must have been 30 or 40 of them in the room, all staring at me. Out on the field Tony Fernandez could have made the greatest play in the history of baseball and no one would have seen it. At first I didn't do anything. I told a couple of guys I wasn't talking, but when they started to turn on the TV lights and click the flashbulbs I started yelling at them to get away from me. Then I asked Jeff Ross, our equipment manager and a good friend, to kick them all out. It took a while and there was some arguing about their rights, but finally they left.

People asked afterwards if Lloyd had talked to me, stirred me up and made me pull the "power play." Others figured I must have been talking to my old friend Damo Garcia. Neither is true. No one suggested the idea. I made the decision on my own. Everyone knew Lloyd was almost as unhappy as I was about being moved. He was still unhappy even after they gave him a one-year contract extension for $1.1 million. Lloyd deserved it: he'd played eight years and his home-run totals hadn't gone down once. Not many guys could say that.

The night I was fined I didn't have David or Randy or anyone else to confide in. I drove my white rental car back to my hotel room at the Ramada Inn feeling as if the whole world was against me. I wasn't hungry so I lay on the brown bedspread surrounded by tan-coloured walls, tan-coloured rugs, with the brown curtains shut tight and stared at the TV. The room was as dark as my mood.

I kept going over and over in my mind what had happened: I had been the MVP in the American League the year before, I hadn't been injured and before we'd even played a game the Blue Jays had decided I wasn't good enough to play in left field anymore. Andre Dawson, the MVP of the National League, was being treated like a hero. I was being treated like a broken-down old man at the end of his career. I'm a proud man and this was more than I could take.

At the time it felt like George Bell against everyone, but later I was told our broadcaster, Tony Kubek, stuck up for me. Kubek and I used to argue back and forth since he was always picking the Yankees to win our division. But it was friendly give-and-take. Anyway, a guy told me about an incident in our bullpen a few innings after I had refused to bat. Kubek was sitting with Rick Leach, who told him that the Blue Jays should fine me a lot of money and suspend me for about a week — $1000 wasn't enough. Kubek pointed out there was no way the Blue Jays could do that since they already had set a precedent.

Leach thought for a moment but couldn't remember one. That's when Kubek reminded him about the previous August.

In August of 1987, we were in Seattle in the middle of a pennant race and Leach was supposed to play in right field because Jesse was in a slump and Seattle was pitching right-hander Mike Moore. Leach didn't show for the game and everyone was worried. The ball club even phoned the police to look for him. Next morning, Leach turned up and when we got back to Toronto he was fined. Kubek said if the Blue Jays hadn't suspended Leach but had given him a fine, they couldn't very well suspend me. So Leach of all people wasn't in any position to knock what I did.

That night David Hendricks was in Abilene, Texas, when he got a call from Gillick. The message said, "George has gone on strike." Reporters were phoning my room, so I had the hotel operator hold all my calls. David tried to reach me, but he couldn't get through. The next morning I talked to both Randy and David. Both listened; neither said I was in the wrong.

That day I went to Plant City with the rest of the team to play the Reds. It was Friday, my turn to play in left field. I soon found out what a big deal my "strike" had become. There are Canadian fans in every city we go to in Florida and they booed me as soon as I walked out to the batting cage before the gates opened. They booed me playing catch before the game and every time I came to bat. The fans were really upset. My picture was in the Florida papers, on the TV and the first item on ESPN. A lot of Dominican reporters were there and they wanted my side of the story. I told them I would never DH again. I meant it. I had had enough.

Now that the issue of me moving to the DH spot had come to a head, a lot of players, like Kelly Gruber and Willie Upshaw, spoke out on my behalf. Gruber said, "There isn't anything wrong with standing up for what you think is right. If you have any principles you have to stand up for them. I have to be behind him, just like umpires stick together and the front office sticks together." Willie said he didn't think I had been treated fairly. Lloyd was on my side too. I heard Lloyd say to a reporter, "Well, how bad a year did he have last year anyway?" Lloyd said I had to be the first MVP winner to come to camp and not have his old job back.

Players supported me, but the ones I really needed support from were older guys like Ernie. All Ernie did was put me deeper in the hole. The Blue Jays even had Ernie Whitt talk to me and he gave me this big speech about how the Blue Jays paid me a lot of money and I should do what they tell me, play wherever they want me to play, do what's best for the team, blah, blah, blah. "No way, Ernie," I told him. "You don't know what I'm going through. Wait until it happens to you." Ernie said that if he were in my position he would do whatever the ball club told him.

Ernie didn't have to wait long to find out how I felt. In '89 the Jays brought up Greg Myers, a left-handed catcher just like Ernie. So Ernie and Myers took turns against right-handers. One would catch and the other would be the DH. After about a week of this Ernie started complaining to the papers about how unhappy he was. He even said he felt like he was "half a player." Where did he get that phrase, I wonder? Ernie said he knew what the initials DH stood for: Dick Head. Now he knew how it felt. It's awful when you know you can play and they give your job away.

Many players and coaches around the league told me the team was wrong the way it was treating me. One coach with the Royals said, "If the Blue Jays were smart they would leave George Bell alone, let him go out there and let him play." In another story a guy who used to manage the Twins was quoted as saying, "We can't understand why the Blue Jays are messing with a good situation. We're not the only team that doesn't understand it. And we're not the only team in the American League laughing at them either."

Saturday I worked out though I was in the group that had the day off. On the Sunday, March 20, we played the Pirates in Dunedin. My turn to be the DH again, our first home game since St. Patrick's Day. Everywhere I went — the batting cage, the clubhouse, the bullpen — writers were asking me whether I would DH. Right up until half an hour before game time they were asking me what I was going to do. I told some I wouldn't DH, so they should stick around. I was having fun with them. I *was* going to DH. The truth is the Jays had threatened me with a $2000 fine and a 30-day suspension if I didn't DH. Randy told me it was best to do what they said.

Everyone stuck around. I didn't sit in the dugout because it was too close to Jimy, but stayed in left field lying on the grass. When I walked in front of the bleachers towards the dugout, the fans booed me and they booed me again every time I was at bat. I was 1-for-4, a single which drove in a run against Pittsburgh's Bob Walk. After I had my turn at bat I'd drop my helmet and bat and head back down to the bullpen. On my way some of those fans down the left-field line yelled some mean things at me, like "See you in three innings, you Dominican jerk"; "Can I buy your glove or are you sending it to Cooperstown?" and "You're not the designated hitter, you're the designated hot head." Of course people around them laughed when they said those things. Sometimes they'd throw in some bad language too even though they were sitting there with their kids beside them. The only cheer they gave me was the Bronx cheer. Later I did get a lot of calls from friends in Toronto who were very supportive. But the only person who would listen to everything I was going through was Randy Hendricks.

On March 22, five days after I had refused to DH against Boston, Randy came back to town and we had a long morning meeting at the Englebert Complex with Beeston, Gillick and Jimy Williams. By this time it was obvious that if they stuck with their plan, the centre fielder would be Sil Campusano. This wasn't anything like our last meeting in New York when we were laughing and joking with each other. It was very serious. I remember Randy arguing, "The Blue Jays will look like a very smart organization if Campy fields like Gary Pettis and hits like Mike Greenwell while George Bell chases Babe Ruth's home-run records as the DH, but they'll look like a stubborn organization if Campy fields like Pettis and hits like Pettis and they play him over George Bell." Randy said if that happened he expected the Jays to be logical and forget the experiment. Greenwell is one of the best-hitting outfielders around, while Pettis doesn't hit a whole lot. It's almost impossible to hit a ball over the head of Pettis when he's playing centre field. Defensively he's one of the best.

At the meeting we reached an agreement although neither we nor the Blue Jays said anything about it at the time. I agreed I wouldn't complain about being the DH and they agreed that if after a month it wasn't working out I would go back to being the regular left fielder.

After the meeting, most of the sportwriters wrote that Jimy won and I lost. I just smiled, I didn't say a thing. I knew where I would be within a month. I'd be back in left. I felt a lot better but I still wasn't happy.

For the final few spring games everything was back to normal, sort of. By now the regulars were playing every day, so I'd DH one game and play left the next. Things settled down and we headed for Denver for our final exhibition games against Minnesota and then on to Kansas City to open the season. In Denver, all the writers wanted to talk about was the DH thing. Lloyd said, "Be prepared. It's going to be this way whatever city we go to. You're big news."

On Opening Day, a Monday afternoon game, I was the designated hitter and hit three homers against Bret Saberhagen and the Royals. We beat them 5-3. I've had good days and bad against Saberhagen, but I wanted to do well. I did, but Jimy wasn't impressed. That day he didn't even shake my hand.

After the game there was the usual crowd of reporters. One of them asked, "Did you know you were the first player to ever hit three homers on Opening Day?" I shook my head no, but I was thinking I was probably the only player to go through a spring like I'd just gone through. I was thinking I'd had something to prove and I'd proved it. After that, every question was about DH-ing, "Did you not prove you could DH by what you did today?" "Were the Blue Jays right in their decision?" and other questions. Since it was Kansas City, the next thing I knew we were back into talking about my comments during the '85 playoffs when I'd said the umps were anti-Dominican, anti-Canadian. That was enough for me, and after about 20 minutes I headed for the showers. After everyone had left, Tom Henke walked by. "What's the big fuss?" Henk asked. "You haven't even got a hit inside the park yet." Even though I was in a bad mood that made me laugh.

We had the next day off and Jimy was up to his old tricks, talking to the press before he had communicated a decision to the player. This time it was Cecil Fielder who got the bad news from a writer. All spring Jimy had said Cecil would platoon at first base with Fred McGriff. Freddie would play against right-handed pitchers and Cecil would be in the lineup against lefties. On the off day he announced that Freddie would play every day, even the next day, against lefty Charlie Leibrandt. I heard a writer ask him, "Even though Cecil had three homers against Leibrandt last year?" Jimy said yes. Big Cecil never got upset but he asked me what was going on, so I told him to talk to Cito. Cito would give him a straight answer. Then on Wednesday, before the game, Jimy changed his mind and put Cecil back in the lineup. So it wound up Cecil had been worried for nothing.

I like playing in Kansas City. The second game, against Leibrandt, I was back in left field and went 5-for-5, had two doubles and drove in a run. As far as Jimy was concerned, however, those first two games in Kansas City might as well not have happened. I might as well have struck out every time or been playing on the moon. Afterwards I thought to myself, "Fine, I'm not playing to please him anyway. I'll just do my job and get back in left as soon as possible."

I was in left field again for our home opener at Exhibition Stadium against the Yankees and right-hander Rick Rhoden. The fans gave me a big ovation as we lined up along the third-baseline during the pre-game introductions. Neil MacCarl of the *Toronto Star* presented me with the Jays' Player of the Year award from 1987 and I got a nice hand then, too. That was a pleasant change after all the boos I'd had in Florida and on the road. In the game I was 3-for-4 with two doubles and I knocked in two runs. We won 17-9. I wasn't letting the controversy hurt my play. After 10 games, five games as the DH and five in left field, we were 4-6 and I was batting 15-for-36 (.417) with seven RBIs. I didn't like the uncertainty but I kept my mouth shut. Every other day the reporters would try to get me going about not liking being the DH, just like in spring training. But I didn't bite.

We split our four-game home series against the Yankees, who had started quickly with eight wins in nine games, and we were already four and a half games back. Then Minnesota came to town. The first game, Friday night, April 15, was cancelled because of freezing weather. I guess they must have had a meeting that day to reconsider their experiment because Saturday morning Lloyd was smiling when I got to Exhibition Stadium. From his expression he didn't have to say anything. He was back in centre and I was back in left and Campy was on the bench as an extra outfielder. All that trouble in the spring for 10 games?

The Blue Jays had put Campy in a difficult position. He was under a lot of pressure and he had struggled, hitting only .130 (3-for-23). The fact Campy hit worse than Gary Pettis, as Randy had predicted, helped change their mind. My keeping my mouth shut also helped. Who knows what else? I was just happy to be back in left field. But I didn't go around gloating because they could have changed their minds any time.

Imagine how many trees died so reporters could write stories about whether it was right or wrong for me to be moved to DH and how many died so they could write I was wrong in not going to the plate that day in Florida! Sometimes I think I sell more newspapers in Toronto than the prime minister.

I still don't understand why Gillick and Williams tried to mess around with a good ball club in 1988. If you couldn't win with that ball club you should have jumped off a bridge. The only thing Jimy had to do with that ball club was write down the lineup. He had three guys in the outfield who went out there every day giving 100 percent. He had good starting pitching, a strong bullpen and finally some men in the infield who knew how to play. Sometimes it seemed that he worried more about things that were happening in the clubhouse than about what happened on the field.

Someone once asked me if I would have been the designated hitter for Coxie when I wouldn't be for Jimy Williams. That's a meaningless question because Coxie never did ask me to DH. The thought of forcing me to be the DH, like Jimy tried to do, would never have entered his mind. He knew I could play and Coxie had respect for his players. If a guy went out and gave 100 percent every single day and did his job, Cox wouldn't mess with that player.

When Coxie was the manager things were different. He told you what spot you were going to be in and left you there. In the home opener of the '84 season against the Orioles, Sammy Stewart was pitching in relief. Jimy was coaching third base. We had runners at first and second with no one out in the bottom of the eighth and the score tied 2-2. So Coxie gave Jimy the signal to give me the bunt sign. I fouled the first pitch off and Rick Dempsey, their catcher, almost caught it. Everyone knows I can't bunt.

Coxie told Jimy to take the bunt sign off. I hit the next pitch into right field for a single. Willie Upshaw scored and we won 3-2. When I got to the dugout Bobby Cox shook my hand.

7

Goodbye, Jimy

"Right now, if Jimy Williams phoned me and said, 'Let's go to Japan, I'm the manager, I'll pay you $10 million a year,' I wouldn't go. I know I can't get along with him."
— *George Bell, November 30, 1989*

THINGS COOLED DOWN A LITTLE AFTER JIMY PUT ME back in left field and Lloyd in centre, but not for long. Now it was Jesse's turn to be unhappy. It didn't look as if "The Best Outfield in Baseball" was going to be together too much longer. Over the winter the Jays had tried to trade Jesse to Los Angeles for right-hander Bob Welch. They tried again in the spring and they were still trying when we went to New York April 22. We were tied with the Yankees, four and a half games out of first place.

Before the series started the newspapers reported that we were going to trade Jesse for Dave Winfield, possibly the Yankees' best hitter and a Gold Glove right fielder. I heard from someone with the Yankees that the trade had been agreed upon two weeks earlier when we had played the Yankees at home. But George Steinbrenner hadn't wanted to finalize the deal until after we'd played the Yankees in New York. He didn't want Winfield to come into Yankee Stadium with us and have all the fans cheering for him. That's what happened in 1983 after Steinbrenner let Reggie Jackson go to the Angels. The fans had chanted, "Steinbrenner sucks! Steinbrenner sucks!"

Winfield was off to a great start, hitting over .350; Jesse was not. What made it even more complicated was that Winfield had 10 years experience and five with the same team so he could veto a trade to any team. Also, when Steinbrenner signed him he had given Dave a no-trade clause to seven cities and we were one of the cities on the list. But the Yankees were now arguing that you can't have a "no-trade clause" at both ends of the contract. One of the Yankee players told me Steinbrenner was so angry with Winfield for some of the things he had written about in his book that he was all set to trade him and let the lawyers argue.

Apart from the trade talk the series pretty much went the way it usually does when we're in New York. We won Friday 6-4 and Saturday 3-2 but lost Sunday 5-3. In the fifth inning on Sunday, Jesse, running in from right field with his head down whispered to Winfield, "Veto the deal." In the end, Steinbrenner didn't show up and Jesse stayed with us — for now.

After the Sunday game in New York we took a charter from La Guardia to Saint John, New Brunswick, where on Monday we were scheduled to play a charity game against the National Baseball Institute from Vancouver, a group of Canadian college prospects. By the time we arrived it was around 11:30 at night and raining, but the people running things had arranged for a seafood restaurant to stay open late so that all the ballplayers could get something to eat. A few of the waiters and waitresses had invited friends there, so it wasn't a closed reception.

I was at a table with Jim Clancy, John Cerutti and Rick Leach. We were telling stories, having a few beers and laughing about what it was like playing in the minors, when all of a sudden a fight broke out in another part of the restaurant. When I heard the noise I went over to try to cool things down. David Wells and Todd Stottlemyre and some of the locals were making all the racket. I don't know what they were arguing about, but they were quickly drawing a crowd.

Suddenly this guy who wanted to fight was after Rick Leach, who was getting a little loud. I tried to take Rick out of the way. The guy took a swing at Rick and he caught me with his follow-through instead. I turned around and popped him. That was it. It was over. We got Stottlemyre and Wells out of there pretty fast. As far as I could tell it hadn't been their fault.

Our game the next day was snowed out. So those poor kids from NBI had flown all the way from the west coast to watch the snow come down and we had flown that far to get in trouble in a bar. Ernie Whitt had already told all the players to keep their mouths shut about the fight. On the bus to the airport David Wells was teasing Stottlemyre; I told him to keep it down because there were writers present. Wells kept singing this song that had a line about how they kept swinging. There wasn't anything in the papers about the fight because no one knew about it.

We were eight and a half games out on May 5, when we lost 8-5 in Oakland. Jose Nunez was charged with the loss. Jose is a hard-throwing young right-hander who had impressed me — and not just because he was Dominican. I was never impressed, though, with the way he was treated. We'd acquired him from the Royals in the major-league draft before the 1987 season, the same way I came over to the Blue Jays. His first year he started a few games, but so far in 1988 he'd been used mostly in relief.

I've seen a lot of guys who came to pitch and didn't have half the stuff Jose had. But over and over again with Jose, Jimy and Al Widmar, our pitching coach, gave Ernie Whitt the sign for what pitch to call. If Jose shook off Ernie a couple of times and didn't want to throw the pitch that Ernie called, Jimy would flash the sign from the dugout and then Ernie would relay it to Jose. There's no way in the world you can play like that. It destroys a pitcher's confidence. Jimy was calling pitches for Jose from the dugout but not for the other guys. Not for David Wells, not for Duane Ward, not for Todd Stottlemyre or any of our other young throwers. Never did he let Jose go out there and do his job the way he's supposed to.

Playing under Jimy as a manager was always like being in the army, but in 1988 it got worse. Even in an army barracks you probably have a TV to watch. In 1988 Jimy restricted the amount of time we could watch the TVs in the clubhouse and lounge before the game. Soon as batting practice started, the TV was off. Guys who were out of the game, or relievers who didn't head down to the bullpen until a couple of innings before it was time for them to work, couldn't even sit in the lounge and watch the game on TV. He thought we'd be switching to another channel. Then he announced we had to quit playing cards at a certain time.

I was trying to do my job in 1988, but it was tougher — and not just because of Jimy. Cito Gaston had warned me that because I'd been MVP, guys would pitch me differently. Actually I was doing okay with my average but not with my home-run swing. I don't know whether the DH experiment had taken its toll or not, but after two months I had only seven homers and 25 runs batted in. By the end of May we were 12 games back, seven games under .500. On June 7, I went hitless against Cleveland and my average was now under .300 for the first time all season.

June 9 was Ernie Whitt's annual charity golf tournament at Nobleton Lakes and that's when the news about the fight in New Brunswick came out. I guess people who worked in the bar were talking about it and eventually the story reached Halifax. Someone from there phoned Toronto, and the next thing you know we're reading it in the paper. They called it a "pier sixer," blood all over the place, women knocked down with punches and all kinds of crazy things. That one punch I threw must have been a big one. Most of the stories concerned me. I got all the ink and I hadn't even started the fight.

Now we were the brawling Blue Jays on and off the field. Todd Stottlemyre, who is a good kid, was embarrassed. He said, "My father played in the major leagues 11 years and never had his picture in the paper for a bar fight and here I'm in there as a rookie."

After being so dominant during most of 1987, we were losing one and winning one at the start of 1988. That's how it was through June, although we were gradually gaining ground. On June 24 when Mike Flanagan beat Detroit 4-1 at Exhibition Stadium, we were 37-37, .500 for only the second time all season. But on July 10, when we won our last game before the All-Star break to move to within 11 and a half games of first, we'd dropped four games below .500.

When we resumed play it was as if Jimy and I were making up for lost time. It all started on July 14 in Oakland, our first game of a 13-game road trip. Before batting practice that day Jimy invited me and a few other players into his office for a closed-door meeting. The other players were Jimmy Key, Mike Flanagan, Kelly Gruber, Lloyd Moseby and Ernie Whitt. Jimy started by saying that we were the veterans, the guys the younger players looked up to. The purpose of the meeting was to make the team better, he told us, and he wanted our help. I sat there quietly and listened to what Jimy was saying but inside I was thinking that I didn't want any part of whatever Jimy Williams was going to decide to do.

The bottom line was that Jimy wanted us to talk to the younger players when they did something wrong, for example, if a guy showed up late or wasn't working hard in batting practice. The other guys at the meeting got into this idea right away. They began to discuss certain players and their problems. It's easy to put the knock on someone not in the same room with you. I didn't say anything. I wasn't going to get involved in talking behind the backs of other players. The one time I opened my mouth I said, "Let's go win some games."

The way I saw it then, and the way I still see it, is that Jimy was trying to pit us against our teammates. I didn't agree with the concept. The meeting had nothing to do with it, but we started the second half strong. We won five out of seven games in Oakland and Anaheim and then on July 21 we went to Seattle. That was when Jimy announced that we were having another meeting. I refused. I said, "I'm sorry, Jimy, but that's not part of my job. It's my job to come to the park, play some cards, have a little fun, take batting practice, get ready, then go out there and win. I don't care about what other guys are doing. I'm going out there to perform for myself. That's not selfish. I try to do the best I can to win, but I can't go into a meeting with a manager behind closed doors and rip somebody else's ass." As far as I'm concerned, Jimy wanted us to do some of his work for him. It was his job to talk with players who were having problems to try to straighten them out.

Jimy was angry and I could tell from the look I got from Ernie that he didn't agree either. Maybe I shouldn't have challenged Jimy in front of other guys, but I didn't need that responsibility. Jimy wanted me to say to Manny Lee, "Hey, you should be hitting the ball to the right side with none out and a man on second." Or tell Pat

Borders, "Pay more attention when you're sitting on the bench; listen to what the pitcher says." They're just examples, but he wanted me to be Big Brother. That's not my style. I enjoy helping a team-mate and I've done it more than once. Kelly Gruber finished the '89 season with the same batting stance I had in '88 because he and I had worked together on his stance in the spring. I can be a terrible fielder but I know what to do with a bat. So I helped Gruber hit the ball. Big deal. If one of our guys is doing something wrong at the plate, I'll suggest he adjust his hands or whatever. But George Bell isn't going to go around telling on other players.

I hadn't fielded the ball well in Anaheim, and Ernie Whitt wrote in his book *Catch* that that's why I refused to go to the second meeting. Ernie wrote, "I didn't think what George did was a class act at all. Jimy had gone out of his way to show confidence in George and to treat him as a leader of this club, then George just turned his back and refused to have anything to do with something that was supposed to help the team turn things around. That told me George was only thinking of himself. But, again, when George has his mind made up about something, no one can change it." Ernie is wrong. Those meetings weren't good for the team and after the first one I made my mind up I'd never go to another.

After Seattle there were no more meetings. I don't know whether Jimy stopped calling them or other guys stopped going, but there were only two meetings of the veterans. Of course I knew Jimy was mad, even though he didn't say anything to me. Looking back, I guess he was just waiting for his chance to get even.

A few days later, on July 26, we were in Minneapolis and we were ahead 3-0 in the sixth inning. Jim Clancy was pitching and the Twins had Kent Hrbek at first and Kirby Puckett on second when Gary Gaetti singled to left. I fielded the bouncing ball and threw home. Ernie was catching, but he didn't even try to catch the high throw and it went all the way to the screen. Although the ball got away from my hand a little bit early, I thought I'd made a good throw. Ernie said it was a bad throw, and I'm sure he thinks that even now.

Puckett scored and Gaetti went to second base on the throw instead of staying at first. Then Todd Stottlemyre came on in relief and walked Gene Larkin, Tim Laudner and Eric Bullock — three guys in a row — to force in two runs and tie the score. The error on the throw gave me six errors in seven games on that road trip. After the inning, when I came into the dugout and placed my glove on the dugout steps, Jimy was there waiting for me. The game was being televised, so everyone watching could see what happened next. He could have waited until later, after the game. Not Jimy. The first thing I remember him saying was, "They pay you two million dollars and you can't even hit the fucking cut-off man with a throw." I yelled back at him, "Do you think I was trying to throw the ball away?" He said, "You're out of the fucking game, you no-good prick! Take a shower! Go home! Get the fuck out of here." Same old story. Jimy yelled at me, so I yelled back at him, "Fuck you, Jimy! You know I want to win." Then I said something I shouldn't have. I said that Ernie should have caught the ball. Jimy didn't notice, he was too steamed. And he said something he shouldn't have: he said if it wasn't for my bat I'd be back home in the Dominican cutting sugarcane. That was going too far.

As I started towards him, Lloyd stepped in between us. Then Cito stood up and started towards me. Cito told me to go to the clubhouse and I did what he asked. I walked up the three levels of stairs with Jimy screaming at me all the way. A couple of times I yelled back, but I was getting a little tired of this. I went down the hallway and into the empty clubhouse.

Later the writers said that I didn't have a chance at the runner at the plate and that I should have hit the cut-off man. That would have kept Gaetti at first base and maybe we could have had a double-play ball. Maybe we would have won that game if I had made the throw Jimy and everyone else wanted, but I know no one else on the field wanted to win more than I did. We got beat 6-3 when the Twins scored in the seventh inning against Duane Ward. That put us 10 games out of first place.

After the game Jimy told the writers he was tired of being shown up by me. What about me? He's the one who didn't care about people's feelings, the one who ran the length of the dugout scream-ing at me in front of players. Then Jimy said the media was too soft on me. Now that's a funny one. Who was ripped more in the papers during the '88 season than I was? I guess Jimy was trying to get writers and TV people to do his job for him, just like he did with the meetings with the veterans when he wanted me to go around spying.

The next day, Wednesday, we had an afternoon game and Jimy benched me. He didn't say a thing, just left my name off the lineup card. I was more concerned that Ernie was upset because I'd said he should have caught the ball. Before the game Ernie asked me if I had said he should have caught the ball. I told him yes. He said, "You messed up and you shouldn't have thought about throwing home. You should have tried to keep the double play in order." Whatever I thought about the play I knew it was wrong to show up a teammate. I apologized to Ernie. I said, "This whole year has been bad from start to finish, nothing has gone right." Ernie didn't say much after that. He just walked away and we didn't speak for a few days.

The club flew home that night and the TV, radio and papers were on my case again. You'd think I was a criminal the way they were talking about me: "Trade him, suspend him, fine him, teach him a lesson, get him out of town."

On Thursday, I phoned Wayne Parrish of the *Toronto Sun*, a writer I trusted. We met at my condo in downtown Toronto. I really poured my heart out for the first time. We talked for hours and I told him some of the things Jimy had said. I wasn't talking to the press in Minneapolis so of course all the writers heard was Jimy's side of it. He denied a lot of the things that had happened. I told Parrish I didn't know how much longer I could take this: if the Blue Jays wanted they could release me. Or maybe I'd just go home to the Dominican and cut sugarcane. I didn't really mean that. Those few days were as tough on me mentally as the spring-training arguments had been.

After that Jimy benched me for two more games. The first game I was sitting at the end of the dugout and someone hit a foul ball, which I fielded on one hop. Next thing I knew the people on the first-base side gave me a standing ovation for the grab. The second game Jimy sent me up to pinch-hit for Lloyd in the eighth inning.

We were losing 2-1 with one out and Manny Lee was on second. Lloyd threw his helmet on the ground and headed for the clubhouse. I popped up and Manny, thinking there were two out, kept on running so I'd hit into a double play, the inning was over and we later lost 3-1.

I started the game July 31 and we lost 6-3 to the Yankees. The fans booed me every time up. The next day, against Minnesota, Frank Viola took a 1-0 lead into the bottom of the eighth when Tony Fernandez led off with a single and Manny Lee beat Greg Gagne's throw to first. Then I came up and hit a 2-1 pitch for a three-run homer off Jeff Reardon and we won 3-1. The ball cleared the 375-foot sign in right centre. The fans had booed me when I came up, but now they gave me a standing ovation and cheered so long Kelly Gruber had to step out. They cheered even louder, so I stepped out of the dugout and waved. It was my first hit since Minneapolis.

In August it seemed like the season was starting to turn around for us and, as so often before, it was on a trip to New York that things got started. On August 9-11 we swept a three-game series, winning the last one in 11 innings to reach the .500 mark for only the third time all season. Then we went in to Kansas City and won our first two games there to make it five straight. We were still nine and a half games behind Boston.

On August 28, I homered against Ed Van de Berg in Texas and it was my first homer in 20 games. The team had fallen back again and we entered September three games below .500, and 10 and a half behind Boston. But the Red Sox were also struggling and again we were playing better. We thought we had a chance.

We started September with seven straight wins, but the fourth game on that streak, September 4, is an especially good memory for me. We were playing the Texas Rangers and Bobby Witt was pitching a great game, carrying a 6-0 lead into the eighth inning at Exhibition Stadium. We scraped back and were down 7-5 in the bottom of the ninth, when Manny Lee reached first on a strike-out pitch that went to the screen. Then Tony hit a single and Lloyd bunted for a base hit to load the bases. Mitch Williams was on in relief and I hit a fastball right on the face. It must have gone 25 rows up into the left-field bleachers. I don't usually stand and watch them like Reggie Jackson used to, but I watched that one. Lloyd said I almost bumped into Mitch when he was walking across the first-base line coming off the mound with his head down. I didn't notice him. I was watching the people in left field jumping up and down. It was my sixth career grand slam and we won 9-7.

Everyone was there waiting for me — Manny, Tony and Lloyd. I told Tony he was getting so old I had to hit the ball out of the park to make sure he'd score — a single wouldn't do. Tony gave that little giggle of his and I gave him a great big bear hug. The fans gave me a standing ovation. They cheered so loud and long I had to come out for a curtain call that hadn't happened since the late July game against the Twins.

That was the happiest I'd been all season. I was interviewed on a radio post-game show and as usual was given a gift certificate. After the interview I gave it to a policeman standing beside the dugout — I always give those things away — and then a CTV cameraman asked me to sign a ball, which I did. As I was walking away he said, "Thanks, George. You're the greatest." We were only six and a half games behind the Tigers and the Red Sox, who were tied for first, and I felt like I was going to turn around my season. I'd had 14 RBIs in my last 39 at bats.

But the season was over for the team. When we arrived in Boston on September 26 we were seven and a half games back and had been eliminated from the race the day before with a loss in Cleveland. Still we didn't want to be the ones to watch Boston win the AL East championship. One Boston win and they'd clinch it. We wanted three wins, but when Jimy announced he was starting three lefties in the series, the papers were full of stories about how everyone knows lefties can't win in Boston. Well, Jeff Musselman, Mike Flanagan and Jimmy Key each won and when we left Boston they were still going back through the records to see the last time that a club had swept Boston at Fenway using nothing but left-handed starters.

We came home and swept Baltimore to finish two games behind in the final standings, just like the year before. Finally, when it didn't matter, we had had a good September. I remember Pat Gillick saying after the one hundred and sixty-second game, "Twenty years from now people will look at the 1987 standings and say how it must have been a marvellous race, tremendous excitement. Then they'll come to 1988 and see the standings and think the same thing, but we'll know different."

A lot of guys think it was all my fault that we didn't win in '88, that the season was lost in spring training. I'll take some of the blame, but I did my job right from the beginning of the season, even as the DH. I don't think anyone can question that. But the team never came together after our bad spring, no question about that. I was unhappy, Lloyd was unhappy and then Jesse was unhappy. He was never traded, but he was platooned with Rick Leach quite a bit. I remember when we came off the field after our last game of the 1988 season at Exhibition Stadium Jesse said, "Well, that's it. That was my last game here. They'll trade me before next season." He was almost right.

I didn't have MVP numbers, but I still drove in 97 runs, which wasn't bad, tenth-best league, and hit 24 home runs. I was the only Blue Jay player to be named AL Player of the Week twice that year, so I couldn't have been that terrible. My numbers were a long way from 1987, though. Anyone could see that. Our problem that year was too many individuals — too many guys figuring out their earned run average while they were sitting on the bench.

I don't think it's just personal animosity when I say that as long as Jimy was the manager something was bound to go wrong. Jimy almost never backed me up; other players felt the same way. A manager's first concern should be the players, the guys who go out there in the field and give 100 percent every day. Jimy's first thoughts always seemed to be the front office. That approach just doesn't work when you run a ball club. I know you have to report to your bosses, but when you lose the respect of your players you're not going to get as much out of them.

Before the '88 season, when everything got blown apart, I was the type of guy to walk into the clubhouse smiling. Everyone knew I had my game face on. I'd play a joke or start needling someone playing cards. There was a good feeling all around. A lot of that left during 1988.

Still, our season wasn't a total loss. We hadn't played as well as we could have in the first half — we had the seventeenth best record in all baseball at the All-Star break — but after the break we were 45-29, tied with Cincinnati for third in all baseball. Only Oakland and the Mets had better records in the second half. So we were optimistic for 1989.

Within a few days of the end of the 1988 season Jimy Williams was rehired for his fourth year as manager of the Toronto Blue Jays. At the same time the Blue Jays refused to give in to free agent Jim Clancy's request for a three-year contract — it was against club policy to give pitchers three-year deals. Clancy's response was to sign with the Houston Astros. Less than two months later the Jays signed Jimmy Key to a five-year deal. The difference turned out to be Clancy's age, 33, compared to Key's, 27. With Clancy headed to Houston, Ernie Whitt became the lone Blue Jay from the expansion draft.

Otherwise the team didn't make any serious alterations in the off-season. John Cerutti would move into Clancy's spot in the rotation to join lefties Mike Flanagan, Jeff Musselman and Jimmy Key, and right-hander Dave Stieb. Five years earlier the Jay rotation had been tilted to the right with Stieb, Clancy, Luis Leal, Jim Gott and Doyle Alexander, all but Alexander hard throwers. Could this rotation — four finesse lefties — work? The party line was to point to the three-game sweep of the Red Sox in Boston the previous September.

Meanwhile everything was pretty quiet on the Dominican front. With no contract to negotiate George could concentrate on enjoying the off-season and spending time with his family.

Maria gave birth to our fourth son on November 12. Again, I went into the delivery room to be with her. First thing Maria said when we began to talk over names was, "Let's call him Randy." It was all her idea to name him after Randy Hendricks. I thought it was a good idea to show our appreciation for what he'd done.

In December we had problems with the ambulance in San Pedro. It broke down when someone needed to get to the hospital. The town couldn't afford to buy a new one. A couple of nights later Alfredo Griffin and I were sitting around sharing a few El Presidentes and we came up with an idea. We had been talking about how dangerous it would be if someone was really sick, needed to get to the hospital and there wasn't an ambulance. Since we were more fortunate than most, why not organize a few of the players and buy a new ambulance?

We all chipped in: Joaquin Andujar and Alfredo — my neighbours — Juan Samuel, Pedro Guerrero and Rafael Ramirez. The ambulance cost around $15 000 and then we had to have it shipped from Miami. You might not hear about athletes buying something like an ambulance for their home town in Canada or the United States, but both of those countries are rich — there isn't as much need for the people to help out their community. Most of the towns in North America have well-organized hospitals and fire departments. In San Pedro, we barely have those facilities. That's why we're trying to make our town a better place.

I enjoy helping out in other ways. The nuns in the Consuelo parish of San Pedro helped Alfredo and me organize a Christmas fund; we both donate to the fund. Each year at Christmas we hand out presents to the kids. There is nothing better than watching a five-year-old take off the wrapping paper and seeing his face light up. We also raise money for the nuns with the George Bell-Alfredo Griffin Celebrity Golf Tournament in late November. We hope to raise enough money so they can make the orphanage larger.

Also before Christmas I provide some food to the poor people of our town. There are still many poor people in the Dominican and our welfare system is not good. I give my uncle a few hundred vouchers and he passes them out to those in need. They turn them in for bags of food or meat. The meat comes from three steers I buy and have killed. Some of the men are the same men who played on my dad's factory team years before when I was the bat boy.

Most people appreciate these acts of charity, but some resent my wealth. That's inevitable, but it still hurts my feelings. There are many people on my island who are richer than I am, who don't do much to help poorer people.

When a Latin player first arrives in North America he can easily get the impression that everyone has plenty of money. In the Dominican we have many rich families, but we have many millions who are very poor. Like most ballplayers from my country, I help out my relatives financially because I have the most income of anyone in my family. I can afford to share. But I don't really like to hand money out to my cousins or my wife Maria's family when I'm helping them. I'd rather go to a grocery store, buy food enough for two weeks and deliver the food. My relatives enjoy that; it's nicer than just throwing a wad of money at someone. I gave my youngest brother, Juan, financial support when he was at Triple A and already married with a son and a daughter, and not making enough money.

This is just one indication of how Latins may be more family oriented than people in some other countries. The way we all grew up so close together makes everything count. American families living in towns the size of San Pedro seem to act different. Say two brothers are living in the same town; they might go two, three months without seeing each other. I just can't imagine acting that way. When I'm in San Pedro I go to see my mom almost every two days, my dad comes to the house almost every day and, if my brothers don't come to my house, then I go to their house. And whenever I'm in New York I see Jose and Rolando.

Your family is one of the most important things in life and the only way you can keep family is if you're close. For the Bell family, life is good. I could quit right now and Maria and the four children would be set for life thanks to the way the Hendricks brothers have looked after my money and thanks to my business investments. Just down the road from where Alfredo and Joaquin live, I started construction on a brand-new house. My school friend, Julio Rivera Lee, was the architect on the project. A few lots down from my new house is a seven-storey office building we're erecting, the tallest structure in all of San Pedro. Joaquin Andujar is supplying the concrete for the structure from his construction company.

I bought a farm for my children in 1986 near Boca de Yuma in the eastern point of our island. It consists of 200 *tareas*, or 44 acres. I don't make much money on the Boca de Yuma farm, but then I didn't buy it to get rich. The farm is for fun — sort of a hobby. And in case there ever is a day I'm desperate for money, I know I could sell the farm at a profit. Also when you have four kids like I have, you have to keep an eye on the future. With the farm I have something my children can depend on if they want to. I know I can't play baseball forever, but the land will be there forever.

The best thing about my farm is that the land is very fertile. One tree after another springs from the jet-black soil at Hacienda Bell. Right now my dad is the boss on the farm, making sure the fruit gets to market and the men water the crops and get the work done. There are often six to eight workers, few of them from Haiti. We grow oranges, bananas, limes, lemons, grapefruit, avocados and mangos. Usually my dad takes the produce from the farm and sells it to Maria's father, who has a place in the open market in San Pedro. Sometimes we sell what we have to the Agricultural Bank and then they sell it to the government.

Our oranges taste sweeter than the ones I buy when I'm in Florida. When we were kids we'd sneak into an orange grove, pick as many as we could carry and then we'd suck the juice out. Now I pull up in my jeep, my man peels the oranges with his machete and cuts them in half for us. Some days we might drink the juice out of 10 or 15 as we're walking around talking. It's funny watching the *gringos* when they try to eat an orange, knocking the seeds out. We suck the juice and spit the seeds out when we're done.

All in all life is pretty good and my kids have nothing to worry about. Right now, I don't know what any of my children will be when they grow up. A writer asked me once what I hoped my kids would grow up to be — baseball player, doctor, lawyer? My answer was: "Whatever they want." But I've already told Pat Gillick how much pop Christopher has in his bat, just like his grandfather. He's 11 years old and only about five years away from being eligible to be signed unless they bring the free-agent draft into the Dominican. When Gillick comes to sign Christopher I'll be the agent, with help from Randy Hendricks. That *will* be a battle.

For now though, I want my kids to learn as much as they can. I want Chris to enrol in a summer hockey school in Toronto. I can't play in Toronto all these years and not even have my kids give hockey a try. Christopher is a good student, Georgie too. Three days a week they go to English school and they speak English really well. Kevvy, my third son, is really something. He's always running around our new house, tackling his brothers, fighting to get the controls of the Nintendo game so he can play Super Mario Brothers. Randy's the baby, so he spends most of the day with Maria or one of her sisters.

Many tourists come to the Dominican from Canada and the United States and it's easy to tell what the biggest difference is between the two North American cultures. The Canadian people — those I meet away from the ballpark in Toronto and those Canadians I meet when I'm at home in the Dominican — are really low key. And they know a lot about countries other than their own. But some American people are ignorant. They think they know everything, but really all they know is one part of the world: the United States. That's it. That's all.

I talk to Canadians all over the place: when they're in the Dominican on vacation or when they're in Florida to see us play, during spring training or when they drive from Vancouver to see us play the Mariners in Seattle or when I'm in Toronto. I talk to people on the street or in restaurants or at the park. Yet wherever I see Canadians, almost never have I heard them tell anyone how great a country Canada is. They don't have to tell me how beautiful it is. I know. I've been coast-to-coast since I started in the minors. I've played in Calgary, Lethbridge and Medicine Hat. I played an exhibition game in Vancouver and I've been to Montreal for the Pearson Cup against the Expos. I've played charity games against the National Baseball Institute in Winnipeg, Regina and Saint John, New Brunswick, and I've travelled all over on the Blue Jay caravan in January. So I know the country pretty well. I'm not saying I know the country as well as most Canadians, but I know enough about it to talk about how beautiful Canada is when I'm in the Dominican or in the U.S. — and I do.

How bad had the relationship between George Bell and Jimy Williams become by spring of 1988? In San Pedro de Macoris that winter, home-town hero Bell had an unusual habit when introducing Canadian visitors to friends at his house. Just as one of his friends was about to shake hands with the stranger, the mischievous Bell would add, "This guy here is one of the best friends Jimy Williams has." Quick as you could say "George Bell" the hand would be withdrawn. Anticipating the reaction, Bell would laugh on cue. Not only did Bell dislike Jimy Williams, so did the whole town of 90 000 — or so it sometimes seemed.

As the 1989 season approached, there wasn't any talk of Bell moving to the designated-hitter spot despite the 15 errors he had committed the year before, a club record that surpassed Rick Bosetti's mark of 13. The Blue Jays had learned their lesson, but it remained to be seen whether Williams could guide his talent-laden team into the playoffs.

I've had my share of run-ins with "mediots" (that's what I call a lot of members of the press — part media, part idiots), but one of the worst run-ins was early in spring training at the Englebert Complex when a guy from a Toronto TV station tried to interview me. I had just finished my running, I was all out of breath. and I politely told him no. But he kept asking me and asking. I didn't walk away into the clubhouse because I was waiting for little Fernando, who one year was the poster boy for the Easter Seals in Clearwater. Fernando has to use a cane to get around. Tony Fernandez met the little boy in 1988 when he was working out at a clinic after he had elbow surgery. Tony introduced him to me and I spent some time with him. I look at Fernando and I think how lucky Maria and I are that we have four healthy boys.

So I kept waiting and the guy kept asking. I'd already told him we would do it later. Finally, I lost my temper. I started swearing at him. He didn't budge. It turned out his cameraman had the camera on, the microphone too, for the whole thing. They put it on the air, bleeping out the swearing. I don't know a whole lot about the TV business, but I know you're not supposed to do that. That's the thing about the media; sometimes they don't realize you want privacy. It happened to me one other time too. The thing I hate is when I tell somebody to stop, and he doesn't. That shows the person doesn't care.

Of course that guy with the camera probably thinks he tricked me. But he didn't trick me, he tricked himself. That's the last interview I ever did with him. I'm sure some people who don't know me think I'm an asshole because of that TV clip. But when somebody says no he has a right to be taken at his word.

At spring training Jimy was at it again. He fined me $500 for being overweight by five pounds. I didn't pay any attention. We had a pretty good start in the spring. Actually it looked like we were unbeatable. We went 21-10 and before we lost the last game of the spring to Philadelphia we had the best record in all of baseball during the exhibition season. But the season didn't start very well for the team. We opened in Kansas City and lost two out of three. In the fourth game of the season against Texas on April 7 we won 10-9 but no one cared about the result. In the eighth inning, Tony Fernandez, who had hit a grand slam earlier, was hit in the right cheek with a fastball from Cecilio Guante. He just fell down flat and lay there. It was pretty scary. Everyone ran out to the plate. Tony had a tiny hole in his cheek, just like when Lynn McGlothen hit me with that pitch at Syracuse in 1982. They took him to hospital in Arlington and operated. It turned out he had a broken cheekbone, which meant he was going to miss five or six weeks. Manny Lee, who was sharing second base with Nelson Liriano, took over at shortstop.

That night in the clubhouse at Arlington Stadium in Texas, I yelled at all the pitchers for not retaliating. Mike Flanagan just looked back at me like I was crazy. You can hear some pitchers figuring out their ERA during the game — that's all they seem to care about. Or a guy will say, "You're only three strikeouts behind me." Stuff like that bothers me.

I get hit a lot and all the pitcher has to say is "The ball slipped" and the league doesn't do a thing. The problem with the Blue Jays is we don't have enough take-charge guys on our pitching staff. Suppose Fred McGriff gets knocked down twice in one game. A pitcher shouldn't have to wait until the manager or pitching coach comes over and tells him to throw at someone on the other team. The pitcher should be thinking right away, "Hey, that's one of the best players we have! We can't let them do that to him."

It hurt to have Tony out of the lineup, but the Jays were bad that spring. On April 30, "The Best Outfield in Baseball" was officially disbanded. On a Sunday morning in Anaheim we traded Jesse to the Yankees for Al Leiter, a hard-throwing lefty. I thought Jesse would be happier in New York. He'd be away from Jimy, and it looked like with Winfield hurt, he was going to get the chance to play every day. I was sorry to see Jesse go, but when I think about it, he took himself out of Toronto. I think he put too much pressure on himself. I remember once in the spring of 1987 after he hit 40 homers we had a game in Winter Haven against the Red Sox. Before the game I heard Jesse telling reporters that he was going to hit 50 homers that year. You can't go around making big predictions like that — the writers remember, the fans remember. You should just play your game. That's what I do. You never hear me saying I'm going to do this, this and this.

Now we had only three outfielders: Lloyd, Rob Ducey and me. Rob had hit better than anyone in spring training, but Jimy hadn't given him much of a chance to play. Now it looked like he would. David Hendricks reminded me that Pat Gillick once told us in Houston — right to my face — that I'd never be the player Jesse was. Maybe it was business talk, but that always bothered me. Now Jesse was gone.

On May 2, we were four and a half games behind Baltimore, when Oakland came into Exhibition Stadium for the first game of a home stand. This was the game when Gene Nelson hit me on purpose with two out in the ninth inning and I charged the mound and bloodied his nose. It all contributed to the bad feelings between the A's and the Jays that year.

Jimy tried to keep peace in the dugout and the clubhouse in 1989, but by that time it was too late. The year before he had restricted our TV use; now we could watch TV when we wanted. He tried to get the players to support him by saying things like "Any problems, come and see me" or "If two players don't feel like you can get along, you both can come talk to me. Let me know if you see anything wrong with one or your teammates." He started a kangaroo court with token fines for basic baseball mistakes like not being able to get a bunt down, or not hitting the ball to the right side with a man on second base and none out. But there were other fines which were supposed to be fun. For example, if you saw someone carrying his bags through the lobby that meant he was too cheap to pay a bellboy. That was a fine. Or if you gave an interview before batting practice once stretching exercises had started, that was a fine. An ugly tie, or stopping by the food table naked on your way to the shower was a fine. I fined Gillick once for coming into the clubhouse when we were having a meeting. The concept sounded good, but after a while it got silly. I think Jimy was trying to say he was sorry and "Let's go and do this together and win this together." But he was two years too late.

On May 10 against Seattle we were almost no-hit for the third time in our first 33 games — that's how bad we were going. Mark Langston was leading 2-0 in the ninth and hadn't given up a base hit. Eventually someone was going to no-hit us. But it wasn't going to be Langston. Tom Lawless, who'd come over from St. Louis as a free-agent, pinch-hit for Lloyd and singled. Then Langston managed to get Nelson Liriano out but Lawless advanced. Then Bob Brenly, who'd come over as a free agent from the Giants, got his first extra-base hit in the American League, a double to left. Alexis Infante, recently called up from Syracuse, pinch-ran for Brenly. Junior Felix, our new outfielder, singled to centre to drive in the tying run and went to second on the throw home. Now the Mariners brought in Mike Schooler, who got Kelly Gruber on a ground ball. Then they walked Tony Fernandez to get to me. Thank you very much, I thought. I hit a ball to left. I didn't get a good hit, but it fell in and Junior scored the game-winner. After dominating us all afternoon

Langston lost the no-hitter, the shutout and the game in a matter of minutes.

But in most games we looked lifeless. On May 10 in Minneapolis we were winning 5-2 in the seventh and ended up losing 6-5 to fall to 12-22. On Saturday night we got beat 10-8 and on Sunday we were terrible, losing 13-1. If there was a worse team in baseball at that time I didn't know which it was.

I had no idea they would fire Jimy. The Blue Jays had never fired a manager during the season. On Monday afternoon, May 15, I was at home when the Blue Jays public relations officer Howie Starkman phoned me to tell me it had happened. He said Cito Gaston was the interim manager. When I got to the park, a lot of writers asked me if I was happy Jimy was fired. They figured I'd be dancing as if it was merengue music to my ears. But I said I wasn't happy; in a way I was down.

When I look back on it, it's kind of sad. I'd known Jimy since spring training in '81, for almost nine seasons, except when I was at Syracuse, and all that time Jimy didn't respect me and I didn't respect him. A few players said Jimy resented the good players on our team because he was a career minor-leaguer like a lot of coaches and managers. I didn't agree with that, but I do know he had more trouble with Dave Stieb, Lloyd Moseby, Jessie Barfield and me than with other players the last couple of years. Jimy the manager wasn't the same as Jimy the likeable coach. He was relaxed as a coach, but tight as a manager. By the end nobody would talk to him, except maybe Ernie, who we used to call "Mr. Prime Minister."

With the teams Jimy had those years, no one else should have won. We should have won the AL East three years in a row: '86, '87 and '88. In '88 the ball club was even better than in '89. The best team, though, had to be our team in '87.

The reason we didn't win was not because Jimy didn't know anything about baseball. Jimy knew baseball. I just don't think he could take the pressure or the heat. If you gave him a job as an infield instructor, he'd do a pretty good job because one-on-one he knows what to do and how to make the decisions. The thing is he can't handle 25 or 26 guys.

Some people probably think I fought with every manager I've ever had. But except for Jim Beauchamp my first year at Syracuse in '82 I've never had any problems. And with Beauchamp our fight must have lasted two hours. So for me, George Bell, the guy everyone calls a problem child, that was the only other time I've caused a manager problems. I play the game hard and most managers like that. Maybe I'm not such a terrible guy to handle after all. And, thinking back on it, I might have been out of baseball if I hadn't fought Jimy over being his designated hitter.

8

The Second Championship

"The Blue Jays have some problems, but despite what you hear or read, George Bell is the least of the team's problems. He's similar to Jeffrey Leonard, who I used to play with. He plays hurt, he runs into walls, he wants to win more than anyone and once in a while says some things that are wrong. But ask anyone in the room who saw him play when he wasn't 100 percent and they'd tell how much he was respected."

— Bob Brenly,
after returning to San Francisco Giants

EVEN THOUGH WE WERE 12-24 AND SIX GAMES OUT when Cito took over, we all thought we had the best talent in the division. With Jimmy Key pitching we won Cito Gaston's first game as interim manager, beating Cleveland 5-3. That was step one. Step two was getting the word "interim" removed from in front of Cito's name. We won two of Cito's first three games at home against the Indians and then we went to Chicago for a three-game series.

As far as I was concerned Cito Gaston was the right man for the manager's job, but then it wasn't my decision. Lloyd, the rest of the hitters and I knew we could win with Cito in charge, but Paul Beeston and Pat Gillick kept saying he wasn't a candidate. Even Cito himself said he wasn't sure he wanted to manage because it would mean time away from his family. I saw him interviewed on TV soon after his appointment and he said he was worried about not being able to have the same relationship with the players he'd had in the past.

Cito is a very patient man. I've known that since I came up from Syracuse in 1983 when he first began to spend a lot of time helping me with my batting. He wasn't strict like the nuns who used to teach me at school, and he wasn't uptight like Jimy. He was easy to talk with and he would listen to your ideas. He always spoke quietly. In some ways he reminded me of Granny Hamner, the Phillies' hitting coach who got me untracked in Spartanburg when I was trying to make it in the minors. I do better with people who speak in low tones, rather than guys that scream at me. In fact over the years the guy on the club I've grown closest to is Cito. Cito is a friend, a good guy, and a good instructor. He's likely the man in baseball I respect the most. I was sure he'd do a good job as manager.

The Blue Jays weren't so sure. While we were in Chicago beating the White Sox, Gillick and Beeston were interviewing a no-name guy — Terry Bevington. The only thing we'd heard about Bevington was how a few weeks earlier he'd started a fight with Don Slaught, a catcher for the Yankees. Slaught had tried to bunt for a base hit when the Yankees were leading 7-2 in the seventh inning. That's considered bad baseball, like rubbing it in the other team's face. The only thing worse would be trying to bunt for a hit in the late innings against a guy who had a no-hit bid going. In those situations you're supposed to hit like a man. So Jeff Torborg and all the coaches in the White Sox dugout began yelling at Slaught and they were still yelling at him when he came out for the start of the next half-inning. Then Slaught started yelling back at Torborg. Just then Bevington, who was heading down the line to coach first, said something back to Slaught. The next thing you knew they were both throwing punches.

Did we need a guy like that? I've never heard of a first-base coach getting into a fight with the other team's catcher. Lloyd and I talked it over a number of times and hoped the Jays would give the job to Cito. We weren't his favourites — Cito doesn't play favourites — but we knew he would treat us fairly. And we didn't want an outsider coming in.

Blue Jay management was torn on the replacement for Jimy Williams. The Jays hadn't talked to anyone before they axed him, so they were starting from square one. They asked the Mets for permis-

sion to talk to Bud Harrelson, but Harrelson declined to be inter-viewed. He said he didn't feel he had enough knowledge of the American League. They interviewed Lou Piniella, the former Yankee manager still under contract to Steinbrenner and chained to the broadcast booth; Terry Bevington, an unknown, but hard-nosed former minor-league manager who had risen rapidly through the White Sox organization with one winning season after another; and ex-Jay Bob Bailor, who was managing at Syracuse. At the beginning no one took Cito seriously as a candidate — including Cito himself.

However the field began to narrow quickly. As soon as the Jays were granted permission to talk to Piniella, owner George Steinbren-ner gave him more responsibilities working with Yankee hitters. Piniella was interested enough to fly from Seattle to Vancouver to Toronto on a red-eye flight to be interviewed. But Steinbrenner, who wanted Piniella to manage the Yankees again, asked for Duane Ward and Todd Stottlemyre in return. That was too high a price to pay. So it was down to Bailor or Bevington — or Cito, who if hired would become only the second black manager in the majors. On May 27 1989, 12 days after Jimy Williams had been let go, the Blue Jays' interim manager Gaston was "more of a non-candidate than he was a candidate," according to Pat Gillick.

May 28, our twelfth game under Cito as interim manager, wasn't just another day at Exhibition Stadium, it was our final game at the old dump. With Cito in charge we'd won 7 of 11 and we were playing the White Sox, a team we'd had some success against. Everyone wanted to say goodbye with a win. There was a big crowd on hand.

I had never liked Exhibition Stadium from the first time I saw it in 1981. It had bad turf, hard as concrete. One night I made a couple of errors and people booed as usual, but that night guys in a private box alongside the Argo football press box threw little cherry tomatoes and pieces of pickled cauliflower down at me. The booing I can take, but I didn't need vegetables on the field during a game. I usually don't pay a whole lot of attention to the fans, but that night I did. That night it was dangerous to be in left field.

Anyway, during the pre-game introductions for Closing Day I was booed by most of the fans. Now that Jimy was gone, any time things weren't going well — we were still nine games under .500 — I was the guy people got angry with. On this occasion they didn't stay angry for long.

We went ahead 5-2 when Lloyd Moseby hit a two-run homer off Jerry Reuss, but the White Sox scored three runs off Dave Stieb and Duane Ward in the eighth to tie the score. In the bottom of the tenth, Kelly Gruber led off with a double against Bobby Thigpen. I thought they might walk me intentionally, but they decided to pitch to me. I hit an 0-1 fastball away up into the left-field seats to win the game and the place went crazy. The ball was long enough and it just snuck inside the foul pole. Years from now I'll be the trivia answer to the question "Who was the last hitter at Exhibition Stadium?"

As soon as the ball landed in the left-field seats the gates opened in the outfield and policemen came riding in on horseback. They didn't want the fans coming onto the field and wrecking things. I don't know what there was to wreck. The grounds crew dug up home plate and gave it to Ernie Whitt — which was a nice goodbye since he was the only remaining original Jay. Rance Mulliniks said Exhibition Stadium wasn't the best place to play, but it had some character. Bob Brenly said that such an exciting win was a great way to leave and then he added, "But I couldn't think of a bad way to leave here."

After the game everyone was talking about Brenly, a DH and back-up catcher who'd come running out of the dugout to see whether my hit was fair or foul and then began jumping up and down like a crazy man — he was more excited about my home run than I was. But in spite of my performance, I didn't enjoy the day. I was still upset over the way the fans booed me before the game, so I wasn't talking to anyone. Still, I was happy that my final at bat in the old place was a good one. More important I was happy for Cito, now that we'd won eight of his first 12 games.

After that we went to Cleveland and we lost our first two, so now our record under Cito was 8-6, which didn't look as good as 8-4. But on May 31, the morning before our final game in Cleveland, the suspense ended. Beeston and Gillick flew in to town and named Cito the manager. Lloyd phoned me in my hotel room when he heard the news. We were both happy for Cito and happy to have the thing finally settled. Now we had a shot at catching the Orioles, even though we were in last place, six and a half games out. I got to the ball park early for the game that night, congratulated Cito and wished him luck.

We already knew what kind of manager we were getting. Cito hadn't changed when he went from being coach to being manager the way a lot of guys do. He stayed down-to-earth and loyal to his players. He told us what he was going to do before he told the press. In that way he reminded me of Bobby Cox. The only thing I regretted was that he didn't have much time to talk to me or any individual player because he was too busy with the job and always talking to reporters.

We lost that final game in Cleveland but then we went to Boston and won all three, including a 13-11 victory in 12 innings after being down 10-0. Junior Felix, our young right fielder, had an inside-the-park grand slam, the first one I'd ever seen.

After sweeping Boston we came home to our new ballpark, the SkyDome. When I got there around four in the afternoon on June 5 the place was a mess. They were still putting up the screen behind home plate. Not all the artificial turf had been laid in foul territory. The American League officials were there inspecting the field, the fences and the foul poles to make sure everything was in proper order. I felt real strange going into the place and it took a long time to find my way to the clubhouse. It was so big and there was so much happening.

The scary thing about the SkyDome for Lloyd and me was how much more ground it looked like we were going to have to cover in the outfield. Exhibition Stadium was 330 feet down the lines, 375 in the power alleys and 400 feet to centre field. The SkyDome was supposed to be about the same size, but Ken Erskine, the director of operations, said the field was actually bigger than they planned. He said the sign markings on the outfield fences were wrong, because the people brought the wrong stencils to paint on the numbers. He said it was 330 feet down the lines, but that it was 385 to the left and right centre and 412 feet to straightaway centre.

We believed him. The outfield certainly seemed bigger than at Exhibition Stadium. The SkyDome people said the numbers were accurate, but Lloyd said he was sticking with Erskine's. So was I. We certainly had trouble hitting the ball out those early days at the Dome. I remember Ernie and Freddie whacking balls to right centre that would carry and then just die at the warning track. It turns out the numbers are close to accurate, but the outfield still seems bigger to me. In fact the fences are 400 feet from home plate in centre field, 330 feet down the foul lines, and 385 feet in both power alleys.

I didn't like the SkyDome when we first moved in. It's nice to look at and I know it's probably 100 percent better for the fans, but some nights I hate the new park worse than the old one. The reason is the lights. In the outfield it's difficult to pick up the ball. At the SkyDome, you can't see properly to play baseball. Exhibition Stadium was rough for night games, in right field just before sun set, but at the SkyDome there is a bank of lights behind the plate where line drives can hide. If you lose the ball for just an instant you could get hit with it. Fortunately, fly balls aren't a problem because you can see the ball going into the lights and then coming out of them. The hitting background is good thanks to a dark, black fishnet over the seats in centre field. But with the roof open you get reflections off the windows of the restaurants and hotel which make it difficult for the hitters.

Don't get me wrong. I'm proud to play at the Dome. The facilities are wonderful. Our clubhouse looks like the old set from "Star Trek." It has plenty of room with four circular marble tables for playing cards or signing baseballs, which we have to do all the time for charities or auctions, or reading the paper. There are six TVs hanging from the ceiling. But I can't help thinking that with so many things going on at the SkyDome — people shopping, eating at the restaurants, drinking in the bars — when you walk into the place you don't have the same atmosphere as walking into an old-time baseball stadium, like at Arlington, or Kansas City or Chicago. In those places, the minute you walk in, you know from the way it looks and from the smell of hot dogs and popcorn that it's a ballpark. After he was traded to Detroit, Lloyd was pretty critical of the new park. He said, "I never felt anything inside the SkyDome. It was like it was all cardboard, even the people. You have a real stadium in Detroit, with real people." I don't agree with that, but the first few games we wondered whether the people were coming to see us play or coming to see the roof move. We watched it and marvelled at it, but I remember Brenly saying that we were just the salad dressing, that the stadium was the main course.

Our first game was against the Brewers and Freddie McGriff hit the first homer in the second inning, a two-run shot. But we were losing 5-2 in the eighth when I hit a homer off Don August. That was all the scoring and we lost our Dome opener 5-4. We lost the next night as well, 6-4, but the third night John Cerutti helped us beat the Brewers 4-2, so the fans finally got to see a win in the new stadium. What's more, we all saw the strangest — and shortest — rain delay ever. We'd started the game under an open roof, but the sky suddenly turned black and it started to rain. Lloyd was batting in the second inning when plate ump Richie Garcia called time. They'd started to close the roof when they saw that the rains were coming but couldn't fully close it before it rained on the field. Home plate is just below the last section of roof to close so it was raining at home plate but not on the mound. Chris Bosio, their pitcher, never even felt a drop, but Lloyd got all wet. The rain delay lasted six minutes. Both teams came out of their dugouts to watch and the crowd gave the roof a standing ovation. After that all the players were dry, but the roof still leaked where the last two seams met and people behind the plate had to leave. The Dome wasn't quite finished yet.

With Cito as manager we were playing well, but I really didn't know how well until I took a look at the standings after we beat the A's in Oakland on June 22. After starting 12-24 under Jimy, we were now 24-12 with Cito. I remember hearing Alan Ryan of the *Toronto Star* asking some of the guys, "If your winning percentage was .333 under Jimy and now your winning percentage is .666 under Cito, why doesn't it round off to 1.000?" Now we were at 36-36, at .500 for the first time since April 16. The team wasn't much different except for Junior Felix, who'd been playing well since he was called up. The big difference was in the way Cito handled everyone. He let us play the game.

After our road trip we returned home June 30 to begin a series with Boston. That's when the Toronto fans started booing me again. I hit only two homers during the whole month and I'd left some runners on base. Also, we'd lost the first three games of the four-game series. Bob Brenly kept asking me if I'd left passes for all those people — Bob was having trouble adjusting to the AL pitchers, but he was a great guy, a great addition to the ball club.

After Boston the first-place Orioles, who'd beaten us two out of three in Baltimore, came into the SkyDome. Everyone said they were playing over their heads and they'd soon fall back, but there was no sign of this on July 4. In the seventh, with one out, two men on base, and the score only 3-0, I grounded into a double play and we finally lost 8-0. So the fans were in a bad mood the next night when Jimmy Key went up against Bob Milacki. The game started out okay — we were ahead 2-1 in the third inning and Key got the first two guys out. He seemed to be cruising. Three hits later the game was tied and they had two men on. Then the Oriole catcher, Bob Melvin, hit a curving drive to the left-field fence. I thought I was going to catch the ball for the final out of the inning, but I hit the fence the same time the ball hit my glove, and it fell loose for a double. Two runs scored and the Orioles were ahead 4-2. After that the fans went crazy, booing me every time I came to bat and any time a ball was hit to left field. Later in the game after I'd reached second base, Cal Ripken, the Oriole shortstop and a classy guy, said, "Rough night." He told me he couldn't believe the fans, that the fans wouldn't have booed an Oriole player like that in Baltimore.

In the end we lost 5-4, so my missed catch was a big play. We had lost and I was upset and frustrated even though I had three hits that game and drove in a run. Of course none of the reporters were interested in my performance. Allan Ryan of the *Toronto Star* asked me about the booing and I said, "You tell those stupid Canadian fans they can kiss my purple butt. I almost kill myself running into the wall and they boo me." I was quoted accurately. I'm not like some players who run around the next day saying like a broken record, "I didn't say that, I didn't say that." I had nearly killed myself trying to catch the ball running into the wall and they had booed me. I was really angry.

Randy Hendricks had me laughing the next day when he phoned from Houston to ask when my butt had turned purple. Later a scout for another team was quoted as saying he couldn't understand Toronto fans: "They boo a guy who runs into the wall and they don't boo Moseby who pulled up short twice on other balls that hit low on the wall." After I had made that "purple butt" comment the fans really started to get on me. I was mad and they were mad. They kept booing me and I kept repeating what I'd said. It was getting out of hand. The fact we beat Baltimore the next two nights to take the series two out of three got lost in all the noise from "the mediots." It was a relief to go on the road.

Next was Detroit and we finished the first half by sweeping the Tigers. Cito and I had a talk in his office. Cito said he didn't think it was such a good idea to talk about the fans the way I had. This wasn't like when Jimy and I went behind closed doors. If someone had been listening at the door they probably would have thought I was talking quietly to myself. That's how low-key Cito is. I said, "But, Cito, you know I'm right. You've been booed before as a player, you know what it's like." But since it was Cito who asked me, I told him I would try to keep things quiet — if the fans laid off me. Maybe Kelly Gruber had a point when he said, "When the boos rain down on George Bell, it's because he usually turns on the tap."

After the All-Star break we were back at the Dome to begin the second half against Oakland, and the fans spent most of the first game booing me. They really had something to scream about in the fifth inning when I lost a Mark McGwire fly ball in the lights. I went down on my knees to keep it in front of me and it hit me in the wrist — it almost got me in the crotch — and I was lucky to keep it from getting past me. As a result, Oakland scored four unearned runs and the scorer gave me an error. When I came up in the bottom of the same inning about 75 percent of the 48 000 people in the stadium were booing. I hadn't planned to do anything but I stepped out of the batter's box, tipped my helmet to the crowd, raised both my arms in the air and then did a deep bow. That's when the place really went crazy. It wasn't any joke: it was my chance to show the fans I have pride in myself. You have to show the fans that they're not your enemy. Down deep I don't think that the Blue Jay fans are my enemy. Fans take out their anger on me when something happens. When I do something wrong, they blow it up like it's the worst thing that ever happened in the history of baseball. They were still mad at me because I wouldn't be the DH in 1988.

Oakland went on to win the game 11-7 and afterwards I again told the reporters that the fans who booed me could kiss my ass. "If they don't know the game after 11 or 12 years of watching the Blue Jays, they don't know shit. Most of those people booing are 21, 23, 25 years old, they drink too much, yell too much and boo too much. I'm 29 years old and I earn $2 million. I don't have to get up at six o'clock in the morning and that upsets them."

The next night, of course, they booed even louder, razzing me when I caught a routine fly ball to left, booing me out onto the field and all the way into the dugout. When people say I'm not in control of my emotions, they're wrong. If I wasn't in control I'd have run right up into the seats like some hockey player and started a fight.

In the fifth inning we were ahead 3-1 when I came up to the plate. Bob Welch, the A's starter, was on the mound and we'd had our run-ins before. So I wasn't surprised when he hit me in the shoulder with a fastball. This time I just trotted to first base, but that didn't mean I wasn't upset. When I got to the bag I was yelling at Welch, "Cut out that shit," and the guys in the Oakland dugout were hooting at me, telling me to stop yelling at Welch. While I was standing at first base hollering, Dave Parker came out of the dugout pointing a big finger at me. As he walked over, Parker called out that he was going to whip my ass, he was going to put his 12-pound fist in my face. I asked him what the hell he was doing on the field, this wasn't any of his business — it was between Welch and myself — and I told him he didn't scare me a bit. No one talks to me like that. By this time both teams were out on the field yelling insults at one another, but there were no fights.

Like magic, the fans stopped booing and began cheering. It was as if they'd suddenly forgotten they were mad at me. Some people said Parker did me a favour, but I think they stopped booing because they saw I was hit with a pitch on purpose and had the self-control not to charge the mound. I still stood up for myself. The umps got everyone back in their dugouts and when I went out to the field to start the seventh inning I saw a large sign in the outfield reading, THE REAL FANS LOVE YOU, GEORGE. When the scoreboard camera caught that one sign there was long, loud applause. That inning I made a good catch against the fence on a ball hit by Parker and the fans cheered. In the bottom of the same inning I hit a run-scoring double and we won the game 4-1. I hoped my quarrel with the fans was over.

Tony La Russa, Oakland's manager, has always thought his pitchers can intimidate me. When La Russa was managing the White Sox the same crap went on one night when the Jays were in Chicago. We were pitching inside, his guys were pitching inside. Anyway, Ernie Whitt and La Russa got into an argument over who was throwing at who. Ernie told me La Russa said, "You guys don't need to throw inside, you're in first place." Does that make sense? The same kind of stuff went on in 1989. Who was throwing at who?

I don't think the fans in Canada are really against me, it's just that they don't really agree with me. They don't understand my personality. A lot of times you'll find a player who is all teeth and smiles, but inside he's nothing. Whatever I feel, I say, and some people don't like that. If to be a popular guy you have to be nice and "smiley" no matter how you feel inside, then I'm never going to be popular. One day I may spend two hours talking with reporters, but tomorrow? Tomorrow they better not even come around me because they've had my time. The next day I feel I have to do something different.

The people I know best, my teammates, seem to appreciate the fact I'm straight with them. I try to be a really true friend and when I say something to a friend I mean it. I don't talk behind anybody's back. When Tony Kubek, for example, would say something I didn't like, I'd tell him. Some of our guys would be like, "Hey, Tony, nice to see you, where you been? Have a nice trip?" then walk 10 feet and dump all over him for what he said on TV. That's not my style.

The way we felt about the SkyDome changed after the Oakland series. In the first 17 games we played in our new home, a total of only 17 homers were hit by both teams and a lot of guys were worried about whether it was a hitter's park or a pitcher's park. In the Oakland series, Oakland hit seven homers and we hit six — 13 in four games. Maybe it wasn't a pitcher's park after all. I didn't care. If I hit them out I hit them out, and if I didn't, there was always next time.

A lot tougher than a batting slump is seeing a teammate you've grown to like get traded or demoted. This year I'd already lost Jesse Barfield. Now I could see the writing on the wall for Bob Brenly. He was hard working. He was having trouble adjusting to the league but he never let it get him down. After a game when we'd won he'd go through the food line and yell, "BOY! You guys SURRRRRE are fun to WATCH!" Usually he'd been watching from the bench.

We started a long road trip in Seattle on July 20 and it turned out to be Brenly's last. He was hitting only .179 as the designated hitter against lefties and he didn't play the first two games because they started right-handers, but he was looking forward to the third game because lefty Randy Johnson would be on the mound. But before the game Cito had Tom Lawless in left field and he asked me to DH against Johnson. That was a bad sign for Bob. After the game, which we lost 5-2, everybody in the locker room was quiet; there was none of the usual joking like you get even after a loss. Cito's door was closed and everybody knew something was up. Before long, out came Brenly. His face was flushed and for the first time since the season started I saw him down. They had released him. I hope I never ever get released like that. I want to decide when my last game is. Tom Henke, John Cerutti, Mike Flanagan and I all waited until the reporters left. Then we went up to Bob and shook hands, wished him well and told him another team would surely pick him up. Sure enough, he found himself back with the Giants.

That season Mike Flanagan continued to be as funny with his mouth as he was good with his arm. The next night we beat Nolan Ryan 4-0 even though we struck out 14 times. In the first inning, with Junior Felix on third, I struck out for what should have been the third out. But the ball rolled a few feet away and Chad Kreuter, the Ranger catcher, couldn't find it so I took off for first. By the time Kreuter had the ball and was going to throw to first he spotted Junior Felix coming home from third. So he hesitated, then threw to first. I beat the throw and Felix scored. Kreuter had a rough night with passed balls and wild pitches, so the fans were booing him. My last time up I told him, "Hang with it, kid, this is nothing." After the game Mike Flanagan said the reason we were playing so much better was the fact we were working more on our RBI strikeouts.

The scene in the clubhouse that night was quite a contrast to the beginning of the season. Everyone was excited we'd beaten Ryan, who had almost no-hit us at home. We were back at .500 with a 50-50 record and now only four and a half games behind Baltimore, but the way the guys were behaving you'd have thought we were in first place by 10. Tony Fernandez was over in one corner of the room singing loudly in Spanish. A couple of guys jokingly told him to keep the noise down, but all Tony did was sing louder. Then Manny Lee started singing along with him. Frank Wills, who is from Louisiana, was only a few seats away. He jumped up and did some kind of Cajun jig. We were all in a happy mood. Then Kelly Gruber yelled as loud as he could, "BOY! You guys SURRRRRE are fun to WATCH!" Gruber looked at Flanagan and smiled, Henke smiled and so did John Cerutti. Then Gruber looked at me and I winked at him. Bob Brenly was gone but we weren't going to forget him.

We went out the next night all set to win and finally get above sea level. But Kevin Brown beat Mike Flanagan 11-1 and for the seventh time we'd failed to get over the hump. This was beginning to seem like a bad habit we couldn't break.

Our next stop on the road was New York, our first visit to Yankee Stadium since Barfield was traded. That was strange, seeing Jesse in Yankee pinstripes. While we were there I heard talk that the Blue Jays were trying to trade me to Houston, that the team couldn't win with me in left field and that I was washed up. I remember telling Lloyd Moseby, "When October rolls around the fans are going to look beside George Bell's name and they're going to see George Bell numbers." And they did.

On July 31 we traded lefty Jeff Musselman to the Mets for a player to be named later. At the time Mike Flanagan jokingly asked how they could make a trade for someone who hadn't been named yet — it would have to be a newborn baby. The next afternoon around two o'clock we found out the player was Mookie Wilson. He was in St. Louis with the Mets so the Jays flew him into Toronto.

Mookie didn't have any hits the first night against Kansas City, but the second night he showed how valuable he was going to be. We were already ahead of Mark Gubicza 1-0 in the fifth inning when Mookie beat out an infield single, went to third on a single by Kelly Gruber and scored after he tagged on my sacrifice fly to left field. Pat Tabler caught the ball and his throw to catcher Bob Boone was ahead of Mookie, but Mookie was safe because he made a great slide. So he was almost out at first, almost out at third and almost out at home, but he was safe all around. When this happened you could feel the bench get excited. The crowd recognized how much Mookie hustled and watching him made everyone else hustle more.

On August 11 we went to Kansas City and Bret Saberhagen beat us 6-2. During that game Tony Fernandez struck out in his first three at bats and left the game. He said he didn't want to play anymore. We were losing only 2-0 in the sixth at the time. After the game I had three or four players come to me and tell me, "You have to talk to Tony and tell him he can't be doing that in close games." I said, "Talk to him about what?" I didn't really know what had happened and didn't want to know. I respected his privacy. If Tony wanted to talk to me, I'd listen.

Tony is a religious man. We've had a lot of people knock our ball club over the years for a number of reasons, but the silliest one I ever heard was that we had trouble winning because we had too many religious guys on our team. There is no question we've had a few religious players: Jesse Barfield, Tony Fernandez, Garth Iorg. Eventually Mark Eichhorn, Kelly Gruber, Jeff Musselman, Rob Ducey. And before '85 Roy Lee Jackson, Jim Gott and Barry Bonnell. But religion hasn't kept us from winning. No way.

In fact, I consider myself religious. I believe in Jesus and I believe the natural things are here because somebody created them, but I'm not a fanatic. I also believe in myself. At different times with the Blue Jays and in Syracuse, a few guys in the organization have tried to convert me to their kind of religion, to get me to become a born-again Christian, but I'm not interested. Some people who get deeply involved in religion don't have confidence in themselves. I'm a crazy guy. I like to have fun, but I know how to take care of myself.

Sometimes I think religion does hurt Tony and some of the other guys when they're on the field. It makes them too nice. If somebody tries to take advantage of Tony Fernandez he doesn't try for revenge. He leaves everything to God. I don't agree. God can only look after so much. Sometimes you have to stand up for yourself. Some guys get hit with a pitch inside and they don't even get mad. There's a time when you have to get angry enough to stand up and say, "Cut the bull." That's the way I play most of the time. A lot of people say I have a mean face when I'm in the field and when I'm running to second base, but the guy who is trying to get you out doesn't care if he breaks your neck or not.

Tony is my friend. He's a good person, a good father and I respect him as much as I do anyone on the team. We're from the same town. But that doesn't mean we have to agree all the time. Tony wants to win as much as I do.

With Jimy the incident when Tony walked out on the team would have been a big crisis. Under Cito it was different. The next night, before we beat the Royals 8-0, Tony apologized to the whole team and it was forgotten.

On August 8 we beat the Texas Rangers at the SkyDome 8-0 and for the first time since April 4 we had a winning record. Not that we hadn't been close: eight times this season we had reached .500 only to lose the next game. That day I had a couple of hits, which turned out to be the beginning of a hitting streak for me and the team. Twenty-two games later on August 31 when my hitting streak ended — the longest in the AL in 1989 — we were in first place to stay. During that stretch I'd had 32 hits in 87 at bats (.368) with six homers and 24 RBIS. During the streak Lynn Gruber, Kelly's wife, told Randy

Hendricks, "It's all a game George plays. He gets the fans excited, they get him excited and then he plays like the greatest player in the game for a month."

All the hitters knew Cito and respected him. We knew that when push came to shove, Cito would stick up for us. The pitchers, though, didn't really know what to expect. They didn't have the same day-to-day familiarity with him as we did. It would have been the same for us if they'd named Al Widmar, our pitching coach that year, the manager.

The pitchers found out August 16, during our hot streak, when we were playing the Red Sox at the SkyDome. We were down 3-2 in the sixth, David Wells was pitching in relief and he was facing Wade Boggs with a man on second and two out. On his second pitch Wells just missed with a ball everyone thought was a strike. So Cito walked out to the mound and just stood there, waiting and waiting. He wasn't going to make a pitching change. He wanted to talk to plate ump Darryl Cousins. When Cousins finally came out to tell Cito to hurry things up, Cito turned and said, "Why don't you just let Boggs start with two balls and no strikes because you never call a strike until he has two balls?" That was enough to get Cito kicked out. Then he really went at Cousins, but it didn't matter. He was out of the game.

Wells came back to strike out Boggs to end the inning. Then Lee Mazzilli hit a two-run single in the eighth and I hit a two-run homer in the ninth and we won 7-3, but that wasn't what everyone remembered. What was important was that Cito had stuck up for a pitcher. That night he gained a lot of respect. I remember one of the pitchers saying after the game, "Cito showed some hair on his ass tonight."

Besides sticking up for the pitchers, Cito was more patient than Jimy. He went to the bullpen less often. Jimy would have relievers up every time the starter got in trouble — four out of five days. It's not just pitching in games that tires out relievers, the "ups" count too. (An up is when a pitcher warms up in the bullpen to the point where he is ready to come into the game. If the guy on the mound gets out of the jam, the reliever sits down again.) Cito was staying with our starters longer, which was good for their confidence and easier on the pen.

Cito kept everyone happy even though we weren't all healthy. My left shoulder had been bothering me since April in Anaheim when I dove and landed on it. And I'd hurt my right shoulder trying to throw out Jody Reed at second on a ball in the gap September 20. So Cito started giving me the hit-and-run sign, which meant I didn't have to try to pull the ball. I could go with the pitch to right. I think he put it on about 30 times and about 23 times we worked it perfectly.

It was close right down to the finish: every game was crucial and some of them were pretty wild. One of the wildest was on September 8 in Cleveland. We had a 5-4 lead with one out in the bottom of the eighth when Joe Carter homered off Duane Ward to send the game into extra innings. After that, each half-inning seemed like it would be the last, but neither team could score despite all kinds of chances. In the thirteenth we looked like we were dead when Frank Wills hit Felix Fermin, the first guy he faced, and Joe Carter singled and went to second on the throw to third. So Cito had Mike Young walked intentionally to load the bases with none out. Mookie Wilson, Lloyd and I all played shallow. A long fly ball meant the guy from third would score anyway. We played in real close and so did infield.

Wills was in a tight spot, but he hung tough. First he got Cory Snyder to bounce a ball to short which Tony Fernandez fielded and threw to Ernie Whitt at the plate for the force. One out, but the bases were still loaded. Then Frank fell behind Brad Komminisk 3-0, so he threw a strike down the middle. Then he pitched inside, Komminisk started to swing, then checked his motion, but the ball hit his bat and rolled towards first. Freddie McGriff was on it quickly and threw home just in time to force Joe Carter. Two out and we all backed up to regular depth. Luis Aguayo popped up. Wills had walked the tightrope and survived.

In the top of the fourteenth I came up with Nelson Liriano in scoring position and Doug Jones on the mound. Richie Garcia was behind the plate and he rung me up on a called strike three on a pitch that was clearly inside. When he made that call I couldn't believe it. So I drew a line in the batter's box where the ball was and Garcia immediately threw me out of the game. Cito and John McLaren, our third-base coach, came out, but I kept arguing with him. I was still angry when they finally got me to the dugout. From there I motioned to Garcia that I'd meet him outside and snap him in two like a twig. Garcia just glared at me and eventually wrote a report on the incident. I think I've had more problems with Richie Garcia than with any other umpire. I don't think he's a fan of mine — maybe because we both have strong Latin tempers.

I wasn't there to see it, but around midnight in the top of the fifteenth, Tony Fernandez lined a one-hopper off Indians' third baseman Luis Aguayo, which hit him right on the cup. Aguayo made the play but the guys on both benches were laughing. In the press box, Ken Fidlin, of the *Toronto Sun*, had the line of the night: "And on the stroke of midnight Luis Aguayo's plums turned into pumpkins." Freddie singled Lloyd home in the sixteenth inning to put us up 6-5 and we held on for one of our toughest wins of the year, but no thanks to Garcia.

A player once asked me the question: Suppose it's the last Saturday night of the season, you're tied for first with another team and the deciding game is the next day. Who would you want working the plate? My answer would be about 15 guys — the American League has many great umpires calling balls and strikes. I joke with a lot of them when I come up to bat and I often chat with them when we're throwing the ball between innings. I've had some problems with Joe Brinkman, but mostly I think that was because Ernie Whitt was always feuding with Joe and knocked him in his book. I've had my share of problems, but I didn't agree with Ernie about Brinkman; he's a good baseball man. In '84 and '85 I used to have problems with Al Clark, but for the last few years we've gotten along well. He's given me some respect. The same thing with Dale Ford.

Sometimes the plate ump puts me in the hole. That's no problem. The only time it bothers me is if the pitcher out there is wild, the bases are loaded and right away I have one ball and two strikes. Then if I say something to an ump, he's mad at me for the whole series. I know I pay for it, but I can't help myself.

Our whole season came down to three games with the second-place Baltimore Orioles at the SkyDome. Going in on Friday, September 29, we were only one game ahead in the standings. So if we beat them the first game we were in command, but the word "choke" was everywhere. Our fans and especially the media from all over North America remembered how we'd blown a 3-1 lead in the playoffs against Kansas City in 1985 and how we'd lost seven straight to end the 1987 season. Brian Holton, a reliever for the Orioles, had said the week before, "Isn't choking the Blue Jays track record?" That kind of talk made us all determined. Our guys would be lining up to hit against Holton — if he ever got into the game.

That night, with Todd Stottlemyre on the mound, the crowd was as noisy as it had been at the old place on the Friday night in 1985 when we played the Yankees and needed one win to clinch. It didn't stay noisy for long. Phil Bradley hit the first pitch Stottlemyre threw for a homer. As the game progressed, that number one on the scoreboard looked bigger and bigger. Jeff Ballard, the Orioles' top pitcher got out of a couple of jams. Entering the eighth with the score still 1-0, Todd loaded the bases with only one out so Cito brought in Jim Acker. Acker had come over in a trade in late August and it was good to have him back. Anyway, he got Craig Worthington to bounce to Tony Fernandez who threw home for the force. Two outs. Then Acker retired Mike Devereaux on a fly ball. We still had a chance.

In the bottom of the eighth Mookie Wilson led off with a single and was forced at second base on a ground ball by Fred McGriff. Cito put in Tom Lawless, the midget, to pinch run for Freddie, and Frank Robinson brought in Gregg Olson to pitch to me. Lawless stole second to make him 12-for-13 stealing bases and when I grounded out he went over to third. So now there were two outs and it looked like the rookie Olson, who was practically unhittable then, was going to escape again. But he threw a wild pitch past catcher Jamie Quirk and Lawless raced home. We were tied.

In the tenth Cal Ripken signed off Duane Ward and Cito immediately went to Tom Henke. He didn't mind using Henk in a tied game, unlike Jimy in 1987 against the Tigers, and Henke got us out of the jam. In the bottom of the inning Junior Felix was at third when John Olerud was due to bat. John, who'd joined the team for September, was a college star from Washington State University drafted by the Jays. I liked him right away. I was on deck as young John walked to the plate and saw some of our guys lowering their heads, figuring the rookie Olerud was overmatched. "Just put it in play," I told him. He put it in play all right, hitting a fly ball to shallow centre. Mike Devereaux caught it and suddenly the same guys who didn't think Olerud could get his bat on the ball were on their feet yelling, "Score him, score him." But third-base coach John McLaren decided to hold up Felix. As the cheers of anticipation died down I was still in the on-deck circle and I could hear "Poppy, Poppy, Poppy!!!!" Maria was there with the boys and Georgie and Kevvy had run down the aisle to cheer me on.

There wasn't much to cheer about — Orioles' manager Frank Robinson walked me intentionally — and then Kelly Gruber grounded out to end the inning. In the eleventh, Henk went out and mowed 'em down again 1-2-3. In his two innings, four of the six outs were strikeouts. Olson had thrown two and two-thirds innings, which Robinson thought was enough for the rookie. He went to Mark Williamson, their set-up man. This is where we had been deeper all year long — our bullpen. With one out Manny Lee singled off Williamson and Nelson Liriano pinch-ran. Ernie Whitt bounced to third with Nelson on the go. Robinson walked Junior Felix intentionally even though he wasn't hitting very well. Now there were men at first and second.

Then Lloyd, who had probably received more boos than I had in the last part of the season, lined a single to left centre to score Nelson and win the game 2-1. With one arm down at his side, motioning the ball down to the ground away from the outfielders, Lloyd looked like Jeffrey Leonard running to first. Why not show some emotion? I knew he didn't want to come back and play on turf anyway, and I didn't know whether the Blue Jays wanted him or not. Thanks to Lloyd we were up two games with two games remaining. We only had to win one to have our second championship.

Saturday afternoon with Jimmy Key pitching, we fell behind early. Except for my single in the first that scored Lloyd, we couldn't get anything going and we went to the bottom of the eighth down 3-1. As we prepared to bat, a lot of guys were talking it up on the bench: there was no way we wanted to go to Baltimore on Monday for a playoff. First up was Nelson Liriano, who walked. Robinson brought in left-hander Kevin Hickey to face Junior Felix so Cito pinch hit Manny Lee. Manny worked the count to 3-2, then drew a walk. How about that! Back-to-back walks by Dominicans! Rob Ducey came in as a pinch-runner.

That put us in great shape for Lloyd, who dropped a perfect bunt down the third-base line. The ball spun in the dirt and looked like it was going foul but then kicked back fair while Ducey and Liriano moved to second and third. Lloyd got quite a reception from the bench; all the people in the stadium were on their feet as Mookie Wilson came to the plate. With the crowd roaring "Moooooo-kee, Moooooo-kee, Moooooo-kee," he lined a single to score Liriano. Then Freddie hit a hard base hit to right field, scoring Ducey. That not only tied the score, but Mookie made it all the way from first to third. The place was going bananas. We'd come all the way back. Now it was up to me.

There was still only one out so I didn't want to strike out — I had to drive the ball somewhere. Williamson had pitched me outside like most of the other teams had been doing down the stretch and he did it again. His first pitch was a fastball on the outside part of the plate and I reached out and poked a long fly ball into right field. Mookie tagged and scored and the place erupted. Now we were three outs away.

In the top of the ninth Cito put in Henk to shut the door. The fans were cheering every strike, booing each time the umpire called a ball. First Henk struck out Mickey Tettleton. Next he got pinch hitter Joe Orsulak on a ground ball to Gruber. Then he fanned Larry Sheets. On the final strike Ernie caught the ball and raised his fist in the air. Then he and Henk both ran towards each other as other players swarmed around them.

The feeling in the locker room is just as difficult to describe the second time as in 1985, but it was just as satisfying for those of us who'd been there before, like Tony Fernandez, Kelly Gruber, Manny Lee, Rance Mulliniks, Lloyd Moseby, Ernie Whitt, Tom Henke, Dave Stieb, Jimmy Key and Jim Acker. Big Henk and Wills were hugging each other like long-lost brothers as champagne ran down from their foreheads. In my corner of the dressing room we unfurled a Dominican flag and hung it over a locker. Manny Lee kept threatening to soak Tony Fernandez with champagne and Tony kept saying he'd be really upset if Manny did it. Tony doesn't drink and didn't want the champagne or beer even on his hair. So Manny came back and soaked Tony with a Diet Coke. I put one arm around Paul Beeston, shook his hand with the other and then soaked him with champagne. I got Gillick too. Pat Borders sprayed Cito. Our trainer, Tommy Craig, was hugging Cito, just as Kenny Carson had done in '85.

In the stretch drive of 1989 my time finally came. I struck out only six times in our last 34 games. In the last 14 games I hit .316 and drove in 11 runs. This time there wasn't any razzing from my brothers like there'd been in 1987.

In the 1989 American League Championship Series, the Oakland A's were just as hungry as the Blue Jays. Lopsided favourites the year before, the A's had been upset by Orel Hershiser, Kirk Gibson and the Los Angeles Dodgers. But then, in 1988, they didn't have Rickey Henderson. In Game One, Henderson's roll block at second not only broke up a double play but broke a 3-3 tie and allowed two runs to score. In Game Two, Henderson stole second when his team was up 5-1 and this set off a war of words with catcher Ernie Whitt, who called Henderson a "hot dog" adding, "Big leaguers don't tiptoe into the bag, they don't show people up." A's manager Tony La Russa responded by labelling Whitt "a fool." Earlier in the same game, Dave Parker had hit a home run off Stottlemyre and then sauntered to first base. Gruber told him he was lucky that he (Gruber) wasn't a pitcher because if he was, "there'd be a lot of heads ducking." Parker asked if Gruber was "running a baseball school of etiquette," and if he was, "had there been any graduates?"

Game Three was in Toronto, and briefly things looked up for the Jays. Ernie Whitt singled in the fourth against Storm Davis to bring home Tony Fernandez and break a 3-3 tie that put the Jays on their way to a 7-3 win. In Game Four, Rickey Henderson hit two homers, and Jose Canseco launched a Mike Flanagan pitch into the fifth deck of the SkyDome to win it 6-5. So the A's entered Sunday's fifth game needing only one victory to repeat as AL pennant winners.

Now we were down 3-1 and our backs were to the wall, but Cito had some extra ammunition we didn't know about. The night before, one of our clubhouse guys from the minor leagues had gone over to the Oakland clubhouse to help with laundry and towels. When he was picking up towels he claimed he saw some sandpaper inside Dennis Eckersley's glove. Eckersley was their stopper, the guy who'd saved the last two wins. But first we had to get Dave Stewart out of the game.

Game Five quickly began to seem like a repeat of the others. In the first inning Rickey Henderson walked, stole second and scored the first run. He tripled home another in the third and Oakland scored two more in the seventh to go up 4-0. But in the eighth Lloyd homered in what turned out to be his final at bat as a Blue Jay and we went into the bottom of the ninth against Dave Stewart trailing 4-1. But the game was far from over.

I was up first. All series they had been pitching me inside, but on a 2-1 pitch Stewart left a fastball over the plate and I hit it hard — over the left-field fence. That was all for Stewart. La Russa brought in Eckersley to hold the lead and put the A's into the World Series. Cito had another idea.

As soon as Eckersley came on, Cito asked the umpires to check his glove for sandpaper. The umpires conducted their search, but they didn't find anything. Cito said Eckersley stuck whatever he had down the front of his pants but they couldn't very well undress him right there on national TV. All the time, third baseman Tony Phillips and Eckersley were standing on the mound, swearing at Cito. Cito was yelling back, saying Eckersley was half a woman because he'd only yell at him from the mound, not come across the line and fight him. I'd never seen Cito so angry.

So Eckersley went to work against Tony, and it turned out we weren't finished yet. Tony singled, stole second, went to third when Ernie grounded out and scored on a fly ball by Gruber. Now it was 4-3 but we were down to one out. Junior Felix stepped in, a rookie with the whole season on his shoulders. When he got the count to 3-2, I'm sure everyone in the Dome was praying he'd come through. But on the next pitch he swung and missed, and that was it — the game, the season and our second shot at playing in the World Series. As the Oakland players crowded onto the field, Eckersley turned and gave our bench the finger.

I agree with those who say that Oakland showed they were better than we were in 1989, but I still think we should have won two or three home games at the SkyDome instead of only one. We should have gone back to Oakland for a Game Six, maybe a Game Seven. After that, who knows what would have happened? I know we did a lot better against Oakland than San Francisco did in the World Series, but that didn't matter much. In the Championship Series the A's put things together and for those five games executed better than we did. They did all the little things necessary to win: sacrificing, stealing bases, hitting cut-off men, throwing to the right bases. We didn't do those things well enough. And we couldn't match their starting pitching.

Still, if you look at the '89 season as a whole, we had a good year. We won our division in spite of a terrible start when we lost 24 of our first 36 games. A lot of people contributed to our turnaround, but we would never have won without Cito and without Tom Henke, who was almost unhittable in the second half.Although I drove in 104 runs I had some dry spells at the plate, one of my worst years ever in left field and one of my worst feuds ever with the fans.

At the end of November we had our third annual George Bell-Alfredo Griffin charity golf tournament at Casa de Campo on the course designed by Pete Dye. The tournament lasts two days and I play a few holes with each foursome. Paul Beeston, who'd become president of the Jays in January 1989, came along with his good friend Mike Firestone, Fergie Olver from CTV and Peter Gammons from *Sports Illustrated*. Peter was doing a story on me, which was to run in their annual swimsuit issue. When Firestone heard this, he predicted that this issue would set a record for circulation. I said, "What do you mean?" He said: "A record low."

The first day of the tournament was the day after Boston signed catcher Tony Pena for $6.4 million. First thing Beeston said that day was, "Well, if it isn't the second highest-paid Dominican baseball player." So I said, "There you go again, Beeston, screwing up the team. We had a chance to get a good catcher and we needed one after the playoffs and you guys didn't go get him." Everyone laughed. Then we all went out and toured the course and a lot of the time we were laughing at Tony Fernandez. Twice he hit balls off the roof of villas that line the fairways. Tony is a great shortstop but he's a terrible golfer.

At the end of November we moved into our new house. It's about 6000 square feet with an in-ground pond in front of the house with fountains and coloured lights at night, sort of likethe kind you might see in a hotel lobby. It's a palace compared to where I grew up. I tell reporters when they come in that the pond is a moat to keep them out. All the furniture, the terrazzo floor, the wood, even the stained glass is from the Dominican and in most cases from San Pedro. Recently we also bought a small farm outside the city so the kids can go there and ride horses.

When I'm home in the off-season my house is always full of people, both my friends and my employees. I have about seven people working for me — helping Maria, keeping up the grounds, working on the cars and the truck. The house seems more like a home when there are plenty of people around. Some days I'll look out and there will be a guy from Toronto with a Blue Jay hat on who wants to talk ball and get me to sign an autograph.

In December, during the Winter Meetings, Lloyd Moseby signed with the Detroit Tigers as a free agent. I was happy for Lloyd since he would get the chance to play every day and would be playing on natural grass instead of the artificial turf which bothered his back. But I knew I was going to miss him. At one time it was hard to imagine the Blue Jays without me in left field, Lloyd in centre and Jesse Barfield in right. Now I was the only one left.

9

Hardball

"The guy George Bell reminds me most of is Frank Robinson. They used to say about Frank when he was with Cincinnati, 'Don't knock him down because he's going to get up and kill you with home runs.'"
— *Cito Gaston, Blue Jays manager and former* NL *All-Star slugger with San Diego*

BECAUSE OF THE OWNER'S LOCKOUT, 1990 SPRING training didn't begin until March 21. We had only five days of workouts and then started playing games on March 26. And with the short spring — 14 games — there wasn't any chance for the fringe guys to make much of an impression. The veterans didn't look real good either. In fact, we were terrible. Tom Henke said we were going to use reverse strategy on the opposition: we were going to sneak up on the other teams and lay an old-fashioned "butt-kicking" on them.

As for me, I didn't start playing until our third game of the training season. My hands weren't in shape to start swinging even though I'd been taking batting practice with my brother Juan at the ballpark my dad helped build in Santa Fe. So I was taking it slow. All that did was make people ask questions about my shoulders and my health. But it seems like they ask those questions every year.

Our season started a week late, on April 9, in Texas, with a single game. Nolan Ryan beat us 4-2. Ryan was another year older but he threw just as hard as he had the year before. Then we went to Toronto for the home opener, the start of a three-game series. In the first one Dave Stieb went six innings and we beat Charlie Hough 2-1. The next night was embarrassing. The Rangers roughed up John Cerutti early: we were losing 10-0 with one man out in the second inning. In the third inning we loaded the bases against Kevin Brown, and I hit a grand slam to left, my first hit of the season, but we got whomped anyway, 11-5. We won the final game of the series 7-1 at Pat Borders; Freddie McGriff and Kelly Gruber all homered. A 2-2 start wasn't what we had in mind, but our starters were suffering from the short spring.

Our first round trip of the season started in Chicago, a place where we usually win. Instead we dropped three straight to fall half a game behind Milwaukee, which was having another one of its fast starts. The only bright spot for me was in the second game when I hit a homer off a rookie named Jerry Kutzler. That's unusual. Most major-league hitters don't like seeing a guy for the first time. It's like walking down a new street and you don't know where you're headed. You don't know how much his breaking ball moves or what kind of pitches he throws. It takes you two or three at bats to find out and by that time his team is usually ahead. Our scouting report didn't contain any news on Kutzler since he'd just been called up, but I guess I just like to play at Comiskey — that was the sixteenth homer I've hit there. I'm going to miss that old park. It's closing at the end of the year and they're building a new stadium across the street.

We finished April with a record of 12-9, which was a so-so start for us, but May soon began to look like a disaster — worst of all we couldn't seem to win at home. There were a few good games. On May 6 we beat the Tigers 11-7 at the Dome, and there were 10 homers, five by each team, which was an indoor record. Ex-Jay Cecil Fielder hit three of them. I hope the Blue Jays received a lot of money when they sold his contract to the Hanskin Tigers of the Japanese League in 1988 because it looked like he was going to have a good year. Our bullpen was overworked because our starting pitchers were still struggling: Mike Flanagan was the first casualty. His record was 2-2 but he had pitched only 20 and a third innings in four starts. Boston offered Flanagan a contract; his arm was hurt and he said no when he could have taken their money. That's the type of guy he is, but he was mostly known for his knowledge of hitters and his sense of humour. He didn't pitch inside enough but he was a good guy to have on our team.

On Mother's Day we were in second place, a game behind Milwaukee. I sent Maria a gift and I also sent flowers to Sue Cannell, Paul Beeston's assistant; to Fran Brown, Pat Gillick's assistant; to Catharine Elwood, who runs the pay office; and to Judy Van Zutphen, Howard Starkman's assistant. I always send them a gift at the end of the year. It's no big deal, but once I received a card from one of the girls saying I was the only player who ever did it.

We needed a gift during our homestand in the middle of May against the west-coast clubs. We managed one win during the eight games, losing two tight games to Oakland and Jose Canseco hit another bullet, a grand slam off Frank Wills that bounced off the top of the slanted glass in Windows Restaurant. Canseco, who hit one into the fifth deck in the 1989 playoffs, said he was going to try to hit the scoreboard next. If anyone can do it he can.

On May 22, we flew west to start an eight-game road trip against the same teams who'd just mowed us down at home, and a lot of the fans and media were knocking the ball club. That tune didn't change after we dropped two to the Angels in Anaheim. We'd now lost nine of our last 10 and had slipped into third place, three and a half games behind the Brewers. But the thing we had to remember is nothing is as bad as it looks, just as no team is ever as good as it looks — including Oakland. Then we headed to Seattle for a three-game series, which wasn't the break it used to be. What with Ken Griffey, Jr., in centre, and two hard-throwing pitchers, Brian Holman and Randy Johnson, they were a lot tougher.

We've had losing streaks before over the years, but this was different. The AL East always used to be the stronger. Now the AL West was better, and we had to get something going soon. That old saying about wins in April and May being as important as those in September is true. But Cito didn't panic. He didn't take any drastic measures. He just kept telling us not to try and win a whole series in one night.

When we got to Seattle it was about three in the morning, but I wasn't tired. I couldn't sleep so I lay there in my hotel room at the Crown Plaza. I started thinking about Maria and the kids. Since it was three o'clock west-coast time it would be seven in the morning in San Pedro. They'd all be getting up: Christopher, Georgie, Kevvy and Randy. Christopher and Georgie would soon be going to school. It was hard to believe that I was old enough to have four kids. I've missed a lot of my kids growing up — that's a price you pay for being a ballplayer. Sometimes when I don't see them for two months or longer I can't believe how much the younger ones have grown. I talk to them on the phone when I call Maria to give her the news, but it's not the same as being there. Sometimes I wonder if I'd have been happier going on to college, becoming an engineer, and playing ball with my *amigos* on the weekends. But if I had it to do all over again, I think I'd make the same decision.

When I look back at my career so far, and when I think about the future, I feel pretty good. There've been some ups and downs, times when I thought the whole world was against me — like at spring training in 1988 when the Jays tried to make me a full-time DH, times when the fans have really got on me — but most of the time I'm glad to be the man with the bat. And the glove.

Since my first year with the team in 1981, the Blue Jays have come a long way and so have I. In 1981 we were playing in a broken-down old ballpark and finished last in both halves of the strike-shortened season. Since I came back up in 1983 we've had a winning record for seven consecutive seasons. No other team in baseball can say that. I'm proud to have played for the Jays, and, if it works out, I'd like to finish my playing career in Toronto.

When I retire from the game I'm going back home. I don't have to hang around and look sad in someone else's face, begging for a job. If they want me to come back and be a coach or something, then they're going to have to invite me. I won't need a job because of the way Randy has looked after my money. Thanks to him, Maria and the kids are set for life.

On a bad day, during a bad week, during a bad month — when the fans are really on me — I sometimes feel like packing it in and going back to my kids. I don't need the money. Some games the fans get angry because they can't understand the way I act, but part of my game, along with hitting homers and driving in runs, is fighting back. If I hit a home run with two men on and the next time up the same pitcher knocks me down, I'm going to get up and charge the mound. I don't care whether it's a home game and the place is sold out, or we're in Cleveland and no one is watching, or the game is the TV Game of the Week. If a pitcher tries to intimidate me I'm going to go out there to kick his ass. That's the way I grew up playing the game.

Some people tell me I should be more like Ernie Whitt who was friendly with everyone, but that's not the way I am. My job is not to win a popularity contest. I'm sure in the history of the Blue Jays no one has ever been booed as much as the fans have booed me. Probably there are two main reasons why I'm booed so often: one is Jimy Williams, who turned a lot of fans against me early, and the other is the fact I'm Latin American. I know that. You only have to walk into a restaurant that won't serve you — this happened to two friends of mine and me in Milwaukee in 1989 — to understand. Or just stand out in left field with me some night when the mood is ugly. At the end of the inning I'll come running into the dugout and a fan will yell: "Get a hit, you shit Dominican!" You can be sure they don't yell "Hit a homer, you dumb Texan," at Kelly Gruber.

A lot of white people identify Latins as troublemakers with hot tempers. That's not the case. I've never met a kinder, more gentle man than Alfredo Griffin. You can't generalize. If I'm such an "out-of-control trouble maker," how come I've never ever started a fight in a Toronto restaurant, never had a fight in the street, never even had an argument with anyone on a Toronto street?

I don't know how many more years I'll play, maybe four or five. I'm 31 and this is the final year of the three-year contract I signed in February of 1988. A lot of players this far into their option year have already had contract talks. Don Mattingly, for instance, gave the Yankees an ultimatum with a few days remaining in spring training. He said either he had a new, long-term deal by Opening Day or this would be his last with the Yankees. Not long after, he signed a five-year deal worth $19.3 million. Glenn Davis, the first baseman with the Houston Astros, is already demanding a new contract and he's not a free agent until 1991.

I want to stay in Toronto, but by the time you read this I may be a free agent or I may have signed another long-term deal. I have a deadline and if I'm not signed by my date then I'm headed for the open market. If we get to the point where I'm putting up the same numbers as last year and there are only a few weeks left in the season, then why not talk to the other 25 teams? I imagine Bobby Cox of the Atlanta Braves would talk to me. Probably a few others.

But we haven't even talked with the Jays so far. Paul Beeston keeps telling Randy, "We'll have to get together." A couple of times Randy has phoned Beeston's office after I've had a good game and left a short message with his assistant Sue Cannell: "Tell him Randy phoned and tell him the price just went up." I can just see Beeston picking up the message and laughing. That's how well the two of them get along. They can tease each other but the meeting never does get set up and I think they're taking a gamble. The longer I go and the better numbers I have, the more money the Blue Jays will have to pay me to re-sign. You'd think they'd know that by now.

During the 1990 spring training Randy was talking to Gillick and Gillick told him he figured I'd re-sign since the Hendricks brothers have a policy of not moving their clients from a city when they're happy. Randy gave him a three-part comeback: "First, Mark Davis left the San Diego Padres after winning a Cy Young award to sign as a free agent with Kansas City Royals; second, Jeff Reardon left the Minnesota Twins to sign with the Boston Red Sox; and third, who says George is happy?" I wish I'd been there to see the look on Gillick's face.

When I do leave Toronto one guy I'll really miss will be Fergie Olver, one of our broadcasters. He's really supportive of the team and me. Some people didn't like the job he did on TV, but I bet the people who didn't like him didn't know him. He's truly a Blue Jays fan, one of the greatest fans the team has ever had. He'll come into the dressing room after a bad night or a tough loss trying to keep the players up.

Whether I retire or I'm traded or I go someplace else as a free agent doesn't matter, there will be two groups of fans. One group, the fans who cheer me, will be angry because they'll be losing a player who plays the game hard. Even some of the people who booed me will probably miss me after I'm gone. When they look down through the Blue Jays stats and compare all the numbers of the roughly 200 position players who've played for the Blue Jays, they'll see one player who had the best total numbers in the history of the organization — George Bell. But the fans who really hate me, the people who have booed me all the time, I know exactly what they'll say: "George Bell is all washed up. See! I told you. I told you he would go downhill. This guy was one of the worst players we've ever had here in the history of the ball club — I've been telling you that for the last five years. I even told you in 1987, when he won the MVP, he wasn't that good."

Writers and deep thinkers are always looking for the two faces of George Bell. I have only the one face. It may not be that good looking, but it's a straight face. That's why I didn't get along with Jimy. I've always been straight and honest with people. I didn't go behind anyone's back like some players did at the veterans' meetings in 1988. I've been honest with all the players, especially the rookies.

I try to treat them the way Big John Mayberry treated me my first year. But the rookies we see these days have bad attitudes. Once, in the eighth inning of a spring-training game at Dunedin in 1987, Jimy told a kid just up from Double A to pinch-run. It was the kid's first major-league camp and he looked at Jimy and said no, he wasn't there to be a pinch-runner. More and more that seems like a typical attitude. I see kids who come up to the big leagues, and when you talk to them it's like they don't really care.

The Blue Jays are partly to blame. They've babied a whole bunch of prospects in the minors, and after they come up, some of them still seem like they're more comfortable with rattles than bats. Too often the club didn't teach them any discipline in the minors. Glenallen Hill was a bad one his first time at spring training in 1987 but he's changed his attitude. And as soon as he changed his attitude you could see guys bending over backwards trying to help him. He learned the hard way that if you don't listen to the veterans, the guys with experience, they'll lose confidence in you.

Rob Ducey was pretty cocky his first time around too. He's a nice guy and everything, but any time anyone tried to give him some advice he made it clear he wasn't interested. He's a lot better now. I'm talking about a situation where you'd tell him, "Don't do that against this pitcher" or "Watch this guy for this." Now he listens. Ducey and Hill weren't the biggest pains, though, by any means. We've had a whole bunch who were worse. Matt Stark, David Wells, Sil Campusano and Junior Felix — Junior was probably the worst of all when he first arrived. He's hard-headed, never listens, and talks back to coaches and older players. He used to play catch between innings with a guy from the bullpen and he'd always be throwing him sliders, breaking balls and bouncing balls at the guy's feet. No one wanted to play catch with him. Some nights when he's in right field the coaches will ask him to move and he won't.

Matt Stark was a talented young catcher, but his bad attitude did him in. One day, early in the 1987 season, at Exhibition Stadium, Stark had a football in the clubhouse and he booted it off the ceiling. BANG! You can probably go there right now and see a big mark where the ball hit. I was at my locker and the noise scared me. I went over and asked him what he thought he was doing. Stark said, "None of your business." I asked him if he was trying to ruin our clubhouse. I said, "If you wreck one of the TVs with your stupid football the ball club is going to charge you for it." His response was, "I don't care. I have money." I also told him if he "didn't act like a professional but acted like an animal" he'd end up back in Triple A. He never came back after they sent him down.

That's what happens to a lot of those players. They get to the big leagues and they don't have the maturity to stay. Talent isn't enough. The way you act in the clubhouse is the same way you're going to act on the field.

Younger players don't respect the older players now the way we did when I broke in. There is too much money and they have things easier. When I broke in I made $45 000. Now rookies earn $100 000 and they have everything. When I came up if I was going to order bats I could only afford to order one dozen bats every two months so I really had to guard my bats. Even now my only superstition is that it's bad luck to let anyone touch my bat before a game. Now rookies order three dozen bats every month. And they have shoe companies giving them shoes. When I came to the big leagues, rookies didn't get free shoes. We waited for one of the veterans to give us an extra pair and we were grateful.

In spite of the money and the spoiling some rookies are great in the clubhouse and that's why they'll go a long way. Pat Borders was the best rookie we've ever had come into camp since I've been here — until John Olerud showed up. Both guys work hard, play hard, keep their mouths shut, listen and do what they are told. Not too many guys knew anything about Olerud when he showed up the last couple of days of August in 1989 without one day of service in the minor leagues. He had had a brain aneurysm the November before and had just turned pro. That first night I teased him when he was running the bases during batting practice. But Olerud didn't mouth off like a smart-ass college kid. I think he'll make a lot of money at this game.

Manny Lee, Nelson Liriano and Todd Stottlemyre were good too. They were the kind of guys you could talk to. That's the way I was as a rookie back in 1981. I might be loud and say plenty of things in the clubhouse now, but in 1981, as a rookie, I listened. I listened to John Mayberry and Alfredo Griffin. I showed respect for the guys with experience. I still think that's the way rookies should behave.

Someone once asked me one of those questions you see in USA Today: "What would you do if you were commissioner of baseball?" First thing I'd do is get rid of the designated-hitter rule in the American League — and not just because I don't want to be a DH. (Who knows, someday I might, if I get the right contract.) In the National League the pitcher gets to bat but he doesn't in the American League; consequently, pitchers in our league are braver. If they had to worry about coming up to the plate after knocking someone down or hitting someone, they would be throwing less at the other team's hitters. It's that simple.

If I was commissioner, I'd also bump the roster up to 26 from 24. We need more men on the roster. The best games the fans see all season are in September when both teams are making moves, when there are extra men on the bench.

Another thing I'd do is start the season in the third week of March instead of the first week of April. That wouldn't be any problem in northern cities like Minneapolis, Seattle, Montreal and Toronto since they now all have domed stadiums. The other northern clubs could start on the road. By starting the regular season two weeks earlier you'd cut down on the long spring training — we don't need six weeks — and you could finish the World Series by the middle of October instead of the end of October. I know I'll never be commissioner — I'd suspend too many pitchers for hitting batters. My job is to stick to driving in runs. Since 1984, I've driven in 649 runs. Don Mattingly is the only player in the major leagues who's batted in more. He has 707.

Next year the All-Star game is in Toronto and I'd like to be there. But I'm at the point where it isn't a big deal for me any more. I set goals for myself but I don't go around saying "I'm going to do this, this and this." I don't tell everyone what my goals are but most years I've gone out and achieved them. I'm not the type of guy who goes around smiling, flashing my teeth and practically begging for interviews. The worst thing I've done all the time I've been with the Blue Jays is refuse to talk to some of the press. So what? They had plenty of other guys to interview.

There is one thing I'd like to accomplish before I'm done: I'd like to retire with the most home runs of any Dominican player. Felipe Alou, my old manager at Escogido, is the current Dominican leader with 206 lifetime homers in the major leagues. My childhood hero, Rico Carty, who used to play for the Blue Jays, is next with 204. Pedro Guerrero, of the St. Louis Cardinals, moved into third place this season with 200. By the time you read this he may be number one. Next is Cesar Cedeno, who my dad took me to see play in Santa Fe when I was a little boy, with 199. At the end of May 1990, I was fifth with 188. Who knows? Maybe I'll even pass Felipe this year. And Pedro is three years older than I am, so after that I'll have a shot at being number one. Tony Perez, from Cuba, is the best of the Latin Americans, with 315 homers. Maybe, if I stay healthy, I have a chance at beating him.

I might not make the Dominican Hall of Fame, but I know I've already made one Hall of Fame. This summer they put me into the Helena Baseball Club Hall of Fame along with Ryne Sandberg and a few others. Next time I see Ryne I'm going to congratulate him and thank him for helping me get used to playing ball in North America.

The most important thing I've learned as a ballplayer is that I don't have to impress anyone. I used to think my season depended on one home stand or maybe one 40-game stretch. But the season is 162 games long and there's plenty of time to do things wrong and plenty of time to do things the proper way. When I came back up in 1983 Cito kept driving that home: "You can't get four hits every night. Tomorrow is another day," he'd say. "You have to be patient. You know that sometimes you will be down and sometimes you will be happy over the course of a long season."

On May 24, 1990, as I lay on my bed in the hotel room in Seattle, the season sure looked like a long one. I was feeling homesick so I called up Maria and talked to the kids before they headed off to school. It was good just to hear their voices. Finally, maybe four in the morning, I got to sleep.

As you know by now that road trip helped turn the first part of our season around. We swept Seattle, who'd beaten us three straight at the Dome, and then beat Oakland two of three. David Wells and Dave Stieb were impressive. So we came home 5-3. Then we split our home stand, taking one of three against the Brewers, who knocked us out of first place, and two out of three against Minnesota. It was June 7, our record was 28-26 and we were one and a half games out as we headed out on the road again for 10 games in 10 days.

That was when we really put it all together and I started to hit. The first night in Milwaukee when we beat the Brewers 11-5 I drove in six runs with a pair of homers — my first multi-homer game since Opening Day in 1988 in Kansas City when I hit three. From there on we just kept winning. When the trip was over we'd won nine of 10 and we were in first place, two games ahead of Boston. It was the best 10-game road trip in the history of the team.

Cito was running a good ship. He didn't lose his cool early when the starters were struggling and he kept giving guys the occasional day off so no one got too tired. He showed faith in his team. For instance, even when Greg Myers went 1-for-24, Cito stuck with him — and Myers broke out on the road trip going 10-for-24. Cito also gave Freddie time off, playing Olerud at first. Freddie played every game but one in 1989 and he was beat at the end of the year. Cito also had Tony Fernandez, Junior Felix, Kelly Gruber and Mookie Wilson off and running with steals and hit-and-runs. I even stole a couple of bases when the guy at the plate missed the pitch when a hit-and-run was on.

So by June 8 we were back in Toronto and things looked pretty good. We were in first place over Boston by a game and a half and everybody seemed to be hitting. Jimmy Key would be off the disabled list soon and if Al Leiter got into shape and came up from Syracuse we'd have a fireballing left-handed starter. As far as I was concerned, if we stayed healthy we could go all the way. We should have been there in 1987 and our team had more experience and more talent than we did in 1985 when we came so close it hurt.

Winning our division isn't enough any more. Before I leave baseball I'd like a World Series ring. Maybe I'll be wearing one before this year is over.

Appendix: George Bell's Stats

Born: October 21, 1959, at San Pedro de Macoris, Dominican Republic. Throws and bats right-handed.

Regular Season

	G	AB	R	H	2B	3B	HR	RBI	Avg.
1978, Helena	33	106	20	33	6	1	0	14	.311
1979, Spartanburg	130	491	78	150	24	15	22	102	.305
1980, Reading	22	55	11	17	5	2	0	11	.309
1981, Toronto	60	163	19	38	2	1	5	12	.233
1982, Syracuse	37	125	11	25	5	4	3	19	.200
1983, Syracuse	85	317	37	86	11	4	15	59	.271
Toronto	39	112	5	30	5	4	2	17	.268
1984, Toronto	159	606	85	177	39	4	26	87	.292
1985, Toronto	157	607	87	167	28	6	28	95	.275
1986, Toronto	159	641	101	198	38	6	31	108	.309
1987, Toronto	156	610	111	188	32	4	47	134	.308
1988, Toronto	156	614	78	165	27	5	24	97	.269
1989, Toronto	153	613	88	182	41	2	18	104	.297
Major league totals	1039	3966	574	1145	212	32	181	654	.289

Championship Series

	G	AB	R	H	2B	3B	HR	RBI	Avg.
1985, Tor./K.C.	7	28	4	9	3	0	0	1	.321
1989, Tor./Oak.	5	20	2	4	0	0	1	2	.200

— Source: *Sporting News*

Acknowledgements

Thanks to our editor, Rick Archbold, who served as the lead guide on this adventure. At our first meeting he said he had a million and one ideas. He was a man of his word. Thanks also to hard-liners Carol Bonnett and Ursula Bollini of the MGA agency, Randy Hendricks of Hendricks Management, and to Patrick Grier, who was a bright young journalist when this aging-process of a project began. I would be negligent not to express my gratitude to Wayne Parrish, Sports Editor of the *Toronto Sun*, a patient man, as well as to my *Sun* colleagues Ken Fidlin, Scott Morrison, Bill Lankhof, Jim O'Leary and Mike Ganter, and to Howard Starkman and Gary Oswald of the Blue Jays and Vicki McKee of Telemedia Broadcast Systems.

Advice, too much of it, came from my sister Elizabeth, inspiration from my parents, both now in another league. When I was growing up in Kingston, Ontario, my father taught me the game: from bat boy to Dizzy and Pee Wee to the long car drives home from Syracuse and Little Britain and every stop in between. He taught me baseball, but not how to spell. After he was called up, second fathers Edward MacCabe and Hewitt Smith took over. I'd be remiss if I didn't acknowledge Greg Walker, Gary Howatt and Bob Jones. This project would not have been completed without help from Eddie Mathews, Willie Hugh Nelson, Wilson Rivera and H.A. Zens.

Finally, I'm eternally grateful to my loving wife Claire, who spent countless hours transcribing tapes and put up with the late nights and odder than usual odd hours, and to Alicia and Bobby, who now can have their computer back.

— Bob Elliott